FIXED

Fixed

HOW GOODFELLAS
BOUGHT
BOSTON COLLEGE
BASKETBALL

DAVID PORTER

TAYLOR TRADE PUBLISHING
DALLAS, TEXAS

Designed by David Timmons

Published by Taylor Publishing Company
1550 West Mockingbird Lane
Dallas, Texas 75235
www.taylorpub.com

Library of Congress Cataloging-in-Publication Data

Porter, David, 1960–
   Fixed : how goodfellas bought Boston College basketball /
David Porter.
      p.   cm.
   Includes index.
   ISBN 0-87833-192-1 (cloth)
      1. Boston College—Basketball—Corrupt practices. 2. Boston College
Eagles (Basketball team). I. Title: How goodfellas bought Boston
College basketball. II. Title.

GV885.43.B68 P67 2000
744.323'.63'0974461—dc21   00-061554

10 9 8 7 6 5 4 3 2 1

Printed in the United States of America

For my parents

Contents

Acknowledgments

Recreating for this book events that happened more than twenty years ago was a challenge made easier by the efforts of many people who deserve more than just these printed words of thanks.

The clerks at U.S. District Court in Brooklyn were uniformly helpful and courteous in responding to my numerous requests for trial transcripts and related materials. In particular, Lourdes Vasquez gave the project a kick-start when I was trying to navigate a sea of paperwork in what was, at the time, a rudderless ship. In addition, Martin Rosenberg and the crew at the Northeast Regional Archives in Manhattan were more than generous in helping me acquire and reproduce mountains of trial materials.

The *New York Times'* reporting of the Boston College investigation and subsequent trials, as well as the Lufthansa robbery, provided valuable context to the story. Articles that ran in the *Washington Post*, *Stamford (Conn.) Advocate*, and *Trenton (N.J.) Times* fleshed out many important details. The *Boston Globe's* coverage effectively captured the tenor of both trials.

I am deeply indebted to those people who shared their reminiscences of what, for some of them, was a less-than-pleasant chapter in their lives. These include Herman Alswanger, Douglas Behm, Jerry Bernstein, George Blaney, Tom Davis, Chris Foy, David Golub, Henry Hill, Kevin Mackey, Mike Mayock, Tom Meggers, Kerry O'Malley, Reid Oslin, Rocco Perla, Leonard Sharon, Robert Simels, Jim Sweeney, Gary Vogler, Gary Zimmerman, and many others. To those few whose vanity or greed precluded them from contributing, I wish nothing but good things.

No less important was the encouragement that came from many corners. Charley Rosen, author of *Scandals of '51*, the definitive book on the CCNY point-shaving scandal and the origin of the quote that opens this book, was a regular source of information and inspiration. George Roy and Steve Stern of Black Canyon Productions and Gary Cohen of Broadway Network Television offered advice and shared their vast expertise with me in the early days of the project.

Nicholas Pileggi's book *Wiseguy*, which introduced the world to Henry Hill, was a valuable tool. It is still the best resource for anyone interested in the inner workings of an organized crime family.

My coworkers at Professional Team Physicians, Inc., were unfailingly supportive and accommodating, particularly Bob Dittmeier, whose editing skills are reflected in these pages; Heather Thompson, who provided the anecdote on sports gambling in ancient Rome as well as research help and encouragement throughout; and Joshua Kurlinski, who never complained.

For helping to make it all happen, I owe a large debt of gratitude to Randy Voorhees and John Monteleone at Mountain Lion, Inc., whose faith in the project sustained me when the light at the end of the tunnel was but a faint flicker. Their efforts helped me realize a dream that was several years in the making.

My parents, David and Rosalie Porter, to whom this book is dedicated, encouraged me in this endeavor as they have in all my endeavors, however half-baked or nonsensical. If a fraction of their generosity and humanity has rubbed off on me, I consider myself fortunate.

Finally, there are no words that can give adequate credit to my wife, Laurie, in the writing of this book. Suffice it to say that her patience and encouragement were beacons that lit the way through many of the difficult days. For that, and for many other reasons, she is a true Hall of Famer.

Introduction

"The American people have a romanticized view of athletics. They want to identify with the entire fantasy that the world of sports has come to represent. Whenever you break a moral code that people are supposed to believe in, you are confronted with a stronger wrath than any burglar or common thief ever faces."
— Ed Roman, a member of City College of New York's disgraced 1950–51 basketball team

When reports leaked out in the winter of 1981 that three former Boston College basketball players were being investigated for shaving points during the 1978–79 season, the reaction from all corners of the sports world was swift and uniform in its condemnation of these heinous acts. This outpouring merely followed protocol that had been established as far back as baseball's Black Sox scandal of 1919 and which continued through college basketball's game-fixing epidemic in the 1950s and early '60s. The intertwining of gambling and sports, two of America's enduring obsessions, seldom fails to inflame public passions whenever the dividing lines blur or cross.

By the following year, when heavy sentences were handed down against former Boston College player Rick Kuhn and four codefendants, it was as if a sense of order had been restored, as if the act of sending five men to spend the next several years behind bars would somehow rid college basketball of a cancerous plague that threatened to eat away at the integrity of the game.

Events later that year cast the penalties in a perplexing light, however. Within six months of Kuhn's sentencing, former University of New Mexico Head Coach Norm Ellenberger was convicted on twenty-one counts of defrauding his school and was given one year of unsupervised probation. And the University of San Francisco's All-American point guard Quintin Dailey was given three years' probation in a plea-bargain agreement on charges of assault with intent to commit rape. Unfathomably, had Dailey been convicted of the original charges he faced, his sentence would have been nearly three years shorter than Kuhn's.

Three men, three crimes, three punishments—but two separate standards for judging behavior, one based on the real world and one based on the fantasy world constructed around the sports arena. Taken together, these three scenarios illuminate, better than any high-minded pronouncements from the overseers of college athletics ever could, the extent to which any sort of chicanery on the playing fields strikes at the heart of our cherished beliefs about sports and sportsmanship. *Do what you will off the court, the message says, but once the whistle blows and the clock starts to tick, give less than your best at your own peril.*

Timing may explain in part the visceral reaction that accompanied news of the Boston College scandal. In 1981 it had been twenty years since college basketball's last major outbreak of point-shaving, enough time for a generation of fans and players to forget about disgraced figures like Sherman White and Eddie Gard of Long Island University, the mess at the University of Kentucky and at City College of New York in 1951, the machinations of master fixer Jack Molinas and the widespread instances of game-fixing in 1960 and '61.

In the fall of 1978, too, college basketball was about to begin a gradual transformation from being a pleasant diversion between the Super Bowl and the beginning of baseball season into a monolith on the American sports scene. Consider what occurred between the meeting at Boston's Logan Airport Hilton in December 1978 that kicked off the Boston College scheme and the trial of Kuhn and four coconspirators in 1981:

The 1979 NCAA championship game between Larry Bird and Magic Johnson—and, nominally, the state universities of Indiana and Michigan that they represented—catapulted college basketball into the national consciousness in the same way that Alan Ameche's overtime touchdown in the 1958 NFL title game added legitimacy to a league that had existed for decades but had not yet fully captured the public imagination. Within a few months, the Big East Conference ushered in the era of the megaleague, which would lead to greater consolidation of power and exponential increases in television rights fees.

Perhaps more significant, Entertainment and Sports Programming Network, known by its acronym, ESPN, began broadcasting out of a small studio in Bristol, Connecticut, and started quietly transforming the depth and breadth of college basketball coverage.

One result of these developments was that by the late 1990s when FBI investigations uncovered point-shaving schemes at Arizona State and Northwestern, a jaded public hardly batted its collective eye at the revelations.

• • •

For anyone who has played organized sports, the thought of a player purposely giving less than his best sticks in the craw. It goes against everything we are programmed to believe in from the first time we play organized sports with referees and a game clock. Yet how many of us would be able to turn down an offer to cut a few corners for the right price? George Blaney brushed up against point-shaving as a player at Holy Cross in the early 1960s and as a coach there during the Boston College scandal. He talks later in this book of his relief that he was not approached by the fixers when he was in college—some of whom were his friends—because he knew that the temptation might have proved too great.

At an even more basic level is a question that is seldom broached: How wrong is it to manipulate the score—but not necessarily the final outcome—of an athletic contest? Think of a laughing Denny McLain lobbing a pitch to Mickey Mantle that Mantle knocked out of the park for his record-breaking 535th home run near the end of his career . . . or tennis players agreeing to split sets at an exhibition event to ensure that the fans get to see a three-set match . . . or a last-place NBA team, in the days before the draft lottery, putting a second-rate team on the floor for a late-season game. Think, even, of an NFL team running out the clock by downing the ball on its opponents' two-yard-line at the end of a game, presumably to avoid "rubbing it in." This sham chivalry obscures the fact that the team with the ball is deliberately trying not to score . . . and, as a result, is shaving points off the final margin of victory.

None of us wants to think that our sports are governed by impure motives, perhaps because we view the games, at least on the collegiate level, as the only corner left untainted by recruiting violations, questionable admissions policies, and ghost-written term papers. In this context, point-shaving acts as the bogey-man, deflecting attention from the blatant lie that much of big-time college sports has become. This only creates more hypocrisy, however; if we do not expect coaches and administrators to obey the rules that govern their activities, how can we expect the same from the players?

Clearly, we cannot. It is not a stretch to say that the same moral deficiencies that could lead a college coach to defraud his school or cause an aspiring NBA prospect to try to rape a woman also extend to the playing field, where nothing more momentous than the outcome of a ball game is at stake. It may be, then, that the only thing separating us from an onslaught of point-shaving is, as Blaney implied, a lack of opportunity on the part of the players.

When presented with that opportunity in 1978, Rick Kuhn, Jim Sweeney, and Ernie Cobb succumbed to the temptation to varying degrees, and suffered terribly for it. If their plight only adds weight to the theory that everyone has his price, then perhaps it is incumbent on us, the people who prime the sports gambling pump, not the players, to exercise prudence and restraint. If we do not, then we become coconspirators, and our shock and outrage when the latest fix is uncovered merely becomes a projection of our own moral deficiencies.

FIXED

CHAPTER ONE

The Odd Couple

J im Sweeney's entry in the Lawrenceville School's 1976 senior yearbook contains, among dedications to several faculty members and coaches, two sayings:

"I thank the Lord for the people I have found."
"Be the one you dream you can be."

The first was a quote from "Mona Lisas and Mad Hatters," a song by pop singer Elton John. The second presumably was of Sweeney's creation. Both phrases—one an homage to the people who had helped get him to where he was and the other a confident look toward the future—provide an insight into the talented, thoughtful, intelligent, good-natured young man who seemed to make enemies of no one, save for the opponents he routinely outshone on the playing fields.

Sweeney grew up in the south end of Trenton, in a rowhouse in a neighborhood that was white, working-class, and predominantly Eastern European. His father, Donald, drove a milk truck for Johanna Farms for twenty years, then worked as a toll collector on the Route 1 bridge, which looks up the Delaware River at a neon sign that says in six-foot-high letters, "Trenton Makes, The World Takes," a tribute to the blue-collar city's manufacturing roots.

Sweeney remembers himself as "a focused kid" who played baseball, soccer, and basketball, and swam competitively. "I had a very good childhood. Very good teenage years," he remembers. "Had an excellent family, very supportive." South Trenton was spared the devastation visited on the north end of the city by the 1968 riots that sent New Jersey's capital city into a tailspin from which it is just now recovering. The Sweeneys had deep roots in the city—Jim's mother was raised in the house he grew up in, and at one time there were three generations living in the house on Dayton Street—and the family did not join the subsequent white flight to the surrounding suburbs.

Sweeney's parents were, however, concerned about his attending Trenton Central High School because of the racial tensions that existed there in the early 1970s. His mother learned about a scholarship program being offered at the prestigious Lawrenceville School located five miles outside Trenton, and Jim enrolled there in the fall of 1972.

It was quite a journey from the blue-collar neighborhood in which he was raised to the verdant campus that was home to the sons and daughters of the privileged class. But Sweeney smoothly made the transition on and off the field at Lawrenceville, and eventually he became one of the most popular students on campus.

On the basketball court, it took eight games of his freshman year for Sweeney to crack the starting lineup, and in his first start he scored thirteen points and led Lawrenceville to an upset win over a local rival, the Hun School. In his junior and senior years, he led the team to New Jersey state prep-school titles.

"He was such an honest, easygoing guy. A hardworking, earnest guy," remembers one teammate. "If you were a coach, a player like Jim Sweeney probably came along once in a generation. . . . A lot of kids, their talent only carries them so far and they have nothing to fall back on. But as Sweeney matured, you could see what a heady, smart player he became."

Fred Gerstell was an assistant basketball coach in the mid-1970s when Sweeney played there, and was one of the people mentioned in Sweeney's yearbook dedication.

"He was basically a sweet guy, super-nice, a scholar-athlete," Gerstell recalled. "Very enthusiastic about the school and enormously grateful (for the opportunity). He was in no sense a troublemaker. He wasn't contentious or rebellious."

Sweeney also excelled on the baseball field, and eventually he earned All-State honors in both sports while at Lawrenceville. He pitched and played centerfield for a Trenton Post 93 team that won the state American Legion championship in 1976, the summer before his freshman year at Boston College. Sweeney's American Legion coach, Gary Vogler, remembers bending the rules for a kid whose talents and personality made the decision almost a no-brainer.

"I remember I wasn't happy with him because he was playing summer league (basketball), but he was the first kid I ever gave an exception to, to play another sport," Vogler recalls. "I had a strict rule about that. But his goal was to play college basketball, and you couldn't deny him that.

"He was probably one of the nicest kids you'd ever want to know. He was one of those kids who you always thought would reach any goal that he wanted to reach. He was almost too nice. You always wanted to praise him, but you didn't do it for fear of favoritism."

It was hard not to come into contact with gambling in some form in Trenton in the late 1960s and early '70s. In the years before state-authorized lotteries and the advent of casino gambling in Atlantic City, backroom bookmaking and numbers operations flourished under the tacit approval of reputed Philadelphia mob boss Angelo Bruno, who reportedly extracted his tribute from the local operators in return for keeping drugs and prostitution off the city's streets.

There is no evidence that Sweeney was involved in gambling during his teenage years. But he certainly was aware of what a point spread was by the time he got to Boston College, and he admitted he would sometimes check the morning newspaper to see what the line was on that night's B.C. game.

• • •

Former Boston College coach Bob Zuffelato, now the head of basketball operations for the NBA's Toronto Raptors, recruited Sweeney in the mid-1970s with an eye toward pairing him with Ernie Cobb, a high-scoring guard out of Stamford, Connecticut. After watching Sweeney play several times and spending time with his family as well as with coaches and counselors at Lawrenceville, Zuffelato knew right away that he had hit the jackpot—and that a coach's normal fear of the admissions office was not going to be an issue. "We were so excited to get him," Zuffelato says. "We knew if we had him and Ernie together, we'd have a dynamic backcourt because you had the scoring (with Ernie) and you had the real point-guard mentality with Jimmy. And academically, I knew I wasn't going to have to worry about him."

• • •

As he had done at Lawrenceville, Sweeney made a quick impression at Boston College. By the 1977–78 season, his sophomore year and Tom Davis's first season as head coach, he was a fixture in the starting lineup. His leadership abilities led Davis to name him a tricaptain along with Bob Bennifield and Cobb. Sweeney was perfect for Davis's system, a versatile player who could score when needed but would willingly give himself up to make his teammates better—and who would not back down an inch in the heat of battle.

"He was a good athlete, a good, tough, hard-nosed kid," Davis remembers. "He could play defense, and he could rebound as well as score."

The freedom of being in college and three hundred miles away from home apparently did not have a negative effect on Sweeney. His peers remember a straight A and B student who was more likely to be found lifting weights on a Saturday night than lifting a bottle of Budweiser. In fact, Sweeney drank so infrequently that he was the quintessential designated driver before that term was even coined. In his spare time, he attended St. Ignatius Church on the B.C. campus and was chosen to be a lector, a member of the congregation who reads passages from the Bible along with the priest.

Mike Mayock, who later became a college football commentator for CBS, played football at Boston College in the late 1970s. For three years he lived in a suite with four other football players and one basketball player— Sweeney. The picture Mayock paints is straight out of *The Odd Couple*, with Sweeney as Felix Unger contending with five Oscar Madisons.

Sweeney's influence apparently went beyond just tidying up after his messy roommates.

"At B.C. back in 1980, you were expected to get your degree, go to class, all those good things," Mayock says. "Jimmy was the one person in the group that never drank, rarely partied, went to church every Sunday, went to every single class when he wasn't on the road for basketball. Then you had these five football players who . . . all liked to hang out. All six of us graduated, but Jimmy was always the one pushing us to go to class.

"Of course, a lot of times he was the one who got pushed naked out in the hallway, because he was the smallest. And we liked to tease him a lot."

Tom Meggers was a senior on the 1978–79 team. He saw in Sweeney a "really great kid" who was destined for the Boston College Hall of Fame, as much for his personality as for his abilities on the court.

"He had an engaging personality," Meggers recalled. "No matter who you were, he could engage you in a great conversation and make you feel good."

Yet by the fall of 1978 and the beginning of his junior season, Sweeney's basketball life and his social life rarely, if ever, intersected.

"I can honestly say I wasn't that friendly with the guys on the team," Sweeney remembers. "I was really friends with the guys that I lived with. If you went back and checked all the people who went in and out of that basketball program, there were a fair amount. I can't say I was unfriendly with people, but the guys that I was living with, they were my buddies."

● ● ●

Friendships between teammates inevitably cut across the artificial boundaries created by playing status, which in part explains the relationship between Sweeney, an established starter since his sophomore year, and Rick Kuhn, a player who some people felt was lucky to be getting any minutes at a Division I school.

The two made an odd pair, but they found enough common ground through basketball to develop a friendship. A former acquaintance characterized them as best friends who "did almost everything together when it came to basketball." During the winter, Sweeney was a regular dinner guest at the apartment Kuhn shared in downtown Boston with his girlfriend, Barbara Reed.

Sweeney and Kuhn had met at a basketball camp in Pennsylvania's Pocono Mountains in the summer of 1976 and entered B.C. together that fall, Sweeney as a freshman and Kuhn as a sophomore. The two could hardly have been more different: Kuhn was older by three years, and at 6-foot-5 and 225 pounds was six inches taller and 45 pounds heavier than Sweeney. Where Sweeney was a gifted athlete though on the small side, Kuhn made up for his marginal physical skills by willingly doing the dirty work required of big men who play basketball: rebounding, defending, setting picks, taking up space under the basket.

Kuhn had grown up in Swissvale, Pennsylvania, a working-class town of about ten thousand residents located seven miles southeast of Pittsburgh. Until the layoffs and eventual closings that ushered in the 1980s, the steel industry was the dominant employer in the region. In 1900, Andrew Carnegie built a railroad bridge that connected Carrie Furnaces of Swissvale with Homestead Steel Works, on the opposite side of the Monongahela River, to form one of the largest steel plants in the country. Union Switch and Signal—which did work for the military until it, too, shut down—also was a major employer.

Swissvale itself was a town that thrived on community-based activities, and the calendar was filled with church bazaars, firemen's bazaars, fairs, and parades. Like thousands of small towns across America, the sports seasons also marked the calendar, from baseball in the spring and summer to football in the fall and basketball in the winter. Baseball in particular was a focus of the community. Despite its relatively small population, Swissvale managed to field about a dozen Little League baseball teams.

During those spring and summer months on the baseball diamond, Rick Kuhn began to carve a reputation for himself. By the time he reached high school, he had developed into a bona fide pro pitching prospect. His successes on the playing fields, while guaranteeing him a certain degree of popularity among his fellow students, apparently did not go to his head.

"He was not really a loudmouth, didn't have a lot of braggadoccio for somebody of the caliber athlete he was," a former classmate recalls. "Not that he was a world-class athlete, particularly in basketball. But when you have a kid from a small town who gets a shot at the pros and plays college basketball, that's big news. But he never really seemed to do that. He was more quiet."

Though Swissvale was overwhelmingly white—by the late 1970s the town population was 94 percent white, according to one survey—Kuhn seemed to move smoothly between the different cliques of the school, a trait he would also exhibit at Boston College. He also is remembered as being particularly popular with members of the opposite sex.

Kuhn's scholastic basketball career was solid, if unspectacular. At Swissvale Area High School, eventually absorbed into neighboring Woodland Hills High in the late 1980s, he averaged fifteen points a game as a junior and eighteen as a senior. He graduated in 1973 and spent that summer and the next pursuing his dream of playing major league baseball in the Cincinnati Reds' farm system.

When shoulder problems derailed his baseball career and the Reds released him in the spring of 1975, Kuhn settled back in Swissvale and began attending the Boyce branch of the Community College of Allegheny County in suburban Monroeville, about fifteen minutes from Swissvale.

Kuhn had a good enough basketball season at CCAC during the winter of 1975–76—under coach Herb Sendek Sr., whose son, Herb Jr., currently is the head coach at North Carolina State—to attract the attention of Zuffelato, who was looking for a big man.

Zuffelato paid a visit to Swissvale and remembers being impressed with Kuhn's family. He also knew that Kuhn had been at a community college and had earned decent grades, which meant he would be able to play right away at Boston College instead of sitting out a season, as he would if he were transferring from another Division I school. Kuhn also would be able to benefit from an NCAA rule that allowed an athlete who had been paid to play one sport to retain his amateur standing and collegiate eligibility in another sport.

Zuffelato felt that Kuhn would fit perfectly with the team he was building.

"He was a bruiser. I thought he had a tremendous upside. In junior college he could score and he could rebound, and I felt that with our guards, it was a perfect match for us. When he came to visit, he liked what he saw. I just thought he was going to be a real fine player. He played right away for us."

By the time Kuhn arrived at Boston College, he had already had a bigger taste of the real world than any of his younger teammates.

"He had a little different take on basketball because of that," former B.C. coach Tom Davis says. "But he was really a good guy. Very willing and very pleasant, very easy to coach. Had a nice way about him. I think he was popular with the other players. I think they all thought a lot of Rick."

This may have been so, yet to some players, it also seemed odd that Kuhn, who never averaged in double figures during his three years at Boston College and didn't make up for it by demonstrating any leadership skills, was given so much playing time.

"You kind of look back and Coach Davis kind of idolized Rick," one teammate says. "He wasn't a great, talented basketball player. He was older than us. I don't know what it was. Maybe it was his age or because he was a little more worldly because he'd spent some time in the minor leagues. But for some reason, Coach would put Rick in the starting lineup. It was very strange.

"Maybe at the time that's what he thought we needed. Maybe he thought (Rick) was providing us with some kind of leadership. But he wasn't a vocal leader in any way."

Then there was the other side of Rick Kuhn, reflected in the people he hung out with, a group that frequently included friends from back home.

"He had some different friends," another teammate says. "He was the kind of guy who could be friendly with different types of people. I would say the core group of his friends were kind of off to the left a little bit, or off to the right. They weren't the mainstream people that most of us would be hanging around with. But that was Rick."

John Feudo was the president of the Boston College band that played at Roberts Center and sometimes accompanied the team on the road. He also did some public relations work for the athletic department. One of his occasional partners on the road was Doug Flutie, a communications major who would later become the school's most famous sports alumnus.

"You have to understand, this was a college atmosphere and the athletes mingled with the students," Feudo says. "For instance, one of the ways the lacrosse team would attract people to come to its games was to have a keg of beer on the sidelines for fans. So you would have half the football and basketball team there, hanging out around the keg."

"If I had to pick a guy I wouldn't trust with my life, (Rick) would be the one. I remember Rick as the kind of guy you wouldn't exactly look at and say, 'There's a guy I'd like to get to know; he looks like a nice guy.' He was not that easy to get close to if you were a fellow student."

Others noticed something a little risque, a little mysterious about Kuhn. Mayock remembers him as the type who "always had something going on the side." Another former B.C. basketball teammate was far from shocked when Kuhn's name was mentioned in early reports about the point-shaving investigation in 1981.

"I can see Rick Kuhn looking you square in the face and saying, 'Yeah, I'm trying my ass off,' and then sleeping like a baby at night," the teammate says. "With Sweeney, I just can't see him looking you straight in the face and telling you that and then throwing the ball off your leg.

"(Kuhn) came from a different crowd. I'm sure there were tough people from Pittsburgh who he knew pretty well. He never really spent a lot of time with guys on the team. He was, what, twenty-four years old? And here we are coming in, seventeen- and eighteen-year-old kids."

By the fall of 1978, Kuhn was even further removed from his teammates by the fact that he did not live on campus, but instead shared an apartment with Barbara Reed on Peterborough Street, a collection of three- and four-story brick walkups that is a long fly ball from the rightfield bleachers of Boston's Fenway Park.

Kuhn had met Reed, an attractive, dark-haired nursing student from Syracuse, at a party the previous fall and begun dating, and the relationship gradually turned serious enough that after Reed graduated from Boston College's School of Nursing in the spring of 1978, she moved back to Boston in the fall to live with Rick and work at a hospital in the working-class neighborhood of Dorchester.

Rocco Perla, a high school friend of Rick's from Swissvale, regularly visited Kuhn in Boston, and on one of these trips in the fall of 1977 he met Barbara Reed at a party at Rick's. He still remembers how on that first night, she told him that her best friend was the sister of William Hayes, the young American who had been arrested in Turkey for drug smuggling and was to be the subject of the movie *Midnight Express*, and how she knew details of the harrowing story before the book came out. Over the course of the next three years, Perla and his girlfriend (and later wife) Georgeanne would develop a close friendship with Reed.

"She was a nice kid, a real family-oriented person, very caring about people in general," Perla remembers. "She didn't really have anything mean to say about anybody, one of those people who's really nice to be around."

That niceness apparently was not always reciprocated, according to another friend who occasionally went to the apartment on Peterborough Street that fall for dinner, and remembered that Reed was a "really nice girl, but I got the impression Rick treated her like shit. He wasn't the greatest guy in the world, the way he treated her. I'll leave it at that. Kind of full of himself a little bit."

For all his swagger and worldliness, though, his former teammates also paint Kuhn as an easygoing, personable fellow. It is possible that this combination of good guy–bad guy was what initially attracted Sweeney to Kuhn. Where Sweeney's upbringing had consisted partly of resisting the temptations that existed all around him, perhaps he saw in Kuhn someone who appeared to have none of the same constraints and who already had sampled some forbidden fruit.

"For some reason, Jim was enthralled by Rick; he idolized him," Meggers remembers. "It's kind of weird. They were just two totally different people. Jimmy was the kind of kid where if you had a daughter, he'd be the guy you'd like to have marry her."

Mayock disputes this analysis of the Sweeney-Kuhn relationship.

"He and Jimmy roomed together on the road a lot, but I don't know if Jimmy ever looked up to him at all," he says. "(Rick) had played minor league baseball, he was a lot older than everybody else, he was streetsmart. I didn't particularly trust Rick, but then I didn't have to."

Trust would become the central issue for Sweeney and Kuhn soon enough, as they would be forced to place their faith in each other or risk the consequences.

CHAPTER TWO

The Meeting

Basketball practice began in mid-October at Boston College in the autumn of 1978, with the first game scheduled for late November. One day a few weeks after the beginning of practice, Sweeney and Kuhn made the short drive from the B.C. campus across the Charles River and into Harvard Square. Their objective was to enjoy the fall afternoon, look in a few stores, and generally take in the bustling atmosphere surrounding the small triangular piece of land that comprised the heart of the Square. It was an uneventful afternoon but for one brief moment. Out of the blue, Kuhn mentioned that he had some friends in Pittsburgh who were interested in betting on college basketball games, and would Sweeney be interested in helping the cause in return for money? In other words, would he be interested in shaving points?

The proposal caught Sweeney off-guard for a moment. Despite the choirboy image he enjoyed among his friends and classmates, he knew what point-shaving was, and he would often open the *Boston Globe* on the day of Boston College's games and look for the point spread to see which way the oddsmakers felt the game was going to turn out. But this was closer to home. This was coming from a teammate, and someone he considered a good friend. Was Rick serious? Was he really considering compromising himself and his teammates for the sake of a few dollars? Maybe he was just kidding around. Either way, Sweeney brushed off the overture, and nothing more was said about it that day.

A few weeks later, not long before the first game of the season, Kuhn approached Sweeney one day after practice and asked him if he'd like to meet some friends from Pittsburgh who were in town for a few days. Sweeney agreed to come along. Sweeney had noticed over the years that Rick seemed to have close ties with friends back home, and Jim had met a few over the years when they'd visited Boston. Just the previous month he had attended a Boston College–Pittsburgh football game with Kuhn and Rocco Perla, one of Rick's high school friends.

• • •

It was November 16, a Thursday, that Reed remembered Kuhn returning to the apartment after basketball practice and asking if he could borrow her van, an old, beat-up vehicle her father had given her for driving back and forth to Boston's Dorchester section, where she worked at a hospital.

Rick was wearing nice clothes that evening and was obviously going out to meet someone. When Reed asked where he was going, he replied offhandedly that he was "going to a meeting" and "going to dinner with some friends." When she asked which friends, Kuhn replied, "Never mind, you're not coming." He seemed excited, though, and his excitement momentarily overcame his attempts to be evasive. What he told her came as a surprise.

"There are some big gamblers in town who want to meet a couple of players," he said. "Sweens (his nickname for Sweeney) and I are going to meet them."

With that, Kuhn left and, after picking up Sweeney at his dorm on the B.C. campus, headed back toward downtown Boston, bypassing the city's clogged streets by taking the Massachusetts Turnpike east toward the airport. They took the Callahan Tunnel toward Logan International Airport, and after they emerged from the tunnel and neared the Logan Airport Hilton, Kuhn parked the van across the street. The two players entered the hotel lobby at about 7 P.M. and, after Kuhn spoke briefly with the desk clerk on duty, took the elevator upstairs.

When they reached the room, their knock was answered by a tall, stocky man with curly dark hair and a mustache. After he and Kuhn exchanged greetings, Kuhn introduced him to Sweeney as Tony Perla. Sweeney recognized the name from his previous meeting with Rocco Perla and figured the two must be brothers, though Tony seemed considerably older than Rocco. There was another man in the room, about 5-foot-9 with dark hair and a wiry build, who appeared keyed up and full of nervous energy. "This is Henry," Kuhn said to Sweeney.

Already, Henry's manner was making Sweeney a little nervous, but he tried to put it out of his mind. They were here to get a free meal and talk basketball, and things didn't get much better than that for two college kids subsisting on dining-commons food. They looked at the room service menu and, encouraged by Henry—who told them to order whatever they liked—chose lobster, the most expensive entrée.

Sweeney's initial impression of Henry can be summed up in one word.

"Unstable. That's the first word that comes to mind," Sweeney remembers. "He was the kind of person that made you nervous when you met him."

After they finished eating, the talk turned to basketball. Henry seemed particularly interested in how Sweeney and Kuhn felt Boston College would fare this year, and as he talked his questions began to get more and more detailed. What was the quality of the teams B.C. would be playing? How did Sweeney see his own role on the team? How much effect did he think he would have on the team's success? The questions seemed odd to Sweeney, who was used to people asking him how the team was going to fare, but never in this manner.

Henry was dominating the conversation at this point, and his slightly impatient manner seemed to indicate he was leading up to something. Eventually, it came.

"Did Rick talk to you about shaving points?" he asked Sweeney.

A look of uncertainty must have crossed Sweeney's face, because Henry began to use a more assuring tone. They weren't asking the two players to lose games, he said; they were only looking for them to hold down the score in games B.C. was going to win anyway.

They could make a lot of money, he told them. If they wanted to do it, it would be fine. If they didn't want to do it, it would be fine also. It was totally up to them.

As Sweeney listened to Henry's words, he noticed Kuhn wasn't saying anything. Suddenly, it all became clear to him. Kuhn, his friend and teammate, had set him up, and had offered him up to these men as someone who would go along with their scheme. Now, he was on the spot.

"I couldn't believe this was happening," Sweeney recalls. "I felt confusion, like, 'What am I doing here? I can't believe I'm having this conversation.'"

As Henry continued, Sweeney's head was spinning. They'd picked him because was he "the perfect front," they were saying, a scholar-athlete no one would ever suspect of being involved in point-shaving. If he cooperated, it would be "extremely financially rewarding"; "extremely powerful people" in New York were backing the operation. All the while, Perla, who had been mostly silent up to this point, kept nodding his head each time Henry made a new point.

"They didn't like the idea of losing games outright," Tony Perla would later say, "but they did indicate [that] on certain games there would be a large enough spread that they would and could very easily keep the games within a certain point spread."

Suddenly, Henry turned to Kuhn with a feigned look of alarm on his face.

"He's not wearing a wire, is he?" he said half-facetiously as he motioned in Sweeney's direction. "Maybe we should take him in the other room and search him." Kuhn and Henry laughed at the thought, while Sweeney managed a weak smile.

• • •

Downstairs, Paul Mazzei sat nursing a drink in the Hilton bar. His day had begun in Pittsburgh, wound its way through New York, and now he was sitting in a hotel in Boston as planes buzzed by, awaiting word on whether this point-shaving scheme was going to fly—and what he would have to do to ensure that it did.

It was then that Henry Hill entered the bar and told him he needed him to come upstairs and talk to Sweeney and Kuhn.

"We've got them all psyched up," Hill told him. "They're eager." Then, Hill told Mazzei he wanted him to pretend he was "the muscle man," or the payoff man from New York. This must have sounded like a joke to Mazzei; if anyone was born to play the part of a New York big shot it was Hill, the Brooklyn native with connections to the Lucchese crime family, not Mazzei (pronounced maze-ee), a small-time drug dealer from suburban Pittsburgh.

Mazzei was a little taken aback, and he told Hill, "I don't know nothing about playing basketball. I know how to bet on games and things like that, but I don't want to go in and talk to these guys. I don't know what to say." Mazzei also had a pretty good buzz going with the booze and the quaaludes he'd taken earlier that evening and was a little wary of going upstairs and flubbing his lines. But Hill assured him it would be fine, and the two men returned to the room.

When they got there, Mazzei found himself in a bizarre situation. There sat Kuhn, whom he knew from Pittsburgh, and Mazzei was supposed to come on like this big-timer from New York, which Kuhn knew he was not. But Mazzei played the part, introducing himself as "Paulie"—a name that struck Sweeney as odd, and which he would remember three years later in court—and began to tell them what he wanted them to do.

"I told them, 'Listen, you guys understand what you have to do,'" Mazzei recalled. "Throw the ball out of bounds, double-dribble . . . you know better than I do." He told the players they would receive twenty-five hundred dollars for each game they fixed, and that they could bet the money they'd earn and double their winnings. Mazzei remembered both of them nodding in agreement.

Remembering some advice he had gotten that afternoon in New York, Mazzei mentioned Ernie Cobb's name, and told them that for the scheme to work, they needed B.C.'s leading scorer on board. Kuhn said they'd "kicked it around" a little bit, and it was decided he would be the one to talk to Cobb. According to Mazzei, both Kuhn and Sweeney agreed to go along with the scheme that night.

He began talking about money, and how he could set up a separate bank account for them to handle the payments. At this point Kuhn began asking questions: How much money would they get for each game? Who would pay them, and how would the payments be made?

Hill spoke up. He reiterated what Mazzei had said, that the payoff would be twenty-five hundred dollars for each game that was successfully fixed. Tony Perla would be the conduit for the money and would pass along the point spreads to Kuhn before each game. Were they in?

At first, Sweeney said nothing. His mind raced, his thoughts jumping from one possibility to another. *What if he said no? Would they let him leave the hotel? What would Rick say? What would his other teammates say? What would Henry's "extremely powerful" friends in New York do?*

Would they threaten his family back in New Jersey? What if he agreed to cooperate but then told Coach Davis?

Sweeney either said, "Okay," or just nodded his head. Hill later said that Sweeney "didn't object" to the proposal. Kuhn remembered Sweeney at first "not knowing what to say," but that once he was offered the money he went along. Sweeney's tone must have betrayed his uncertainty, however, because when Kuhn and Perla left the room for a few minutes, Hill made an attempt to soothe Sweeney's frayed nerves.

"Don't worry," Hill said, "just cooperate with us and everything will be fine. Just don't breathe a word of this to anyone." Sweeney recalled Mazzei repeating to him, "I like you, I like you. We've got the perfect front in you. We did our homework. Nobody's going to suspect someone like you."

Sweeney also remembered Henry adding a warning: "Don't make matters difficult for yourself, or we can make matters difficult for you."

• • •

Henry Hill offered a slightly different description of Sweeney and Kuhn when he talked to *Sports Illustrated*'s Doug Looney in 1981. He remembered both players telling him how they felt they weren't going to make the pros, so they might as well make some money while they could. He also described them as savvy, eager, and fully aware of what they were about to do.

"They couldn't wait," he claimed. "You talk about being ready. . . . They knew who I was and why I was there. They knew I was the one with the connections to get the bets down, and they kept asking me to make sure to get bets down for them in addition to the twenty-five hundred we promised for every game. They talked about shaving points and betting lines and the odds so casually, I had the feeling they had been doing this stuff since high school.

"The thing that got me was they were familiar with the betting, they knew about spreads, they were not dumb kids. They knew how to shave, because when I tried to explain to them they said, 'Naw, we know all that shit.'"

When Kuhn and Perla returned to the room, someone—later there would be much ado over exactly who—produced a Boston College schedule card, the wallet-sized kind the school's athletic department printed in the thousands, for players and fans to carry in their wallets. Hill immediately began to circle the games for which a gambling line would be set in Las Vegas, games against major schools like Connecticut and Holy Cross as opposed to smaller schools like Bentley or Stonehill, B.C.'s first two opponents. For the latter games, bookmakers wouldn't bother to set a point spread, chiefly because it was impossible for them to be familiar enough with every tiny school in the country to make an accurate line, and betting interest would probably be minimal anyway.

"I asked which of the upcoming games they felt we could shave," Hill recalled later. "Sweeney took out one of those little schedule cards, circled the games he thought we could fool around with, and gave the card to me. They kept saying that they liked the idea of just shaving points and not blowing the games."

Hill sticks to his story that it was Sweeney who circled the games on the schedule. He also claims that Sweeney accepted five hundred dollars from him—as did Kuhn—as a "good faith" gesture from the gamblers.

"I'm positive," Hill says. "He denied taking the five hundred dollars. . . . I gave him five hundred dollars and I gave Kuhn five hundred dollars that night. And I gave Kuhn about an ounce of coke also. Sweeney circled the games that he felt that price was going to be enough where he could shave (points). Because it wasn't every game that they'd be favored enough that they could shave four or five points. Because that's all we were looking for. We weren't looking for them to dump any games."

• • •

Hill noticed that B.C.'s first major opponent was Providence College, on December 6. The Friars had been a perennial New England power during the early- to mid-1970s—with players like Ernie DiGregorio, Marvin Barnes, and Kevin Stacom—but had slipped during the latter part of the decade. Still, they were a big enough name that there would be a point spread on the game, and that was all Hill and Perla needed to know.

They agreed that the Providence game would be a test, a trial game to see if the scheme would work. Perla told Kuhn he would call him on the afternoon of the game and relay the point spread to him. The rest was up to the players.

As they were getting ready to leave, Sweeney saw Hill hand Kuhn some money, though he couldn't see how much. Hill would testify he gave Kuhn six hundred dollars as good-faith money, "because he was a nice guy. And I was trying to be a nice guy." He also said he gave Kuhn a quarter-ounce of cocaine. Kuhn, meanwhile, gave Hill his phone number in Boston.

• • •

By the time Kuhn and Sweeney left the Hilton it was after 11 o'clock, and Kuhn was in an animated mood, talking excitedly about all the money they were going to make and how easy it would be. Sweeney could tell from his friend's demeanor that he had been looking forward to this night, probably for quite some time.

Sweeney, meanwhile, was still having a hard time believing what he'd just seen and heard. But he was sure of one thing: He'd just gotten himself into something that was bigger and scarier than anything else he'd ever done. He'd let this Henry, this fast-talking con man, talk him into doing something that went against everything he stood for.

"I've played that scenario over a hundred times in my mind," Sweeney says today. "I may have been young and impressionable, but I certainly wasn't so blind that I couldn't figure out the makeup of this individual."

Kuhn, on the other hand, seemed jubilant, as if they'd just won a big game. When they got to where Barbara's van was parked across from the Hilton, he pointed to a Cadillac parked across the street. "See that?" he said. "We can make enough money to buy one of those in cash."

As they rode home, Sweeney remembered Kuhn pulling out a wad of bills from his pocket that Henry had given him. He offered Sweeney three hundred dollars, which he said was half of the total amount. Sweeney declined. Years later, Kuhn would claim he had only been given one hundred dollars by Perla and then offered Sweeney fifty, but to Sweeney, taking the money in any amount would have been like signing his name on the bottom of a contract. He wanted more than anything for the events of the previous few hours to become a distant memory as soon as possible. He swears he refused the money.

It was after midnight when Kuhn returned to the apartment on Peterborough Street. Reed couldn't help but notice his excitement.

"Kid"—that was his nickname for her—"I had a good time," he said. "These guys treated us great," recounting how "Paul" had gotten him high.

Reed saw him count out "at least" $250. He showed her the money Henry had given him and assured her, "The future is going to be better. Bills are going to be paid." He told her "there would be more where that came from," and that "over the summer he had discussed an idea with his friend Rocco and Rocco's brother Tony for the upcoming season that involved betting."

Reed apparently bought Kuhn's explanation of what would be referred to for the rest of the season as "the betting thing." She assumed that Rick meant he would be offering the Perlas inside information on the games, giving his opinion on which teams he thought Boston College had a good chance to beat so they could win their bets. He had played the year before, after all, and would know the strengths and weaknesses of the teams on B.C.'s schedule.

Gradually, though, Reed would realize that much more was afoot, but for now, it seemed harmless enough. Besides, Rick had told her that Jim Sweeney was involved in the plan, and the Jim Sweeney she watched on the court and occasionally cooked dinner for at the apartment hardly seemed like the kind of person who would do anything improper.

"I asked him if he was doing something wrong, and he said that he would tell people how he thought the team looked in practice or how they had done the last time they played, and he'd give them his idea of who would win the game," Reed said later. "These men were gamblers and they bet on games based on his advice, and if they won, they'd share some of the money with him and Sweeney."

Then Kuhn asked her, "Would Sweeney do anything wrong?"

Over the next few days, Kuhn took Reed on a shopping spree to the Natick Mall outside of Boston and began thinking of what he was going to buy when the rest of the money came in. Sweeney, meanwhile, was thinking of how he wished he could go back to that Thursday evening and the meeting with Perla and Henry and tell them that no, he really wasn't interested in doing what they wanted him to do. But he knew that wasn't going to happen, so he went about his business and prayed that somehow the whole thing would blow over. And all the while he counted the days until December 6, when Boston College would face Providence.

• • •

What Sweeney and Kuhn probably did not know on November 16, 1978, was that they had already committed a crime just by being at the meeting and giving their assent to the plan put forth by Perla and Hill. What they should have known was that they had just set in motion events that would irrevocably alter the rest of their lives, and that would ultimately land five men behind bars.

Furthermore, from that evening forward the relationship between the two friends would be fundamentally altered. Kuhn's and Sweeney's paths would diverge drastically as time went on, until ultimately, Kuhn—the guy who seemed to always have an angle—would pay the heaviest price for his loyalty to his friends, while Sweeney would emerge unpunished largely because he blew the whistle on his former buddy.

For nearly two years, though, no one breathed a word about what had happened at the hotel that night, except to a few close friends. If the strain of keeping such a damaging secret weighed heavily on Kuhn, it must have been a crushing burden for Sweeney, whose life had always been defined by doing the right thing, the responsible thing, the proper thing, to get where he wanted to go and to please the many people who had come to expect so much from him.

Now, suddenly, he found himself confronted with a situation where he was not in control of his own destiny, and where divulging his participation in something so sordid and so against his principles would have shattered not only the image others had of him, but the image he had of himself.

CHAPTER THREE

The Man from New York

In the summer of 1978, eight years before he would become history's most famous Mafia turncoat with the publication of *Wiseguy*, Henry Hill was just another mobster in prison, languishing in a federal penitentiary in Lewisburg, Pennsylvania, a stone's throw from prestigious Bucknell University but hundreds of miles and a world away from his natural habitat.

Hill's connections to the Mafia dated back to his early teenage years in the 1950s, when Brooklyn was fully in the grip of organized crime. It did not take long for the enterprising youngster to fill up a lengthy and varied rap sheet with entries for an army court martial (in 1962), larceny, transporting untaxed cigarettes, bookmaking, loan-sharking, assault, arson, robbery, truck hijacking, and extortion. It was the latter crime that earned him a prison sentence of ten years, of which he served four (1974–78) at Lewisburg and nearby Allenwood, where, among other hobbies, he dealt in narcotics and bribed prison officials.

That Hill was able to operate for so long with such relative impunity—the extortion conviction was the only real time he served—was due to his connection with the Lucchese family, one of New York's six organized crime families that had controlled the city's rackets since the early 1930s. Heavily involved in the garment industry as well as in the traditional Mafia strongholds of loan-sharking, gambling, and labor racketeering, the Lucchese family in 1978 was headed by Anthony "Tony Ducks" Corallo, whose nickname allegedly stemmed from his knack for ducking the authorities—though he, too, would eventually wind up behind bars in 1987 on a racketeering conviction.

Douglas Behm was a young prosecutor in the Brooklyn DA's office in the late 1970s when he was chosen to work with the Organized Crime Strike Force of the Eastern District of New York, part of a nationwide network of agencies established between 1967 and 1971 and designed to monitor and prosecute mob activity. In the spring and summer of 1980, one of Behm's primary projects was Henry Hill, who by then had come in from the cold and was preparing to begin a second career as the government's star witness in a host of trials.

Behm remembers a character who bore little resemblance to the one portrayed in print and on the big screen.

"I watched (the movie) *Goodfellas*, and he kind of came off as a lovable schlemiel. Henry was not a lovable schlemiel," Behm says. "Henry was a dangerous guy, and there was an atmosphere of danger around him. I remember when we first met with the FBI agents, one of the first things I said to them was, 'This guy's got a shtick, and he's good at it, but be careful with this guy.' He was a street guy in the ultimate sense of the word. He was a creature of the street. He was a creature of the environment that he grew up in, and which, to a certain extent, he chose for himself."

Early in his two-decade odyssey of crime, Hill met James Burke, who would become his partner and confidant and whom he ultimately would help put behind bars for the rest of Burke's life. Burke was something of a paradox, a man who by many accounts was a loving husband and doting father who helped out with his son Jesse's Cub Scout troop, but who also was considered to be as ruthless and cold-blooded as anyone operating in organized crime in New York.

Burke, who was thirteen years Hill's senior, was something of a mentor to the young, aspiring hood. His childhood, as described by lawyer Anthony Lombardino at a sentence reduction hearing in 1984, made Hill's seem blessed by comparison. It began with an assault at the hands of his father when Burke was an infant. The father soon deserted the family, and the young Burke spent the next several years in a succession of foster homes until finally, by age fourteen, he was essentially fending for himself. By the time Hill was five, Burke, after numerous scrapes as a juvenile, already was serving five years in an upstate prison for passing bad checks.

"Jimmy taught me every bad habit I had," Hill recalls. "I was like a brother to the guy. We used to be at the racetrack six days a week. From the racetrack we'd go to the crap games, from the crap games we'd be looking for bookmakers.

"We were together literally every day of our life from (the mid-'60s) on. He was one of the most feared guys in New York City at the time. No one fucked with Jimmy Burke. Plus he had the Queens District Attorney's office in the palm of his hand. There were twelve special investigators out of the DA's office, and Jimmy had every one of them on the payroll. The day it came out that I was in the Witness Protection Program, four of them put resignations in."

Burke became something of a legendary figure in mob and law enforcement circles in the 1960s and '70s, partly for his cold-blooded demeanor, but also for the scope of his criminal activity and the zeal with which he approached his work. FBI mob informants portrayed Burke as a one-man crime wave in Brooklyn and Queens whose résumé included running a truck hijacking crew for Lucchese family capo Paul Vario, among other highlights. Though Burke's Irish ancestry precluded his becoming a full-fledged member of the Lucchese family, he was apparently considered such a good earner that he commanded more respect than most of the family's ranking members. One informant went so far as to call Burke the largest importer of untaxed cigarettes in New York City in the 1960s.

Had their day-to-day business not consisted primarily of figuring out new and creative ways to circumvent the law and occasionally busting a few heads along the way, Burke and Hill might have seemed like any other buddies living and working and socializing in any one of a hundred working-class neighborhoods in New York City's outer boroughs.

Burke lived with his wife, Frances, and their four children in a one-family house on 160th Avenue in Howard Beach, Queens, about a ten-minute drive from Hill's childhood home in Brooklyn. Ten minutes to the south, in Canarsie, was Geffkens, the bar/restaurant where Vario worked as a cook after his release from prison in the mid-1970s. Ten minutes to the north of the Burke home was Robert's Lounge, on Lefferts Boulevard in Ozone Park, where authorities videotaped Hill and Burke meeting frequently with other Lucchese family associates. Fifteen minutes east of Robert's sat Hill's house in the quiet residential community of Rockville Centre, Long Island, where he lived with his wife, Karen, and their two daughters.

The backstretch of Aqueduct Racetrack was practically within walking distance of both Burke's house and Robert's, but it was nearby John F. Kennedy Airport and the innumerable money-making opportunities it represented that was of primary importance.

Much has been written and depicted about the extent of truck hijacking and other crimes against property that occurred at JFK during the 1960s and '70s. But according to Behm, who was in charge of investigations into corruption and racketeering at the airport, the Wild West, shoot-'em-up exploits of Hill and Burke were hardly the primary focus of the feds.

"There was a lot of that, but that was Henry's street view," Behm said. "That's what Henry saw. Henry saw the robbing and the hijacking and the cargo theft. And there certainly was a lot of that. But from the federal standpoint, we felt the locals could deal with that. What they couldn't handle, what nobody could handle up until that point, was the labor racketeering that was going on at Kennedy Airport."

The Lucchese family controlled the labor rackets at the airport, extorting millions of dollars in payments from shipping companies who ultimately threatened to desert the airport and use Boston or Philadelphia instead. Compared to the prospect of New York's major international airport withering up and dying in the face of the power wielded by the mob-controlled labor rackets, even the $5.8 million Lufthansa robbery late in 1978 took on less importance.

"Lufthansa, as glamorous as it was, was just a glamorous low-level theft," Behm continued. "Henry was getting to see the stuff that was falling off the back of a truck. Vario and those guys were at a much higher level. Henry was a street guy. Henry was not sophisticated. Henry did what Henry was told to do.

"People look [at Henry Hill] and say, 'Oh, wow, he's that big mob guy.' And I say, 'Yeah, but compared to the real guys, he was nothing.'"

• • •

Hill's and Burke's luck ran out in 1972 when both were arrested and convicted of extortion, stemming from a trip to Florida in which they had strong-armed a gambler who was delinquent on his payments. Hill's ten-year sentence landed him in Lewisburg, where he came to know another man who would eventually become a close friend and partner, and who would interest Hill in a scheme to fix college basketball games.

Shorter and stockier than Hill and lacking enough hair to earn the nickname "Kojak," Paul Mazzei was in his early thirties and serving a five-year sentence for selling LSD in Pittsburgh when he met Henry Hill at Lewisburg in the mid-1970s. Before going to jail, Mazzei had trained to be a court stenographer, but this early brush with the right side of the law apparently did little to dampen his enthusiasm for participating in a wide assortment of criminal activities, ranging from dealing in illegal weapons and robbery to receiving stolen property.

Before mentioning the point-shaving scheme, Mazzei began cultivating a friendship with Hill that he eventually was able to exploit for his own ends when he got out of jail in 1977 and returned to Pittsburgh to resume selling drugs. But Hill made out well on the deal, too; all he did was allow Mazzei to use his name as a reference to gain credibility with some of the other drug dealers in Pittsburgh. In return, Hill would get fifteen hundred or two thousand dollars every few weeks from Mazzei. (Hill later found out that the Pittsburgh people thought Mazzei, who called Hill "Paul from New York," was connected to New York mob kingpin Paul Castellano.)

It was a sweetheart deal for Hill. "I figured, 'Look at this fucking guy—how sweet is this?'" he remembers.

According to Mazzei's description, life at Lewisburg was not unlike summer camp. He spoke in 1984 of how every so often he would climb a fence—the prison had no bars or barbed wire—and walk about a mile to a place where he would pick up a duffel bag filled with vodka, whiskey, salami, and cheese. Frequently there would be another bag containing an ounce or two of marijuana alongside the duffel bag, which Mazzei recalled Hill using to pay off the gambling debts he habitually incurred.

When Mazzei was paroled in the spring of 1977, he went back to Pittsburgh and enrolled in dog-grooming classes at Professional Beauty Supplies, with an eye on starting his own business. He trained on the job for nine months, and ultimately secured a loan to buy a business called Plush Puppy, which he would later describe, apparently without irony, as "a sophisticated dog-grooming school, something like on the style of Harvard."

Unfortunately for Mazzei, the old habits died hard, and after his release from prison he had been unable to stay away from the drug business even as he pursued his dog-grooming career. Once Hill was released from prison in the summer of '78, Mazzei became Hill's Pittsburgh connection in a drug operation that authorities would later estimate handled more than $1.5 million worth of product by early 1980.

The underground drug economy requires an army of lower-level operators to make it thrive, like twenty-eight-year-old Anthony Perla, a resident of the Pittsburgh suburb of Wilkinsburg. In a way, Perla's life was the American Dream gone awry. On the surface, he was an upstanding citizen who held three college degrees from Edinboro University and the University of Pittsburgh and worked as a librarian at General Braddock Junior High in Braddock, Pennsylvania. But much of his spare time was spent augmenting his modest librarian's salary through various extralegal means.

Perla owned a restaurant-lounge in suburban Swissvale in the mid-1970s, and once was arrested (but not charged) for possession of an illegal horoscope machine. By 1980 he owned 25 percent of a vending-machine business with his father and two of his three sons that purveyed games like Pac-Man and video poker machines.

It was in drugs and gambling, however, that Tony Perla demonstrated true business acumen. While he earned approximately eleven thousand dollars a year as a librarian, Perla estimated that his drug business brought in an extra twenty thousand dollars a year, and that his bookmaking operation was even more lucrative, earning him about thirty or forty thousand dollars annually. Perla had been a partner of Paul Mazzei's since the early '70s, and admitted selling marijuana by the pound during his heyday, though he claimed he never sold it to students in the school district where he worked.

Rocco Perla was eight years younger than his brother Tony, and in the summer of '78 was working at the Maytag appliance store that his father, Rocco Sr., owned in Swissvale. He had gone to Swissvale Area High School, where he had an undistinguished athletic career as a junior-varsity basketball player. Rocco was involved peripherally, if at all, in his brother's various schemes and scams, but he would play an important role in the Boston College point-shaving conspiracy because of his friendship with a star pitcher and basketball player from Swissvale named Rick Kuhn.

• • •

Rocco Perla remembers hanging out with Kuhn during the summer of 1978, sometimes at Tony's house and sometimes at Rocco's parents'. One day, Paul Mazzei was over at Tony's and noticed the hulking Kuhn. His gambler's mind put two and two together, and just like that, the Boston College point-shaving conspiracy was born.

"He looked at this guy and said, 'Man, this guy is a monster, what's he do?'" Rocco remembers. "Paul was always looking for an edge, always looking for an angle to do something, and I think that's what spawned the idea. It was more by happenstance than anything else. I would have to say

Paul Mazzei was the one who dreamt up the whole thing. I can certainly say it was not me, and it was not Rick. And I'm pretty certain it wasn't my brother who thought of it initially."

Whether or not Tony Perla spent the summer of 1978 "cultivating" Kuhn for his role in the point-shaving scheme is up to debate. Both men denied a father-son or mentor-pupil relationship that newspaper and magazine reports would later describe. When it came out in 1981 that Kuhn had been driving a pink Cadillac in the summer of '78, it was theorized that he had been given the car by Perla as an inducement to join the plot; but Barbara Reed remembered Kuhn telling her that the car had come from David Ludwig, a contractor who employed Rick during part of the summer. Whether it had been bought, borrowed, or stolen depended on which story Rick was telling at the time.

After three brief discussions with Perla during July and August, Kuhn claimed he did not discuss the plot again until the week of the meeting at the Logan Airport Hilton in mid-November. On one of those three occasions, Perla dropped Kuhn at Paul Mazzei's house in the Pittsburgh suburbs where Mazzei lived with his girlfriend, Joan Thompson. Perla left soon after dropping Kuhn off, and Kuhn assumed he went to talk to someone else about the scheme; but even if that assumption was incorrect, it was clear that Mazzei, an inveterate gambler who was hardly likely to turn away a chance to indulge his vice, was the latest player in a drama that now extended from Pittsburgh to Lewisburg and was making its way toward New York.

• • •

Four hundred miles to the east, Hill was back in business in Brooklyn, set up with a no-show job by Paul Vario at a nightclub run by Philip Basile, another character who within a few years would join the ranks of those convicted on the strength of Hill's testimony.

Hill had been released from Lewisburg in the middle of July, and he was eager to make up for lost time and begin earning again. Mazzei, his former prison buddy, had a steady supply of marijuana and cocaine that Hill could sell back in New York. There was no time to waste, so Hill slipped out of the Community Treatment Center in Manhattan, a halfway house where, in his words, "for ten dollars you could walk out anytime you wanted," and flew to Pittsburgh within a day or two of his release.

Though it is not clear whether the point-shaving scheme was discussed during Hill's initial trip to Pittsburgh or on a subsequent one, at some point in late July or August, Hill met Tony Perla over drinks at Mazzei's duplex and the basics were laid out for him. Perla told Hill his younger brother had gone to high school with one of the Boston College players who "wanted to do business" for the upcoming season. Mazzei and Perla also told Hill that they needed him to add some muscle to the operation because, in Hill's words, they couldn't bet enough money in Pittsburgh to pay the players without the local bookies getting suspicious. Mazzei, at least, would have known by now that Hill was connected with people like Vario and Burke in New York, and it seemed logical to use those connections to further the scheme.

One can imagine Hill in all his glory, playing the role of big-city tough guy to the hilt as the two rubes from the back country essentially asked for his blessing on the plot. Conversely, Perla might not have known Jimmy Burke or Paul Vario if they showed up on his doorstep, but he must have thought that he was finally entering the big time, for here was a real, live New York mobster having a drink with him and listening to his plan.

"Tony, I thought, was pretty hip," Hill remembered. "He was a sharp kid. At that point I thought I could do some business with these guys. I was a little skeptical of Paul. But when I met Perla and I met Kuhn, I knew this thing was going to fly."

Hill's suspicions about Mazzei lend an insight into wiseguy etiquette. There was a story going around that Mazzei had testified against some people in Pittsburgh before he went to prison, and Hill had been advised to stay away from Mazzei by a member of the Pittsburgh mob who also was doing time in Lewisburg. Yet the prospect of a new revenue stream from the B.C. scheme seemed to override any second thoughts Hill and Burke might have had.

"That basically is a rule of thumb with all greedy wiseguys," Hill says. "It's the truth. They didn't give a fuck if he was a rat bastard, as long as he never ratted on them. And Jimmy heard the story, too, because I was whacking up what I was getting from him to Jimmy. He didn't give a fuck if this kid ratted on some pot dealer in Pittsburgh. Who gave a fuck?

"Paul was a quaalude addict and a coke addict, a pretty loose horse. . . . But I figured we got something big here, if we played it right. I knew we could make a nice score with these kids. And then when I met Kuhn and he said he could get the captain, I said, 'Wow, that's it. This is a fucking sure thing.'"

The basic plan was for Hill to handle the money and Perla to handle the players, with Mazzei as the go-between. It sounded easy enough, except that Hill's end was somewhat more complicated. Betting on college basketball in the late 1970s was not nearly as heavy as it is today, which meant that any bookmaker probably would spot something suspicious the second time big money came in against Boston College from one of his regular customers.

In order for the scheme to work, then, Hill would have to set up a network of bookmakers, all of whom were in on the scam, who could handle large bets and "lay them off"—trade bets, basically—with other unsuspecting bookmakers around the country without arousing suspicion. If there was one group of people Hill was familiar with, it was bookies, but it would still be a daunting task. And, if there were any difficulties with any of the bookies, all of whom had goons at their disposal to collect unpaid debts—Hill himself had been one at one time—Hill would have to provide protection for the players and gamblers involved in the scheme. The New

York faction, represented by Hill, Burke, and others connected to the Lucchese family, would front the money initially to pay the players. Mazzei would deliver the money to Pittsburgh to Tony Perla, who would funnel it to the players directly or through his brother Rocco. The same process would be used for the passing of the point spread from Burke and Hill to the players.

In theory, it sounded simple enough. In practice, however, it became something else entirely. To start with, the bookmakers all wanted a piece of the action, and, according to Hill, their numbers swelled as the season progressed, to the point where it became increasingly difficult for the gamblers to spread their money around. Even when things worked smoothly, it took a concerted effort.

• • •

As summer turned to autumn and Sweeney and Kuhn and their teammates returned to Boston for the fall semester, Mazzei was chewing up the miles between Pittsburgh and New York, traveling about four or five times a month to meet with Hill and oversee the drug operation. Meanwhile, Hill mentioned the point-shaving plan to Burke, who had returned from prison in Atlanta in mid-October to a hero's welcome from the old gang. Hill described the mechanics of the scheme, and remembered Burke being "very enthused" about the idea. Burke told him to "keep it quiet," and that he would speak to Paul Vario about giving his approval to the plan.

The Pittsburgh–New York connection moved one step closer to being realized on the weekend of November 4 when Mazzei flew to New York to meet with Hill. One of the highlights of the weekend was a party at Burke's house celebrating his return from prison. One of the partiers at Burke's that night was Peter Vario, Paul Vario's son.

"There was a lot of hugging and kissing going on," Mazzei said later. "Everybody was kind of glad that Jimmy had gotten out of prison and was home with his family."

The day after Burke's party, Mazzei and Hill went to Robert's Lounge, where they met Burke as well as bookmakers Nick "Iron Shoes" Botta and Martin Krugman. At this meeting, Mazzei said he went into the men's room with Burke and gave him five thousand dollars—"I knew he had just gotten out of prison and knew he could use a few dollars," Mazzei said. When the discussion got around to the point-shaving scheme, Burke said he wanted to meet Tony Perla and get the story from "the horse's mouth."

Later on the same day, Mazzei and Hill went to Geffken's, the bar where Paul Vario had been working since his release from prison. Though Mazzei was excluded from their conversation, on the way back to the Holiday Inn in Rockville Centre, Hill told Mazzei that Vario had given him the okay to set up a network of bookies to execute the plot, but that they would have to run the proposition past Peter Vario, and also Richard Perry, a Lucchese associate whose specialty was gambling.

After Mazzei returned to Pittsburgh, Hill had several discussions with various bookies at Robert's Lounge and at Bobby's Restaurant at twenty-seventh Street and Seventh Avenue in Manhattan, an establishment owned by bookmaker Milton Wekar. Wekar was skeptical about the scheme initially, but agreed to go along.

A week and a half later, the curtain officially rose on the plot. Hotel records from the Sunrise Motor Inn in Lynbrook, not far from Hill's home in Rockville Centre, reflect that Mazzei and Perla arrived in town on Wednesday, November 15. By this time the word from Kuhn was that Sweeney was interested in participating. This statement would later be contested by Sweeney, making it possible that Kuhn had already started to embellish the truth when he spoke to Perla—or that Sweeney was doing a good job of disguising his true intentions.

Hill picked the two men up at the hotel on Thursday morning, November 16, and drove to Robert's, arriving around 11:00. By noon, several other people had arrived, including Burke, Krugman, Botta, and Peter Vario, whom Mazzei recognized from the party at Burke's two weeks earlier. Mazzei told Burke and Vario that his friend Tony, "the horse's mouth," was here, if they wanted to talk to him.

"We're looking for Richie Perry," Mazzei remembered Burke saying. "We don't know where he is right now." Vario added, "He was supposed to have been here. We have to find him."

Vario also said something to Mazzei that caught Mazzei off-guard.

"I'm not sure about your friend over there at the bar," Vario said, referring to Perla. "He looks like a cop to me."

Mazzei was incredulous.

"A cop? You mean I flew all the way up to New York and brought a cop here?" he asked angrily. The remark stung Mazzei. "That's crazy. Listen, I'm going to sit at the bar with my friend and you guys decide what you want to do here and let me know," Mazzei said, and went over to sit with Perla.

When he told Perla about the conversation that had just transpired, the whole scheme nearly collapsed before it started. "Let's get out of here," an angry Perla said. But Mazzei, perhaps envisioning his carefully laid plan about to go up in smoke, urged Perla to reconsider.

"Let's wait and see what happens," he pleaded. Perla relented, and decided to go out and get something to eat. He was gone about twenty minutes, and by the time he returned, eating a sandwich, Richie Perry had been located at Aqueduct, and they were going to follow Vario there to meet with him. Hill told his Pittsburgh guests that Perry "knew all about basketball and knew about fixing." Perla and Mazzei went in Hill's car and followed Vario to Aqueduct.

For a man whose gambling instincts were held in such high regard by his peers, thirty-three-year-old Richard Perry seemed to have an uncanny habit of being in the wrong place at the wrong time. In 1974, he was one of only two people convicted out of twenty-eight who were indicted on charges of fixing horse races at Yonkers Raceway, and served six months in jail. By the late 1980s he would be involved in bringing unwanted publicity to the Nevada–Las Vegas program through various indiscretions. But Perry, who sometimes went by "Sam Perry" but was referred to by those who knew him as "Richie the Fixer," had coached in the New York–area summer leagues that fed the big-time college programs and developed a reputation as a shrewd judge of basketball talent. He also was an inveterate gambler who always seemed to have an angle on whatever big games were going on around the country. Hill and others considered him a handicapping genius.

When the entourage arrived at Aqueduct, Hill found Perry near the betting windows and brought Mazzei over and introduced him, while Perla took a seat on a bench about fifteen or twenty feet away. Mazzei then described the scheme to Perry and said he hoped Perry would accompany them to Boston that night to meet the players. Perry replied that although he was busy that night, he was interested.

Perry was holding a college basketball preseason magazine, the kind that listed all the teams' rosters and the scoring averages of their returning players. He suggested to Mazzei that they get Ernie Cobb involved, seeing as Cobb was the team's leading returning scorer. At this point, Mazzei did not even know who Cobb was—which couldn't have impressed Perry—but the advice sounded reasonable. Mazzei also asked Perry if paying the players twenty-five hundred dollars per game—which is what he, Perla, and Hill had agreed to so far—was fair, and Perry agreed that it was. Perry also said he would be able to bet in the vicinity of twenty to twenty-five hundred dollars per game, and perhaps as much as thirty-five hundred, which sounded great to Mazzei.

Tony Perla, meanwhile, watched from his bench a short distance away and tried to decipher what was being said by reading hand signals and body language. Perla already had decided that the tall, lanky Perry, who towered over the other men, and the shorter, chunkier Vario resembled Laurel and Hardy.

The four men spoke for close to an hour, a good portion of which was spent trying to convince Perry to go to Boston with them to meet the players, according to Mazzei. At one point Mazzei began to relay questions to Perla and give the answers back to Perry and Vario. Perry wanted to know which players were involved, and Perla answered, through Mazzei, that the players' names were Kuhn and Sweeney. Perry heard this and asked if Cobb was involved, and Perla remembered Perry saying, "You've got to get him."

Mazzei then made a bold move, or so he later claimed. He told Perry how Perla had been unfairly maligned back at Robert's, and that now Perry was claiming he was too busy to go up to Boston. "I don't know how serious you guys are about this," Mazzei later said he told Perry and Vario. "As far as I'm concerned I think you're serious about it, but to show good faith, I've got to ask you for a few dollars for some expense money. This money, you'll make me feel good, and [show me] you want to get involved in this thing."

Mazzei claimed that Perry and Vario then reached into their pockets and came up with about three or four hundred dollars between them. Mazzei, Hill, and Perla, who had gone out to the parking lot about fifteen or twenty minutes earlier, then left the racetrack and went to the airport to get the shuttle to Boston. Hill announced that he would be going to Boston instead of Perry.

The three men arrived in Boston before dinnertime. Perla, using his father's address of 1211 Kings Avenue, Pittsburgh, registered for two adjoining rooms and paid in cash. Identification, however, was given by Hill, who produced a government ID numbered 178-30-6241—no small irony in itself, as it certainly was not the last time Hill would use the government to further his ends.

• • •

After the players left the hotel at about 10:30 or 11:00 that night, Hill, Perla, and Mazzei ordered some more drinks from room service, then snorted some cocaine. Hill called Burke in New York to give him the report of the meeting, but Burke wasn't home, so Hill left the Hilton's phone number and went to sleep at about 3 or 4 A.M.

The phone rang the next morning a little before 8 A.M. It was Burke asking how things had gone the night before.

"I met the kids," Hill told him. "Everything is good."

CHAPTER FOUR

The Scene

To anyone weaned on college basketball in the late 1990s, the 1970s might as well be the 1870s for all their perceived relevance to today's game. Form-fitting shorts—Daisy Dukes, in hoop slang— are the dominant nostalgic image offered from an era that came before the shot clock and the three-point line sucked most of the variety out of the college game and produced the homogenized version fans are spoon-fed today.

Yet there was something wonderfully unpredictable about college basketball in the Me Decade. Combination defenses, box-and-ones, full-court pressure, the four-corners stall, matchup zones, weaves, even basic maneuvers such as the pick-and-roll still had some currency, long before the game turned into a slam-dunk contest for players making one- and two-year stopovers on their way to the NBA.

The differences in playing styles meant that on a Saturday night in Worcester, Massachusetts, Holy Cross could score 95 points and lose, while two hundred miles south in New Jersey, Princeton could score 42 points and win. Or, two teams might each decide to slow things down and produce a 12–7 game, which happened every so often.

"The beauty of college basketball has always been its variety," says George Blaney, who coached those Holy Cross teams for more than twenty years spanning the '70s, '80s, and '90s. "John Thompson was pressure, Dave Gavitt was mixing defenses, John Chaney was the zone, Dean Smith was the innovator. All those kinds of things. But as you put the clock in, and as you put in the three-point line, it brings about a sameness.

"The threat of (Princeton coach) Pete Carril holding the ball for three minutes was greater than the fact that he actually held the ball. Most of the time he actually held the ball about twenty-five seconds, but the threat of them holding it for fifty seconds made you play a different kind of defense. So there was tremendous variety in the game, and I think the game was better at that time."

It also was a time when a Division I coach could earn thirty thousand dollars a year, and command a recruiting budget that would not even buy a hot-shot point guard a decent new compact car today . . . a time when some schools' entire basketball budgets were roughly equal to what many head coaches would earn in base pay within a matter of years. Yet it was also a time when there was a measure of camaraderie among rival coaches, partly due to the fact that, as Blaney points out, with no NCAA restrictions on scouting, "every night you'd be at a game, so the coaches got to know each other very well."

And it was an eclectic assortment of talent that prowled the sidelines in New England in the mid- to late 1970s. There were established coaches such as Gavitt and the University of Rhode Island's Jack Kraft, both of whom had taken teams to the Final Four, and UMass's Jack Leaman, forever known as Julius Erving's college coach but also a thirteen-year veteran with a lifetime winning percentage of .633. There were solid achievers like Holy Cross's Blaney and Dom Perno at Connecticut, and two relative youngsters who would each go on to win a national championship a decade later, Jim Calhoun at Northeastern and Rick Pitino at Boston University.

Together, their schools comprised New England's version of the Big East before the real Big East was minted in the summer of 1979. The Boston College–Holy Cross rivalry was among the most bitter in the country, and the two teams would routinely draw more than ten thousand fans to Boston Garden. If the UMass–UConn clashes were less intense, it was only by degrees. Fairfield, Northeastern, Maine, Boston University, Harvard, and Yale formed the remainder of the core of Division I basketball in the region.

And it was all about to change. While the NCAA's introduction of the three-point shot and the shot clock in the mid-1980s would alter the game in profound ways, there were other fundamental changes brewing in New England hoops in the fall of 1978.

UMass, one of the region's dominant teams well after Erving left school, had already taken the plunge in 1976 and joined the Eastern Eight Conference along with Villanova, Duquesne, Penn State, West Virginia, Rutgers, George Washington, and Pittsburgh. In 1979, spurred on by the Eastern College Athletic Conference's (ECAC) edict that member schools had to schedule home-and-home series with each other, Gavitt would join forces with the athletic directors of Georgetown, Syracuse, and St. John's to propose a new, multisport conference that would be able to control its own scheduling and television contracts. No one, perhaps not even Gavitt, could have envisioned the Big East as it is today, or even predicted the effect it had almost immediately upon its inaugural season in the 1979–80 school year.

Still, college hoops was always a slightly tougher sell in Boston, a city that was, is, and always will be obsessed with its professional sports teams. As the college basketball season approached in the fall of 1978, there was plenty of residual anguish from the late-season collapse of the Red Sox that had culminated in a wrenching, one-game playoff loss to the Yankees on a bright October afternoon at Fenway Park.

Yet even if men and women of letters were not yet inspired to compare Boston College's basketball team to tragic figures in Greek mythology as they routinely did with city's cursed baseball team, the small Jesuit school on the city's western border would soon catch the attention of the city's sports *cognoscenti.*

• • •

Boston College was founded by a group of fathers of the Society of Jesuits during the Civil War as a small college for boys in Boston's South End. The campus was eventually relocated to farmland in Chestnut Hill, on the western edge of the city. Known as "The Heights" for the steep inclines that divide its upper and lower portions, the campus is a mix of modern architecture balanced by a heavy Gothic influence. Boston College is bordered on the north by Commonwealth Avenue, the road made famous as the route that brings Boston Marathon runners into the city each April (B.C. is right at the beginning of "Heartbreak Hill") and on the east by the Chestnut Hill Reservoir, which separates the eastern end of campus from Cleveland Circle in Boston proper.

The modern era of basketball at Boston College dates back to 1963, when former Boston Celtic guard and NBA Hall of Famer Bob Cousy took over as head coach. Cousy actually had been signed to coach B.C. the previous year, but Celtics owner Walter Brown, upon hearing this, reportedly convinced his star guard to play one more year. That left B.C. assistant Frank Power to coach the Eagles for the 1962–63 season, and the team won nine games and lost sixteen.

Cousy took over the next season and soon Boston College began to carve out a reputation that spread beyond the New England region. His 1964–65 team earned the school's first NIT berth, and the next season beat a Louisville team led by Wes Unseld in the NIT's first round before losing to Villanova. The Eagles made the NCAA Tournament the following two seasons, and the 1968–69 team led by Terry Driscoll and future B.C. coach Jim O'Brien was ranked in the national top ten and made it to the NIT championship game, where it lost to Temple.

Cousy's successor, Chuck Daly, couldn't replicate his predecessor's winning ways, and after two seasons left to coach the University of Pennsylvania. He was replaced by one of his assistants, Bob Zuffelato, who quickly set about plumbing the depths of the city's fertile basketball talent pool and before long had commitments from Bob Carrington, Bill Collins, and Will Morrison, three prize Boston-area recruits.

After a mediocre first two seasons, Zuffelato's teams won twenty-one games in 1973–74 and finished third in the National Invitation Tournament, then duplicated that win total in 1974–75, winning the ECAC New England tournament, qualifying for the NCAA Tournament for the first time in eight years and defeating Furman in the first round before losing to Kansas State and North Carolina, the latter in a consolation game.

The Zuffelato era at Boston College quickly took a downturn, however.

In 1975–76, the senior year for Carrington, Morrison, and Collins, the Eagles won only nine of twenty-six games, and nine of the seventeen losses were by margins of five points or fewer. The next season brought more of the same: an 8–18 record, with losses in nine of the season's final ten games. Zuffelato resigned in 1977, and he was replaced by Dr. Tom Davis, a relative unknown who was hired away from Lafayette of the East Coast Conference.

Davis's impact was felt immediately. Using mostly the same players from the previous year's team, he coached the Eagles to a 15–11 record. Tom Meggers, a senior on the 1978–79 team who played three years under Zuffelato before Davis took over, remembers a distinct change in style.

"There was a little bit more discipline and structure," according to Meggers. "The talent pool had gone down (the year before), and we struggled. But (Davis) took the same team and brought in some freshman, who didn't really have much of an impact, and we won fifteen games."

Davis had grown up in the tiny town of Ridgeway, Wisconsin, and as a player captained two University of Wisconsin–Platteville teams to the NAIA tournament. His coaching itinerary included high school jobs in Illinois and Wisconsin before he accepted an unpaid assistant's job under Bud Milliken at the University of Maryland while working on his doctoral thesis on the role of sports and exercise in Colonial times.

Davis had already begun to develop his own style of coaching, which stressed pressure defense all over the court and by necessity required willing players, and lots of them, to carry it out. It was a style he had employed with his high school teams, and one he continued to perfect when, after a short stint as an assistant at American University under Tom Young, he landed the job at Lafayette in 1971. In six years at the small school in Easton, Pennsylvania, Davis averaged nearly twenty wins per season and twice coached the Leopards to berths in the National Invitation Tournament.

By the time Davis got to Boston College in 1977 and moved into a house four doors up Heartbreak Hill from the school library with his wife, Sharon, and their infant son, he had developed a reputation as a coach who never sent his team onto the court unprepared.

"If you ever played for a Davis team, he put the fear of God in you," sophomore forward Chris Foy recalls. "He was a firm believer that you didn't win the game on the day of the game, you start winning the game at practice. Anybody you played, it was like you were playing UCLA; that was the way he prepared. He was an unbelievably anal guy. (Merrimack's) Eddie Murphy and Dana Skinner were Pete Maravich 1 and Pete Maravich 2. I mean, they were great players, but they went to Merrimack for a reason. But he'd beat that point into you: any game you go into, you have a chance of losing.

"Every year it was the same thing. We never lost to a team we should have beaten. I mean, *never* in my four years."

Meggers remembers one of Davis's unorthodox motivational ploys.

"We were playing our biggest game of the year, at home against St. John's, and I'm starting and Rick (Kuhn) is starting, and so is Michael (Bowie), and he brings us in and he says, 'I think there's a time for every player in their career to decide when it's over. You can just hang up your sneakers.' This was before the biggest game we were playing! And he's saying, 'I think it's time you guys just hang it up.'"

The Boston College program Davis inherited was a step up from Lafayette—B.C. offered athletic scholarships, for one thing—but seemed to be operated on coupons and petty cash. For instance, the Eagles had only one paid assistant coach until they joined the Big East for the 1979–80 season. That was Gary Williams, who would later succeed Davis at B.C. and go on to head coaching jobs at Ohio State and Maryland.

If Davis thought that moving to the big city would bring more coverage over the airwaves, he soon found out he was mistaken.

"When I took the Boston College job, forget television, our games weren't even on radio," Davis recalls. "There were no radio broadcasts. Then a local lawyer said, 'I'm going to try and get a radio contract for B.C.,' so he bought the time on a country music station in Waltham and put it on the air, and he became a broadcaster himself."

The lawyer was Len DeLuca, who is now a senior vice president in charge of programming development at ESPN.

The school's basketball facilities were on a par with the other New England schools they played. Boston College played its games at Roberts Center, a quaint little brick bandbox of a gym that held about four thousand fans and had a rubberized floor that the players tolerated but were not overly enthusiastic about. When the place was packed and loud, it made for a hellish experience for visiting teams since the bleachers were right up on the court; when it was half-full or worse, it could resemble a glorified high school gym.

• • •

Practically from the time he first picked up a whistle, Kevin Mackey had a sixth sense for detecting the big-time player from the small fry who would never make it past the asphalt playgrounds. Often it came down to desire, and Mackey could smell that desire a city block away, could see it not only in a kid's eyes but in the way the kid carried himself, the way he reacted with the ball in his hands and the clock ticking toward zero. It was this eye for talent that caught Tom Davis's attention when Davis took over at Boston College in 1977.

Mackey reveled in his role as the outsider, and he portrayed himself as someone who was unafraid of going to neighborhoods where he often would be the only white face that wasn't peering out of the window of a police cruiser. He loved to describe himself as a "poor Irish street kid" who had grown up in the Winter Hill section of Boston, an area notorious for being a center of mob activities in the city. Barely out of Saint Anselm's

College in Vermont, he took the head coaching job at Boston's Cathedral High and built the program into a New England Catholic School Class B champion. He accomplished this by first convincing school officials to admit students from the housing projects, then by exploding the racist notion that inner-city black players were incapable of playing disciplined, "team" basketball.

His successes continued at Don Bosco Tech, where he coached future Boston College starters Dwan Chandler and Joe Beaulieu on a team that won a state title and was ranked in the national top ten.

By the time he got to Boston College, Mackey was avowedly seeking out players who played, in his words, "like sharks after blood," players who often had been passed over by larger schools because of academic deficiencies or irregular body types. His formula was deceptively simple: look for the kid "who went to the wrong high school, had the wrong coach, went to the wrong summer camp—or maybe didn't go to summer camp at all," he would say, the kid who didn't fit the IBM computer printouts used by all the other coaches. Mackey specialized in small, scrappy point guards, and he would recruit several over the next few years at B.C. who would go on to play in the National Basketball Association, including Dana Barros, John Bagley, and Michael Adams.

"I don't know if I've ever known a person who could evaluate talent better than Kevin Mackey, as far as looking at a prospect and projecting how good he was going to be," Davis says today. "Kevin may be the best. In fact, I think he is the best I've ever seen. And he would rank with anybody."

Davis remembers Mackey being so eager to make the jump from high school to college coaching that he came on staff and, initially, worked part-time for practically no pay.

• • •

For the 1978–79 season, Mackey and Davis had assembled a promising group of veterans and newcomers who either could be counted on to fit into Davis's system or who had already had a year to become used to his up-tempo style.

"Tom was such a substituter, almost more so than anyone else in college basketball," Mackey recalled. "We pressed, we changed defenses, and Tom ran guys in and out. He used his bench better than just about anyone in the country."

The team's heart was the backcourt duo of cocaptains Sweeney and Cobb, two players whose talents complemented each other perfectly. Cobb was a scorer with a sweet shooting stroke who was so sure of his ability to put the ball in the basket that he felt no single opponent could hold him in check.

"Ernie was a pure scorer," Mackey recalled. "Anything he could do to score a basket, he'd do it. That was his reason for being."

Sweeney, on the other hand, derived satisfaction from setting up his teammates with well-timed passes, and usually took shots only when the opposing team's defense gave him a clear opening. The two players' statistical averages reflected these propensities: While Sweeney finished his career averaging less than 10 points per game, by the end of the 1990s he still owned the fifth-highest assist total in school history. Cobb, meanwhile, averaged 22.8 and 21.3 points per game, respectively, in his junior and senior seasons and finished his career as the third-leading scorer in Boston College history.

"I really enjoyed them from a coaching point of view," Davis said. "They were both good workers. It was my first year at Boston College, and we were attempting to turn around a situation where they hadn't been very effective. I think they were appreciative that B.C. was making the commitment to get the program going in the right direction."

Chandler and Beaulieu, meanwhile, were rejoining Mackey, their high school mentor, at Boston College after each taking a detour. Chandler, a 6-foot-2 leaper who had had a standout scholastic career at Don Bosco, had taken a year at Maine Central Institute to get his grades up. "I don't know that you would say he was an NBA prospect," Davis says, "but in crunch time in a game, he was the kind of guy who would give you what he had."

When Mackey was at Don Bosco, he had found Beaulieu living with his mother in an apartment in Cambridge. When Beaulieu was considering enrolling at Harvard, Mackey initially tried to dissuade him by telling him, "It won't be like high school. No one goes to the games at Harvard." Mackey's master plan was to get an assistant's job with Chuck Daly at the University of Pennsylvania and bring Beaulieu with him. But when he failed to get the Penn job and was hired by B.C., he convinced Beaulieu to make the move from Cambridge to Chestnut Hill.

Beaulieu was something of an enigma to his teammates and coaches. Big and strong at 6-foot-8 and 240 pounds, he had the size and skills to be a dominant player but was a classic underachiever on a team of overachievers. He also was a gifted student—he had earned admission to Harvard, after all—but underperformed in that sphere as well, according to some of his former teammates.

"Intellectually he was a very bright kid who just got lost somewhere along the way," one teammate says. "He was the kind of kid who could have had a better basketball career than he did, and he could have had a better academic career than he did. He never took advantage of what Boston College had to offer. That's my opinion. He was a bright kid who had a lot of talent."

Davis will only say that Beaulieu was "a very, very interesting guy. Very complex. Very bright, very talented. He had a lot of real positives, but he was just sort of trying to find his way, trying to find his niche."

Backing up Beaulieu at center would be Kuhn, who had earned a reputation as a banger under the boards during the previous two seasons.

Beaulieu's opposite on the B.C. team was 6-foot-4 sophomore forward Chris Foy, an overachiever who was one of Davis's first recruits. Scrambling for players after his hiring in May 1977, Davis called Dick Weiss, now a college basketball columnist for the *New York Daily News* but then a coach in the Conshohocken summer league in suburban Philadelphia.

"I need players. I need somebody hard-nosed who can do the job," Davis remembers telling Weiss, and Weiss recommended Foy, who had gone to St. Joseph's Prep in Philadelphia and had not been heavily recruited by other Division I schools. By his senior year at B.C. in 1980–81, Foy was named team captain.

One Boston College player who achieved far less notoriety than his talents deserved was 6-foot-6 senior swingman Michael Bowie, whose smooth, fluid style made him an inside as well as outside threat. Bowie hadn't played much in his first two years at B.C., but then he began to make strides his junior year before coming into his own as a senior. Davis remembers him as "an athletic player who could do a lot of things." Teammates regarded him as a loner who didn't socialize much with the rest of the team.

Chandler was not the only freshman to have an impact at Boston College during the 1978–79 season. Six-foot-six forward Vin Caraher, the son of a Long Island policeman, steadily increased his playing time as the season progressed and provided valuable scoring punch for the Eagles. Like Beaulieu, though, Caraher's work ethic left a little to be desired.

"He was an easygoing guy who wanted to have a good time," Mackey recalls. "We used to try and push him, and he'd laugh at us. I think we wanted him to be better than he wanted to be."

Team chemistry is an elusive quality that usually requires a player—or perhaps more than one—with a dominant personality to act as the fulcrum around which the rest of the team is balanced. That player or players seemed to be absent from the 1978–79 Boston College team. Of the regulars, Cobb and Bowie pretty much went their own way, while Kuhn seemed to have his own agenda and certainly wasn't suited to be a rah-rah guy.

Sweeney might have been the most logical choice, given his personality and his position as point guard, but he was not a consistently vocal leader either. The underclassmen—Foy, Caraher, Chandler, Rich Shrigley—would eventually grow into their roles, but not for another year.

"It wasn't like there was any animosity," Meggers recalls, "but it wasn't like people were running around going, 'Hey, want to go to the movies?'"

Three of the starting slots were givens: Sweeney and Cobb at the guards and Bowie at one forward. Beaulieu and Kuhn alternated at the center spot, and Caraher, Chandler, Foy, Meggers, or Shrigley, a 6-foot-4 freshman, split time at the other forward position.

On another level, there were two sets of rules, one for Cobb and one for the rest of the players. While Cobb could miss his first seven shots of the game and still wind up playing thirty-eight minutes, any other player, with the possible exception of Sweeney, had to earn his playing time. Meggers refers to it as the "Eight Club"—the eight players other than Cobb or

Sweeney who would get between fifteen and twenty-five minutes of playing time. If you fell out of the Eight Club, you might play four minutes—or no minutes at all.

"He was the kind of guy that if you had a good game, you played the next game," Meggers says of Davis. "Or, if your practices were good, you played in the next game. But if you played a lousy game, chances are you were not in the starting lineup. You had to earn it back in practice again. You could go from twenty minutes to zero. It was a tough way to play."

• • •

As Boston College prepared for its season opener against Stonehill College on November 27, Rick Kuhn was making plans of his own. He had gone home to Swissvale for the weekend around the time that basketball practice started in mid-October, and when he returned he told his girlfriend, Barbara Reed, that they were going to have a phone installed in the apartment. Until then, when either of them had to make a phone call, they would use a pay phone outside the apartment building on Peterborough Street.

Reed had no illusions as to why they were getting the phone; soon, she noticed Rick made and received a lot of phone calls to and from Pittsburgh. Rick even insisted that she not answer the phone if they were both in the apartment, since it would always be for him. He also told her not to worry about the cost of the phone line or the long-distance calls that he was making in increasing numbers. On Sundays it would usually be Rick's brother, Fred, or his parents, but more often than not it was Rocco or Tony Perla.

Barbara and Rick were having other troubles around that time, stemming from his weekend trip to Swissvale. Reed, who admitted she did not trust Rick when it came to being faithful, had noticed some phone messages left for him at the B.C. gym from a girl named Valerie whom he had dated while he was at community college in Pittsburgh, and she was convinced the two were going to hook up when Rick went home.

Rocco Perla, Rick's friend from Swissvale, was in Boston frequently over the next several weekends, and on one of the trips ran into Sweeney at a B.C.–Pittsburgh football game. According to Sweeney, who had met Rocco on campus a few times over the years, there was no discussion of gambling during that encounter.

That was not the case in mid-November, according to Ernie Cobb. As he described it, he was doing some extra shooting in the gym one day after practice ended when Kuhn, who had already dressed and showered, came upstairs from the locker room accompanied by Rocco, who began to ask him how the team looked that year. Then, he asked Ernie how he thought the Eagles would do against Stonehill in the season opener in two weeks.

Cobb told him he could not guarantee a win, but that B.C. had beaten Stonehill easily the year before and would probably do the same this year.

"Great," Cobb says Rocco told him, because he was planning on betting on the game. He asked Cobb if he was interested in betting any money, and Cobb explained that he didn't have any money to bet. Perla offered to put up the money, but Cobb wasn't interested.

Cobb recalled Perla saying that if Boston College won the Stonehill game, he would pay him one thousand dollars.

"I thought it was just talk," Cobb said later. "I hadn't known the guy prior to Rick Kuhn introducing him to me, and I basically thought he was just BS'ing."

On the night of November 27, Boston College defeated Stonehill, 89–76, though not without some indications that the Eagles were not quite operating like a well-oiled machine just yet. Stonehill actually led at half-time, 39–36, after making 60 percent of its shots in the first half, before B.C.'s pressure defense took over in the second half.

Cobb scored twenty-four points and made good on his prediction, but there was no word from Rocco. This did not surprise Cobb, since he wasn't really expecting anything to come from Rocco's offer anyway.

Boston College won its next two games, one of them a surprisingly difficult 80–77 decision over Bentley College on November 30, and the other a 93–70 breather against LeMoyne on December 3. That set the stage for the Eagles' game against Providence on December 6, which would pose the first test of the season for Davis's team . . . and the first test for the scheme that had been laid out just weeks earlier.

• • •

As Boston College prepared to face Providence College on Wednesday night, December 6, the pace of communications between Pittsburgh, New York, and Boston picked up dramatically. On Tuesday night, Tony Perla called Kuhn to see if everything was still all set for the game; it had been three weeks since the meeting at the Logan Airport Hilton, after all, and it was a wise move to see if anyone had gotten cold feet in between.

Kuhn assured Perla that Sweeney was still with the program, and that with Sweeney handling the ball there would not be a problem with keeping the score down against Providence. Perla dutifully passed this information on to Paul Mazzei, who in turn told Henry Hill in New York. By early Wednesday afternoon, when Jimmy Burke got the point spread and relayed it to Hill, everything seemed set: the Eagles were favored by between seven and nine points, meaning they could still win by any amount less than that and still pick up money for the gamblers. Hill recalled that they placed about five thousand dollars on the game, spread out among several book-makers who had knowledge of the scheme.

The first inkling that things were not going to go as planned came on the afternoon of the game. Sweeney remembered Kuhn telling him that he had talked to Tony Perla and that Tony had said they needed to win the game by "less than eight or nine points," because people in New York would be betting on the game.

"Are you serious? Do you really want to go through with this?" Sweeney said. Kuhn, who had already told Perla that everything was all set, replied that he did. Kuhn would say later that Sweeney agreed to shave points in the game, but Sweeney's actions several hours later demonstrated that he was in fact doing the opposite.

Playing at Roberts Center that evening, Boston College pressured the Friars into sixteen turnovers in the first half, and took a twelve-point lead at intermission. The visitors stayed within eight or ten points until the final minutes, however, until consecutive baskets by Kuhn, Cobb, Vin Caraher, and Joe Beaulieu turned a 62–54 lead into a 70–54 advantage with 2:19 left in the game.

While B.C.'s rally revved up the Roberts Center crowd, on the court Kuhn was watching a nightmare unfold as the Eagles' lead kept increasing. During a timeout in the second half, he confronted Sweeney out of earshot of the rest of the team.

"What are you doing?" Kuhn demanded.

"I'm playing," Sweeney said. "I'm trying my hardest to win."

By the end of the game, which B.C. won, 83–64, Kuhn knew he was in trouble. He had told Tony Perla that he could count on him and Sweeney keeping the score within the point spread, and now they had not only defeated Providence, but had obliterated the seven- to nine-point spread.

In the locker room after the game, Kuhn was visibly upset.

"Are you crazy?" Kuhn said to him. "I have to go back and face a phone call from Tony Perla."

Hill was not pleased, either. Even though he had lost only a few thousand dollars on the game, he already was beginning to wonder if he was going to be able to rely on a couple of college kids to do his bidding. There was also the embarrassment of being on the losing end of anything, which rankled him.

Burke also was angry and wanting answers. This prompted a flurry of phone calls between Pittsburgh, Boston, and New York, during which Paul Mazzei, who had only lost a few hundred dollars on the game, explained that the problem was Cobb, who had scored twenty-five points. They would have to get him involved, or the scheme wasn't going to work. Hill, relaying the official word from New York, told Mazzei to get word to Kuhn that Cobb had to be recruited for the Harvard game on December 16.

It did not take a genius to figure out what was needed, and Kuhn already knew that Sweeney's unreliability meant he was going to have to widen his search for another player (or players) who would cooperate. Cobb was a given; Joe Beaulieu was another possibility, since he played the center position and frequently got more minutes than Kuhn. Besides, like Kuhn, it was not unheard of for Beaulieu to unwind after a tough practice with various mood-altering substances, and he might be persuaded to join up for the promise of a steady supply.

Around this time, Kuhn also hit upon a way to play both sides against the middle: he would skim the payoffs to Cobb or Beaulieu, or whomever else he could convince to go along with the scheme, by telling them he was only being paid fifteen hundred dollars when the actual figure was twenty-five hundred.

Either way, Kuhn was going to have to play salesman again.

Back in New York, Hill and Burke were not the only ones who were beginning to view the scheme with suspicion. Perhaps sensing a losing proposition, Richard Perry told Hill after the Providence game that he would not be putting up any more of his money for the scheme, though he would continue to book bets.

Worried that their network of bookies would stage a revolt after the Providence fiasco, Hill and Burke visited Milton Wekar at Bobby's Restaurant in Manhattan a few days after the game. Wekar, an experienced bookmaker, was skeptical. Even after Hill told him about the recruitment of Cobb, Wekar told him, "They're full of shit, those kids. They'll take your money and run and you can't trust them—period." Hill went so far as to call Mazzei in Pittsburgh from Bobby's so that Mazzei could explain to Burke about Cobb. By the time Hill and Burke left Bobby's, Wekar agreed to continue to play his part.

They also stopped in to see Martin Krugman, another bookie in the network, at 40 Yards, a bar-restaurant on Queens Boulevard. They assured Krugman that the Providence game was an aberration, and that with Cobb on board everything would proceed as planned.

• • •

In Pittsburgh, Tony Perla had gotten the message loud and clear: the New York faction did not want any more games discussed until more players were involved, specifically Cobb.

The problem was, Perla already was beginning to have suspicions about Kuhn. Rick could say he had talked to Ernie and that everything was set, but how would Perla know that Kuhn was not holding out on him? He also knew that a month earlier at the Logan Airport Hilton meeting, Kuhn had expressed a reluctance to approach Cobb anyway. So, Tony Perla turned to his brother.

In contrast to Cobb's assertion that he did not know Rocco Perla before being introduced to him by Kuhn after basketball practice in November, Rocco remembered meeting Cobb the year before, when Ernie was living near Kuhn's campus dorm, and possibly on one other occasion.

Tony Perla issued his brother explicit instructions.

"Offer him money, ask him if he'll go along, but don't threaten him; don't bother him," he told him. "If he threatens you or turns on you, back away from him and say you're kidding."

Rocco Perla arrived in Boston on Saturday night, December 9. He recalled that Kuhn and Sweeney picked him up at the airport and took him to the Chestnut Hill Mall for lunch, though since records showed his plane left Pittsburgh at 7:40 P.M. on Saturday it is doubtful the Mall was still open for lunch by the time he arrived in Boston.

According to Kuhn, he and Sweeney had a conversation with Rocco in which Sweeney said he didn't want to be the one to approach Cobb, and that if anyone else approached Cobb, that Sweeney didn't want Cobb to know he was involved. Kuhn said he didn't feel like approaching Cobb either, so it was decided Rocco would speak to him.

Kuhn said Sweeney also told him he had already spoken to Joe Beaulieu about the Harvard game, and that Beaulieu "hadn't disagreed" with the idea of shaving points but wanted to talk about it further before committing. (How Sweeney went from refusing to participate in the scheme in the Providence game to acting as Kuhn's recruiter for the Harvard game strains credulity.)

Rocco recalled dropping Sweeney off at his dorm at around 10 o'clock and continuing on with Kuhn to the Westgate Apartments, where Cobb lived with his girlfriend, Laverne Mosley, and a German shepherd named Thunder.

According to Rocco, after some small talk he broached the idea of shaving points in the Harvard game to Cobb, and specifically mentioned that he would get twenty-five hundred for doing his part. He remembered Cobb "at first was very skeptical. He didn't want to go along with it at first for fear that somebody would find out. . . . He was concerned that if anyone found out, it would hurt his chances of playing professional basketball."

Eventually, Perla said, Cobb agreed, but on the condition that only Kuhn and Rocco were to know about his involvement. He specifically did not want Sweeney to know, which was substantially the same request Sweeney had allegedly made a few hours earlier regarding Cobb.

During the time when Rocco actually proposed shaving points to Cobb, Kuhn drifted away to another room in the apartment, and later said that this was because he did not want to be connected with the proposal in case Cobb said no. That way it would look like the offer came from Rocco alone. Kuhn remembered Cobb was leery of the proposal, but eventually agreed to it.

Rocco called his brother before he returned to Pittsburgh and told him that Cobb had agreed to go along with the scheme for the Harvard game, but that he wanted to be paid by Rocco and did not want to deal with any other players on the team.

For his part, Ernie Cobb denied ever meeting Rocco Perla the week before the Harvard game and claimed that he only met Rocco at the gym the one time with Kuhn after practice in November, though he concedes he might have "seen him around" campus on other occasions.

Rocco Perla, however, is unequivocal in his recollection of going to Cobb's apartment that evening and getting Cobb's commitment to shave points in the Harvard game. And he adds a bit of information that was not divulged at either trial and that reveals much about Cobb's possible motivations.

"Somebody that we had connections to had some friends in a scouting combine that used to scout college games throughout the country," Perla recalls. "I don't know if it was me or Rick, but [Cobb] was promised that in addition to money, that his name would be drawn into the eyesights, if you will, of the scouts in this scouting combine. He was concerned that although he was well-known at Boston College, he wasn't really known as a pro prospect, and he thought he should have been.

"At some point we actually had the scouting report from one of these combines, and we shared it with him. I remember it distinctly; it said 'offensive skills okay, lacks defensive skills to guard pro-type players.'"

• • •

A few days before the Harvard game during the week of December 11, Joe Beaulieu and Rick Kuhn went back to Kuhn's apartment one night after practice to unwind. Beaulieu arrived at about 8:30 and stayed until 2 A.M., during which time the two players drank Tanqueray gin and smoked some grass.

At about 1 A.M., Kuhn turned to Beaulieu.

"You know, we're both playing the center position," Kuhn said. "I have some friends who are interested in betting on the games."

This did not exactly sound like front-page news to Beaulieu. People were always betting on the games. But he listened as Kuhn continued.

"Since . . . one of us would always be in the game, we would have a pretty good opportunity to be able to affect the outcome of the game," he pointed out.

Beaulieu agreed.

"Well, my friends said maybe we can make some money doing this," Kuhn offered.

"I don't want to get involved in anything," Beaulieu said. "That is out of my league."

Kuhn kept pressing, however, telling Beaulieu that these friends would "bring them down to New York some weekend and talk to us down there, and there would be cocaine and women. . . ." Kuhn added that his friends did not want them to actually throw a game, just keep it close.

But Beaulieu was not moved. Though he was not known among his teammates for being someone who let responsibilities stand in the way of having a good time, he was not about to let his friendship with Rick lead him into this kind of trouble. Plus, he was concerned about even having had a conversation with Kuhn about point-shaving, since NCAA rules required that players report any approaches from gamblers.

Still, Beaulieu, like Jim Sweeney, did not report Kuhn's overture to anyone at Boston College, let alone the NCAA, partly because of his friendship with Rick, partly because he did not "think it was necessary" to do it, and frankly, as he said, "I didn't think there was any substance to what he told me."

As time went on and no more mention was made of the proposal, Beaulieu figured there really had been nothing to it. Besides, he assumed that Kuhn did not have the kind of relationship with anyone else on the team that would allow him to make any other approaches without getting himself into trouble.

• • •

In the early morning hours of December 11, 1978, five days before the Boston College–Harvard game, seven masked gunmen forced their way into the Lufthansa Airlines cargo terminal at New York's JFK Airport and, after handcuffing nine employees and beating up a tenth, made off with what was originally reported to be $3 million in cash and $2 million in jewelry.

Within a few days of the brazen heist, as the FBI, the New York City Police Department, and the U.S. Customs Service wrestled over jurisdiction in the case, sources in local and federal law enforcement claimed to already know the identities of four of the thieves: Angelo Sepe, Thomas DeSimone, and Anthony Rodriguez—all reputed or known associates of the Lucchese family—and Jimmy Burke.

The story unfolded over the next several days: Lufthansa employees offered sketches of two of the bandits; the amount of money stolen was upgraded to $5 million, making it the largest cash robbery in U.S. history; and the black Ford Econoline van allegedly used in the robbery was found abandoned in the Canarsie section of Brooklyn.

While all this was going on, Henry Hill had other business to take care of. Burke, who was going to go to Ft. Lauderdale before the weekend, gave Hill instructions to call him there to get the point spread for the Harvard game on Saturday. According to Hill, Burke also gave him five thousand dollars to pay the players after the game if they were successful in shaving points, and told Hill to "make sure the players saw him in the stands" at Boston Garden Saturday night.

Instead of going straight to Boston, however, Hill first flew to Pittsburgh on Friday, December 15, where he met up with Mazzei, Tony Perla, and a young blonde woman introduced as a friend of Tony's named Judy Wicks, a graphic artist who frequently ran drugs for the two men. Hill apparently made enough of an impression on Wicks that she decided to accompany him, Mazzei, and Rocco Perla to Boston the next morning to watch her first college basketball game in person. Boston College was playing Harvard in the first game of a doubleheader at Boston Garden, and her newfound friend was talking about making a big score.

CHAPTER FIVE

"Winning in Smaller Ways"

Today, "rival" would be too strong a term to describe the basketball relationship between Harvard and Boston College, so wide is the talent gap between the Ivy League and the Big East. But in 1978, the rivalry was real; though Boston College had won eight of the schools' previous ten meetings, five of those wins were by four points or fewer.

The December 16, 1978, meeting between the two schools held to form, with B.C. winning, 86–83, in the first game of a doubleheader at Boston Garden. After the game, Mike Mayock was surprised when his roommate Jim Sweeney approached him with an urgent request.

"Jimmy came up to me and said, 'I need to talk to you. Let's go to Mary Ann's,' which was a popular bar that I hung out at. I knew it was serious because Jimmy didn't drink, and he didn't go to Mary Ann's."

During the course of a long conversation that night, Sweeney told Mayock everything: that he had been approached by people who wanted him to shave points in the Harvard game, and that they had threatened him. He also said he was scared to death and did not know what to do.

When he had gotten over his initial shock, Mayock realized there was only one thing to do.

"My reaction was, pretty much immediately, that we needed to go see (B.C. athletic director) Bill Flynn, who (Jimmy) and I both knew well because we were athletes," Mayock said. "I said, 'Jimmy, tomorrow, you and I are going to go see him. We've got to get this out there right now and get you protected.'"

But Sweeney stopped him.

"Mike, you weren't the one being threatened," Mayock remembers Sweeney saying. "I want to play pro ball in Europe. What happens?"

Had Sweeney heeded his roommate's advice, the course of his life and the lives of several other people over the next twenty years might have been fundamentally altered. But caught in a spot east of a rock and west of a hard place, he chose to stay silent. His rationale reveals a crack in the façade of the Boston College athletic "family."

"I didn't have a relationship with those people, even though one guy was my coach and the other was the AD," Sweeney explains, referring to Davis and athletic director Bill Flynn. "History shows that they were successful at what they did, and they were good men, but I was one of hundreds of athletes. And I didn't have a strong relationship with them. I don't want to say anything that's disparaging because that's not my intent. It's just that I didn't have a relationship with them, and I didn't feel I had the confidence that I could go there and they would listen. . . . I could be 100 percent wrong in my perception, but that's what I was feeling at the time. Feelings are neither right or wrong, they're just reality."

• • •

The Hill-Mazzei entourage flew on Allegheny Airlines to Boston's Logan Airport on the morning of December 16, rented a car at the airport, and arrived downtown at the Sheraton Prudential Center in mid-afternoon. The hotel registration card showed a "Tony" Perla checked in at 3:15 P.M. and reserved rooms 1840 and 1841, with two guests in each room. "Tony" was actually Rocco Perla, who left a credit card imprint with his name on it and further confused things by signing his father's address, 1306 Schoyer Avenue, Pittsburgh, when he registered.

Not long after the arrival at the Sheraton, Hill called Burke in Florida to get the early line on the B.C.–Harvard game, which he then relayed to Rocco Perla to give to Kuhn. The Eagles were favored by thirteen points, a large spread but not uncommon for a game against an Ivy League team. Rocco called Rick at his apartment to make sure that there would be enough tickets for everybody and also to pass along the point spread to Rick so that he, in turn, could pass it along to Sweeney and Cobb.

Normally on game days, Barbara Reed would drive Rick over to campus in the old van her father had given to her, but on this day Rick said he would be going to the arena in the team van, and that Rocco would pick her up in a cab. "You go with him," Reed remembered Kuhn telling her. "There are other people coming, and I want you to get tickets for them. I left them in your name."

Early that evening, Rocco called from the Sheraton, and twenty minutes later showed up at Reed's apartment, which was a short distance away by cab. Reed rode with Rocco to the hotel, and when they got there Rocco introduced Reed to three people, "two men and a girl with blonde hair," Reed later recalled. The men were introduced as Henry and Paul; she did not remember the girl's name.

After the introductions, Rocco said he had to go upstairs to the room for a few minutes, so Reed sat on a couch in the hotel lobby with Wicks. The two women sat there for about fifteen minutes, during which time Reed observed Henry and Paul making numerous phone calls from the pay phones in the lobby, and conferring with each other in between.

When Rocco returned, the five of them went in two cabs to Boston Garden. Reed rode in one cab with Hill and Wicks, and recalled that once they got inside the arena, Henry, Paul, and Rocco seemed "very nervous," and spent most of the time before the game walking around the lobby and making more phone calls before going in to their seats. Rocco actually spent most of the game pacing back and forth between the concourse area and the row of seats the group occupied behind one baseline, in the middle of the Boston College cheering section.

• • •

A few days before the Harvard game, Kuhn had brought up the scheme again to the reluctant Sweeney, who says he told him, "I don't want any part of it." This irked Kuhn, who responded, "Are you crazy? These people just lost money. They're looking to win it back. You've got to cooperate."

At that point, Sweeney agreed to go along, though he would later claim that he did so while fully intending to play his hardest against the Crimson.

That afternoon, Kuhn told Sweeney that Rocco Perla, Hill, Mazzei, and a friend of Mazzei's would be coming to Boston to "make sure all the people were cooperating" in the scheme. Hill's and Mazzei's presence may have solidified Sweeney's decision to keep his lips sealed about the scheme; after all, if they were serious enough to come all the way to Boston to make sure things went as planned, they certainly would not hesitate to back up with action the threats they had made to Sweeney at the Hilton meeting. No doubt for similar reasons, Sweeney declined Kuhn's invitation to come to the Sheraton that afternoon to meet with Hill and Mazzei.

As the teams took shooting practice at Boston Garden about an hour before the game, Kuhn approached Sweeney and told him the point spread, and added that he had spoken to Cobb, and that Cobb would be cooperating. As testimony would later reveal, Kuhn may have been bluffing; either way, it was important to have Sweeney at least think that Cobb was on board.

Kuhn also gestured toward the stands, where Reed was sitting with Hill, Mazzei, Rocco Perla, and Wicks. Sweeney would later say he recognized Hill, but not Mazzei, in the crowd. Regardless, the implication was clear.

"See, these people are here," Kuhn told him. "We've got to please them."

• • •

The game looked like it would be one-sided when Boston College scored the first nine points, seven by Chris Foy and two by Joe Beaulieu. But Harvard, a team featuring only nine players who had any varsity experience before the 1978–79 season, rallied and actually took the lead twice during the first half before heading into the intermission trailing, 48–45.

The Crimson took a page out of B.C. coach Tom Davis's playbook and applied defensive pressure all over the floor, and the tactic worked for most of the game. Harvard took a 56–55 lead with 14:44 left in the game on a jumper by Dave Coatsworth, before B.C. slowly began to take control. Two jumpers by Beaulieu made it 72–66, but Harvard kept scrapping, and when Glenn Fine drove the length of the floor for an uncontested layup in the last ten seconds, B.C.'s lead was down to one, 84–83. The Crimson were forced to foul Foy, and the sophomore made both foul shots with :02 left to seal the win for the Eagles.

The Eagles had won and now sported a perfect 7–0 record, but it wasn't enough to stop Davis from lambasting them in the locker room after the game, Sweeney remembered. For public consumption, Davis was typically complimentary of the opponents.

"You have to give Harvard credit," he told reporters after the game. "They played good man-to-man defense. They shut down a lot of things we've been doing against other people. Nobody's saying we're a great team, because we're not. We're just a nice little undefeated ball club. But I knew Harvard would be tough. I've seen them play. I don't know if my players expected them to be so tough. I tried to tell them. Maybe now they'll learn that their old coach knows at least a little bit."

Beaulieu produced an inspired performance in his first game against his former school, scoring seventeen points. Having been approached by Kuhn and asked to participate in the fixing of the game, he also was one of a select few people who actually knew what had just happened. His post-game statement to a *Boston Globe* reporter suddenly took on a double meaning:

"A lot of people expected us to blow them out, but they've got a good ball club," Beaulieu was quoted in the newspaper the next day. "I don't think I had any score to settle or anything like that, but I know I had a lot riding on the game. I've got a million friends at Harvard. My girlfriend goes there. I knew I was going to get a lot of ribbing either way."

At least one B.C. player thought the final margin was closer than it should have been. Foy, who jokes today about being "the worst athlete on the team," remembers having his best game of the season with thirteen points—in front of his parents, no less, who had driven up from Philadelphia for the game—but also remembers wondering how the Eagles could have let the Ivy Leaguers come so close to defeating them.

"Looking back on it, Harvard sucked. I was a better athlete than the kids that played for Harvard. You look back and say, 'How did we only beat those guys by three? They suck.'"

• • •

Once the scheme was exposed more than two years later, there would be much scrutiny focused on the Harvard game and specifically on the performances of Sweeney, Cobb, and Kuhn. But the clues seem to lead in opposite directions.

According to Kuhn, Sweeney was in on the fix for the Harvard game; yet Sweeney says he was pretending to go along with the scheme while playing to the best of his abilities. The latter statement is buttressed by the fact that Sweeney scored eighteen points, more than any of his teammates, in one of his best scoring games of the season.

Cobb also steadfastly denies any point-shaving in the Harvard game, despite Kuhn's contention that Cobb had told Rocco Perla the week before at his apartment that he would go along with the scheme for one thousand dollars. Yet Cobb's performance in the game raises doubt as to whether he was indeed playing his best. Playing against an inferior team—and one certainly possessing no player (or players) who could come close to guarding him—Cobb scored just twelve points and committed seven turnovers, one number well below his season average and the other well above.

Even today, it is difficult to fathom that Cobb, who accounted for more than 25 percent of B.C.'s scoring production that season, could score nineteen points against Rhode Island, the best team in New England; twenty against UCLA; and thirty-one against Holy Cross—all far superior teams to Harvard—yet could manage such a lackluster effort against a bunch of Ivy Leaguers, particularly in a game in which both teams scored in the eighties. The performance is even more puzzling given that Cobb's former high school coach was in attendance along with another couple from Stamford that Ernie knew.

• • •

While B.C. and Harvard battled on the Garden's famed parquet floor, in the Boston College cheering section there was action of a different kind. Reed was becoming increasingly annoyed with Hill and Mazzei, who were sitting several seats down from her in the same row.

Reed remembered Hill and Mazzei drawing attention to themselves early in the game by aggressively rooting for Harvard and cheering for every Boston College mistake. These were the people she had given tickets to; in a way, they were her responsibility, and she worried that the other fans in the Boston College section—many of whom knew her from her association with Rick—would assume that they were friends of hers, which they most certainly were not.

"The whole section was upset," Reed said later. "We were all Boston College fans, but these two men who Rocco introduced me to were clapping and laughing and cheering against Boston College. They were laughing at mistakes made on the court and waving and clapping their hands and (being) very obnoxious."

Needless to say, Hill and Mazzei were quite pleased with themselves when the final buzzer sounded and the final margin fell well under the point spread. By this time, Reed, who had been doing a slow burn throughout the game, was fuming. She confronted Kuhn outside the locker room after the game.

"Who the heck are these people?" she demanded. "They acted really strangely." But Kuhn was in a hurry, and he answered with a curt "Shut up," and went off to look for Rocco, Hill, and Mazzei, who were waiting for him.

Reed continued her complaints about the behavior of Hill and Mazzei when she and Rick returned home to the apartment, and an argument developed.

"Look, they're errand boys for the man from New York," Kuhn told her. "Paul is Henry's errand boy. Henry is the errand boy for the man from New York. Don't pay attention to them."

"But you almost lost the game," Reed said. "What happened?"

"I'm really happy with what happened," Kuhn replied. "I'm glad (about) how I played." He then explained that this was a test game for "the betting thing," and that the men were pleased because they had won their bets.

Reed then accused Kuhn of trying to lose the game on purpose, to which Kuhn gave the immortal reply:

"We are not trying to lose. We are trying to win in smaller ways."

• • •

Several versions of what transpired outside the locker room after the B.C.–Harvard game would be offered over the next few years. Hill alone would provide several accounts, each one slightly different than the one before it.

What emerges is that money changed hands between the gamblers and players; how much money was handed over and what exactly it was being handed over for depends on whose version you believe.

Like the rest of the team, Sweeney listened to Davis's five-minute harangue in the locker room after the game, then showered and dressed and got ready to meet his girlfriend, Maura, and his father, who had come up from Trenton for the game. As he was preparing to leave the locker room, Kuhn told him there were some people he wanted him to meet.

Sweeney and Kuhn walked out of the locker room and into the concourse area, which had a hallway that curved around so that if you walked far enough away you would be out of sight of the locker-room door. About two dozen people were milling around in the area outside the locker room, mostly friends and family of the Boston College players, and Sweeney noticed Barbara Reed among them.

Then he saw Henry and Paul, the two men he had met in the hotel a month earlier, and whom he had seen in the stands before the game. They approached him, and Hill shook his hand and congratulated him on "throwing a pass out of bounds at the end of the game"—assuming, obviously, that Sweeney had committed the mistake on purpose. Sweeney said nothing in reply, and Henry and Paul soon walked down the hallway with Kuhn, around the corner and out of Sweeney's sight.

Sweeney never saw any money change hands, nor did he accept any money from Hill or Mazzei. He left with his father and Maura, but did not mention to them who the two strange-looking characters were, or what they had said to him . . . or how tied up in knots he felt about what had just happened.

"I thought I could work it out on my own, and that nothing would ever come of this," Sweeney said later. He also would say that at this point he felt that he had not done anything wrong. After all, he had scored eighteen points, Boston College had won the game, and he had put forth his best effort. So what if these lowlifes thought he was helping them out? He knew he was not.

Barbara Reed was waiting just outside the locker room, to the left of the locker-room door, and she saw Sweeney come out but could not remember if Kuhn was with him. She did recall seeing Kuhn go around the corner with Rocco, Mazzei, and Hill. When Rick reappeared five minutes later, he was alone.

What happened during this brief encounter is perhaps not as important from a legal standpoint as it is from a moral one. Going by the letter of the law, the players and the gamblers could have been found guilty of conspiracy to commit sports bribery even if no points were shaved and no money changed hands. Certainly the amount of money that was passed between Hill and his minions and Kuhn, Cobb, and Sweeney was not an issue that ultimately determined anyone's guilt or innocence in court.

Yet the image it conjured was a potent one. Here was a college basketball player—a student-athlete presumably bound by the bylaws of amateurism and fair play—sneaking around a corner and accepting money from a convicted felon after allegedly altering the outcome of a game. It was the realization of every coach and administrator's worst fear, and it would provide a convenient moral peg on which the government prosecutors would eventually hang their case.

• • •

Fueled by an elixir of quaaludes, cocaine, booze, and the adrenaline rush that always accompanies a winning bet, Henry Hill and Paul Mazzei were riding high by the time the final buzzer sounded on B.C.'s win. They had just spent the last two hours watching their investment pay off handsomely, and now it was time to pay the players, which meant Kuhn, who had been nominated as paymaster.

Hill, in various accounts, claimed that he and Burke won between fifteen and twenty-five thousand dollars on the game. But they would not see any of that money until midway through the next week, when they would collect from Perry, who had gotten most of their money down for them with various New York bookmakers. But they needed to have money for the players now. Hill claimed Burke took care of this by giving him five thousand dollars before Hill left for Boston.

How much money was given, to whom and by whom, after the game seemed to change each time Hill told the story. First, he told FBI agents in July 1980 that he paid Kuhn himself in the hallway outside the locker room. Then he told *Sports Illustrated*'s Doug Looney in early 1981 that he "gave Rocco Perla five thousand dollars, all in hundreds" to give to the players. By the time Hill appeared before a grand jury in June 1981, he was omitting that Rocco Perla and Mazzei were even at the game, and instead was claiming that he gave Tony Perla the money in the men's room at the Garden after the game to give to Kuhn—only this time it was three thousand instead of five thousand dollars. (Tony Perla was, in fact, back in Pittsburgh awaiting news of the game.)

Five months later, at Kuhn's trial, Hill's facts changed again. Now, he claimed that he counted out three thousand dollars before he went to the locker-room area with Mazzei. Once down there they found Kuhn in street clothes among the hubbub, and Hill and Kuhn walked around the corner from the locker room near a men's room entrance, where Hill gave Kuhn the three thousand dollars and told him, "Here's three thousand, you'll get another two Monday or Tuesday."

Kuhn then allegedly told Hill, "I've got to take care of Cobb's man," and walked away around the corner, Hill said, in the company of a man Hill did not recognize, though he was sure it was not Cobb.

Mazzei's version corroborates Hill's in some aspects but not in others. When the game ended, Mazzei immediately went to a phone and called Tony Perla in Pittsburgh to give him the good news. Then, he testified, he gave "either Rocco Perla or Henry Hill" fifteen hundred dollars before he and Hill walked down to the locker room. Mazzei believed Hill had another fifteen hundred dollars on him, and that Hill gave the entire three thousand dollars to Kuhn.

While Hill spoke to Kuhn, Mazzei saw Cobb emerge from the locker room, and he went over to him and said, "Nice game." Mazzei knew he was not supposed to approach Cobb, since Tony Perla had told him that Rocco was the one who was to pay Cobb through Laverne. But he was having trouble containing his enthusiasm after making such a big score, and he wanted to thank Cobb personally.

• • •

Rick Kuhn's box-score line for the Harvard game was a model of symmetry: no field goals, no foul shots, no points. Yet, according to Hill, he had had a subtle effect on the game that only those lucky few who stood to gain from Kuhn's mistakes could appreciate. In the *Sports Illustrated* piece, Hill described Kuhn "fumbling the ball out of bounds," and, later, fouling a Harvard player on a made basket and then, after the free throw was missed, allowing the same player to go around him and score.

Nevertheless, if Kuhn's efforts had enriched the gamblers, he claimed not to have benefited himself, at least not on that night. He would later claim that Hill's version of the postgame meeting was erroneous, and that he never received three thousand dollars from Hill or anybody else that night. He did admit to getting five hundred dollars, however, from Rocco later on that evening at his apartment.

Not surprisingly, Kuhn's version was supported by his friend Rocco Perla. Perla testified that after the game ended, he went to the men's room with Hill and Mazzei, where Mazzei gave him fifteen hundred dollars to give to the players. Hill, observing the transfer, put his two cents in, saying, "Give them some partying money," until the rest of the money could be collected from the bookies in a few days and wired to Boston.

Perla's chief role on this evening was as liaison to Cobb, and to show Ernie that the gamblers could be trusted to keep their end of the agreement. The first thing Rocco did after leaving the men's room was to head to the locker-room area to find Cobb. When he did, he told Cobb, "I have something for you."

But Cobb didn't want to take the money just yet. "Not now," he told Rocco, and said he would get the money later, at Rick's apartment.

But Laverne Mosley, Cobb's girlfriend, approached Rocco and said they weren't sure if they were going to be able to go to Kuhn's—and also mentioned that Ernie had told her Rocco had something for him.

"Yeah, I do," Rocco said, and handed her one thousand dollars in fifty-dollar bills.

Perla said he then went back to the hotel before going over to Rick's, where he claimed he found a crowd that included Rick, Barbara, Jim Sweeney, Laverne and Ernie, and a few other people he didn't know. Reed, Sweeney, and Cobb all denied that there was a party at the apartment, but it was here that Perla said he gave Kuhn the five hundred dollars, which would seem to fit in with Mazzei's statement that he gave Rocco fifteen hundred dollars, of which one thousand had gone to Cobb through Laverne and the remaining five hundred had gone to Kuhn—not three thousand, as Hill suggested.

• • •

The first people Ernie Cobb saw after the game were Herman Alswanger, Cobb's high school coach, and his wife and son, and the DeMarcos, another couple from Stamford. They had driven up from Stamford for the game, and afterward came down to the locker room to meet Ernie before going back inside to watch Holy Cross play Cincinnati in the second game of the doubleheader. Cobb was particularly interested in watching Holy Cross guard Ronnie Perry, who was considered one of the best players in New England, and who played the same position as Cobb.

Cobb was visiting with his guests when Rocco Perla gave Laverne Mosley the one thousand dollars. The group then went inside the arena and watched the second game, and saw Holy Cross drub a Cincinnati team featuring future New York Knick Pat Cummings, 110–88, behind twenty-four points by Perry and twenty-three from Gary Witts. Afterward, they returned to the Parker House, where the Alswangers and the DeMarcos were staying. Ernie and Laverne returned to their apartment at about 12:30 A.M.

Cobb denied going to Kuhn's apartment after the game and denied seeing Rocco after leaving Boston Garden. He did not deny receiving the money, however, and said that transaction occurred after he and Laverne arrived home at the Westgate Apartments, when Laverne produced an envelope containing the twenty fifty-dollar bills Rocco had given her.

Cobb could not believe that Rocco had actually come through on his promise, and that he was now holding one thousand dollars in his hands.

"Wow, I was pretty surprised," Cobb recalled. "I didn't expect it. But at the time that I had it, I said, 'Well, he wasn't lying after all.'"

Like Sweeney, then, Cobb accepted money from someone he knew was involved in gambling, and not just gambling on college basketball games in general, but on Boston College games that he was involved in. Unlike Sweeney, however, who said he was just pretending to go along with the scheme, Cobb would later contend that the money was in return for information he had given the gamblers on the Bentley and Stonehill games earlier in the season. For this reason, Cobb rationalized, it was okay to accept the one thousand dollars.

When asked at his trial more than five years later why he had no apparent qualms about taking the money, Cobb explained, "Because really, it was just something that happened. If Rocco had been there at the time, maybe I would have questioned, but the way it was given to me and the way I had received it later on in the evening, I just didn't give it much thought. I felt that I didn't do anything wrong to get this money.

"It was around Christmas time, and I could think of many things to do with the money at that time. It went very quickly."

Rocco Perla, meanwhile, says he is certain the money he gave to Laverne Mosley that night to give to Ernie was in return for fixing the Harvard game.

• • •

Hill, Mazzei, and the rest of the group were on a high when they left Boston Garden and went to one of the bars across the street from the arena to celebrate with a few drinks. The fiasco of the Providence game was forgotten, and all was well for the time being.

The party continued late into the evening back at the hotel, and the next morning, the Perlas flew back to Pittsburgh while Mazzei, Hill, and Wicks flew back to New York. Once there, Hill and Mazzei met Richard Perry at a bowling alley near Aqueduct Racetrack. Perry gave Hill the remainder of the players' money for Mazzei to bring back to Pittsburgh, though Hill's memory wavered on whether it was fifteen hundred, two thousand, or twenty-five hundred dollars that he received.

This would be the only time Perry gave Hill money for the players; he already had expressed his skepticism about the scheme and had indicated he would not be betting his own money anymore, though he would continue to book bets for Hill and Burke.

Mazzei went back to Pittsburgh and gave Tony Perla one thousand dollars, and on December 19, a Tuesday, a money order totaling two thousand dollars was wired to Rick Kuhn in Boston. Added to the three thousand that Hill said he paid Kuhn at Boston Garden, this would make a total of five thousand dollars. Assuming that the original plan of paying the players twenty-five hundred dollars each was being adhered to, that would mean there was enough to pay two players, not three, a fact that would eventually be brought out in court and would have the government scrambling for an explanation.

• • •

When Mayock and Sweeney returned to the Boston College campus that night, Mayock still held out hope that Sweeney would change his mind and go to see Flynn the next day. But the next day came, and Sweeney did not go. What he told Mayock then was what he told prosecutors in 1981 at Kuhn's trial and what he continues to say today: that he had already resolved to just try and forget the whole thing existed and play as hard as he could play for the rest of the season, the gamblers be damned.

The dilemma would deepen for Sweeney within a few days, when money entered the equation and formalized his involvement in the scheme. Now, more evidence existed than just a meeting in a hotel room where plans and ideas were tossed back and forth.

Mayock again urged Sweeney to go to Flynn and tell him everything, but Mayock was politely but firmly rebuffed. At that point, Mayock realized that Sweeney had made up his mind, and nothing was going to change it.

"I don't blame him, I wasn't in the situation," Mayock says today. "And basically, that was the last conversation he and I ever had [about it], because I respected his privacy. I told him the next day we had to go see Mr. Flynn, I told him when the money showed up that we had to go, and at that point I couldn't do anything more, because he had made his mind up. Once he shot that down, I tried to respect that and stay out of his way.

"He was going to play every game as hard as he could play and hope the thing went away. And I could understand why he said it, but I didn't agree with it. I think he just had a course of action in his mind, and when Jimmy did that, you knew he was going to go through with it."

A month earlier, Sweeney had sat in a hotel room and listened as men he had never met before intimidated him into agreeing to go against everything he had been taught to do as an athlete. Now, instead of exposing the plot and risking the censure of his family, friends, and teammates, he was going to grit his teeth and proceed as if nothing had happened . . . a decision he would spend the rest of the season—and his life—trying to rationalize.

In the meantime, Mayock and roommate Dan Conway, who also was told about the scheme by Sweeney, became amateur detectives in reverse, looking for clues to a crime that they knew was being committed while they watched—but that they were powerless to stop.

"Conway and I went to every home game and every game we could drive to," Mayock recalled. "We loved hoops anyway, and now we had this added intrigue. We watched Jimmy as closely as we could, and he seemed to be under more strain than ever, but we thought he played as well as he could, as hard as he could, everywhere.

"It looked to us that if anything was going on, the guy they had to bring in was Cobb. He was the logical guy, because Kuhn couldn't do anything. He was on the end of the bench. We didn't know anything about the Pittsburgh conduit at that point. So we ended up scrutinizing Cobb for the rest of the year. And Ernie was an erratic shooter. He was one of those guys who could just get hot, and you could forget about it; or he might miss his first nine shots. But we thought some sloppy things happened down toward the end of the season."

Yet even with advance knowledge of what was afoot, Mayock and Conway would sit in the stands each game and still not be able to say with assurance which mistakes, which offensive foul or turnover or missed shot, were committed intentionally and with the aim of abetting the point-shaving scheme. It just was too difficult.

"How do you figure it out?" Mayock asks today. "You can't read into people's intentions. Even with inside information and looking for things, we couldn't figure it out."

CHAPTER SIX

Hoop Dreams

Anyone setting odds on young Ernie Cobb's future at the beginning of the 1970s might have been justified in making failure a prohibitive favorite. Cobb suffered from hyperactivity as a child, and later was found to have asthma. His father, James, who did occasional work as a paver, was rarely around when Ernie was growing up, leaving his wife, Hattie, who worked as a domestic, to support Ernie, his brother, and two sisters.

In the 1960s, the family lived in the housing projects in the south end of Stamford, Connecticut, a city that by the 1980s and '90s would become home to scores of corporations seeking to tap the New York marketplace without paying the city's exorbitant office rates. But before the influx of cash and people, Stamford was a small, grimy, relatively undistinguished city that was overshadowed to the south by the upscale suburbs of Westchester County, New York, and to the north by the blue-blood enclaves that dot the Connecticut coastline.

By the time Cobb reached high school, the family had moved to an apartment building on Merrill Avenue, which was a step up from south Stamford. A YMCA was close by, and there was a park across the street. And it was a short downhill ride into the center of the city.

Like many urban kids whose family lives are unsettled, sports, particularly basketball, were a stabilizing influence in Ernie Cobb's life. Yet many of those same kids fail to succeed on organized teams once they reach high school age because of the rawness of their games, a by-product of hours spent playing on cracked asphalt courts with forgiving rims and few rules, where the macho code of "no blood, no foul" is balanced by the fact that playing defense is an occasional thing at best.

It was just such a player who showed up at Herman Alswanger's office one day in the fall of 1971. The young Stamford High School basketball coach had been around long enough to see all types of players pass through his door, but this one seemed different. Alswanger could see the eagerness in the freshman's eyes and feel the determination in the way he spoke of his basketball goals. Cobb had been cut by his junior high coach the year before, but told Alswanger that he wanted to try out for the high school varsity that winter.

The coach was impressed enough that he gave the kid some assignments—running and weightlifting routines and some preseason conditioning drills—that would get him ready once practice began in December.

Thus began a friendship between Cobb and Alswanger that endures today, even though their contacts are few and fleeting. Thirty years ago, Alswanger's interest in the young Cobb went far beyond the gym.

"The father was out of the picture, he was back and forth," Alswanger remembers. "When I got involved, I got the father, picked him up, got him to different things. . . . Once he knew his son, he tried. The mom was there, but she had her hands full. So Ernie was pretty much on his own.

"He was a raw talent. He just loved to go out there and play, and face any challenge. And he did whatever you asked him to do. He truly loved the game."

Cobb made the Stamford High varsity in his freshman year and began to slowly carve a reputation as a player whose work ethic bordered on the obsessive. After practice, while the rest of the team showered and changed after one of Alswanger's typically tough, two-and-a-half-hour sessions, Ernie would have Joel Hollander, the team manager, or anyone else he could grab for the job, feed him passes as he moved around the court, shooting from different spots, one after another, perfecting his stroke, until the number of shots reached well into the hundreds. Were it not for the night janitors kicking him out of the gym, Cobb might have stayed in there all night, firing away.

He was no slouch in the off-season, either. He lifted weights religiously, and soon his 5-foot-11 frame was tightly muscled. To maintain his conditioning for basketball, in the fall he ran on the school's cross-country team. The running helped his asthma, so that by the time he was a senior he was able to discontinue using the inhaler that Alswanger had given him.

Cobb and Alswanger both knew that what Ernie did on the basketball court was only half the equation, though. The city's playgrounds were littered with players whose inability to measure up academically cost them a chance to go to college and receive the kind of exposure that could lead to an NBA contract. So, with the same kind of determination that drove him to shoot those five hundred jump shots each day after practice, Cobb set about making himself a better student.

It was tougher than anything he had to do on a basketball court, mainly because, as Alswanger recalls it, Cobb could barely read by the time he entered high school. But if basketball was his obsession, his schoolwork became his love, as if he was discovering a new world after years in the dark. He studied reading with a tutor five days a week, during seventh period, while most other students were leaving for the day.

"He loved it like he loved basketball, because he realized what he missed," Alswanger recalls. "He was very bright. Once he picked it up, it was like you gave him a new toy. And he got better and better with his grades."

• • •

Teaming with his cousin, Gary Cobb, who later would earn a football scholarship to Southern Cal and play linebacker in the NFL, Ernie was averaging thirty-eight points per game by his junior season, including a fifty-six-point performance against rival Danbury.

That day in Alswanger's office two years earlier, Cobb had said his goals were to make the team as a freshman, make the starting lineup as a sophomore, be a team leader by his junior year, and make All-American and earn a college scholarship as a senior. The final piece of the puzzle fell into place during the 1974–75 season, when Stamford, led by the Cobb cousins, finished 24–2. Ernie averaged twenty-eight points per game—he would have put up gaudier numbers if Alswanger had not showed some mercy on Stamford's opponents by resting Cobb in the fourth quarter of many games—and was named All-State and All-American. At a high school All-American game at Kutsher's Country Club in the Catskills, Cobb beat out Roy Hamilton and Brad Holland, both UCLA-bound seniors, to gain a starting spot on a team that also included a young center named Bill Cartwright.

College recruiters had already begun taking notice, and scouts were frequent visitors to the Stamford High gym to see Ernie and Gary. One of them was Bob Zuffelato, who had attended Central Connecticut State and now was the head coach at Boston College. Zuffelato knew that the state of Connecticut was a fertile ground for basketball talent despite its small size, and had produced players such as Calvin Murphy, Rick Mahorn, Mike Gminski, John Williamson, and Sly Williams in recent years.

Zuffelato was impressed with Cobb's intensity and work habits, but he also knew that the academic part of the admission process was going to be an uphill battle. Still, something told him it would be worth it. It certainly wasn't the counselors at Stamford High, though; Zuffelato remembered that they gave Cobb "hardly any chance whatsoever" of making it at Boston College.

"When you recruit somebody, you don't know what's going to happen down the road," Zuffelato said. "We knew he had a difficult background, but we felt we could work with him. He knew we were really going to work with him (academically). Getting a degree was important to him. It didn't come easy to him, but it was really important to him. I think they bent a little bit—and I don't mean bent the rules, because he did qualify— but I think they maybe took a player that I felt could make it with a lot of help, and they gave me a chance to work with him."

Cobb also knew what he wanted in a college. If he was going to be the first one in his family to pursue a college degree, he wanted to be sure it was at a school that met his criteria. He liked B.C. because of its academic tradition and because its campus was centrally located and he would not have to travel too far between classes, his dorm, and basketball practice. He also would be able to study with a tutor, as he had done in high school. When the University of Connecticut eventually entered the recruiting race, Cobb had all but made up his mind to go to B.C.

Cobb arrived at Boston College just as the program's fortunes began to plummet, which turned out to be a fortuitous time for a player who had become accustomed to carrying a team on his back. The 1975–76 season was a disaster, as the senior-led unit of Bob Morrison, Will Carrington, and Billy Collins stumbled to a 9–17 record that included ten losses by margins of five points or less. Cobb played at both point guard and shooting guard and averaged 4.5 points per game in limited action. The next season, an 8–18 debacle that cost Zuffelato his job, featured a fifty-two-point loss to Clemson in the Milwaukee Classic, a twenty-point defeat at the hands of rival Holy Cross, and an embarrassing twenty-five-point loss to Fairfield in the season finale. Cobb, however, finished the season averaging over seventeen points per game and was clearly beginning to stamp himself as a player who could score whenever he had the ball in his hands.

• • •

Of the six freshmen that Zuffelato recruited for the 1975–76 season, only Cobb and Tom Meggers, a forward out of Chicago, remained when Dr. Tom Davis arrived in Boston before the 1977–78 season. With Davis's tighter reins and stricter practices came a new style of play as well: an offense that was based around motion, bounce passes, and finding the open man. This would be an ongoing source of frustration for Cobb, who was just getting accustomed to being the centerpiece of the B.C. offense.

Cobb also chafed under Davis's rule for other reasons. "He always used me as an example," he once said. "Certain ballplayers were late and he never said anything, and me being the leader, I was automatically benched if I was late. I faced that discrimination throughout my career. If I did something, someone would say, 'You always let Cobb get away with it.'"

Nevertheless, Cobb was content where he was, and he resisted the temptation to transfer. He had adjusted well academically, met some nice people—including his girlfriend, Laverne Mosley—and felt it was in his best interests to stay in Boston for the next two years.

There was another factor at work though. Cobb's master plan included the NBA, and he had reconciled himself to the fact that he was going to have to get there on his own merits. Whereas a decent player from one of the major programs—UCLA, Kentucky, Indiana, North Carolina—would stand a good chance of getting drafted by an NBA team, Cobb felt that playing at Boston College, he would have to be that much better to earn the same consideration. Yet this only made him more determined to be the team's leader, the player who would have the ball in his hands when a clutch basket was needed. It also gave him extra motivation when B.C. played against the elite teams and players. Cobb viewed these matchups in personal terms, which occasionally caused friction between him and his teammates when it appeared he was trying to shoulder too much of the load.

Undaunted, Cobb pushed himself relentlessly. He would play all day on the weekends during the off-season, against whoever would give him a game. He lifted weights four or five times a week, and ran the mile and a half around Chestnut Hill Reservoir on the east end of campus. As his backcourt mate Jim Sweeney remembers, "He had no body fat; it was like he was chiseled out of rock."

Cobb also resurrected the shooting ritual he had followed in high school.

"Ernie poured his heart and soul into scoring points," assistant coach Kevin Mackey remembers. "He used to come into the gym (in the off-season) and he'd stand in one spot and get his girlfriend, or some little kid he'd given a dollar to, to be a feeder. And he'd shoot jump shot after jump shot. You had to see it to believe it."

The hard work paid off, and in 1977–78, his junior season, Davis named him a tricaptain along with Sweeney and Bob Bennifield. Cobb responded by averaging 22.8 points per game and shooting better than 50 percent from the field, an outstanding shooting percentage for a guard. He was named to the All-ECAC team and was the MVP of the All-College Tournament in Oklahoma City during the Christmas break.

"He was one of the true scorers," Davis remembered. "He had terrific range and great scoring ability."

• • •

By the beginning of his senior year in the fall of 1978, Cobb was living in an off-campus apartment in Boston with Mosley. He kept to himself for the most part, according to his teammates; Sweeney, who saw him every day at basketball practice for nearly five months each year, can barely recall having a real conversation with Cobb during their three years together on the team.

A picture would emerge several years later, after the whole mess became public, of Cobb as a naïve innocent swept up in a situation he did not fully understand. But that version ignores the truth, which was that even though Ernie Cobb did not necessarily have the educational background of his teammates, he was by no means dumb. On the contrary, it was his shrewdness and determination that had gotten him to where he was. His thirst for an NBA career was what nourished him, and he had made all the right moves to position himself to attain that goal.

That is, until the winter of 1978–79, when fifty twenty-dollar bills were too much to pass up.

"To be honest, I've got to figure Ernie knew exactly what was going on," says one former teammate. "He kind of knew the drill. Sweeney was incredibly book-smart, his common sense traded at a ten. Ernie's street smarts traded at a ten. He knew what was going on. Nothing comes for free. A thousand bucks? I mean, I didn't spend a thousand bucks in a whole year back then."

CHAPTER SEVEN

Disorder on the Court

In the end, it was visions of palm trees and sandy beaches that did it for Chris Foy. The senior at Philadelphia's St. Joseph's Prep was deciding on where to spend the next four years of his life in early 1977, and first-year head coach Tom Davis was dangling a trip to Hawaii and the Rainbow Classic in front of him like an uncontested layup. Foy took the bait and, in December 1978, midway through his sophomore season, he was eagerly anticipating the two-week trip that would take the Boston College team halfway around the world.

Like many schools before and since, B.C. used the trip as an inducement for high school seniors who might be wavering about spending the next four winters in frigid Boston. By the 1978–79 season, the school had sweetened the trip by scheduling a West Coast stopover that included two games, one of which was to take place at storied Pauley Pavilion against UCLA.

Before the team plane even left Logan Airport, however, Foy began to notice some things that did not really make sense until later.

"I get on the plane and Kuhn's got this full-length leather coat, and Cobb's got the biggest boom box I've ever seen," Foy remembers. "Sweeney didn't do anything out of the ordinary except for the fact that he hung around a lot with Kuhn on that trip, and we hardly ever saw them.

"I found it kind of peculiar that those three guys in particular just lived a different lifestyle than we did on that trip. As we're getting the eighteen-dollar per diem and eating at McDonald's and getting an Egg McMuffin sandwich, these guys are living large."

Just how large Kuhn was living was something Foy and his teammates might not have been able to fathom, even if they had been privy to the details of the scheme. In addition to the three thousand dollars Kuhn had received at Boston Garden after the Harvard game—one thousand of which had gone to Cobb and five hundred to Sweeney—more money had been wired from Pittsburgh a few days after the game.

After basketball practice on Tuesday, December 19, Rick and Barbara

Reed looked up the address of the nearest Western Union office and drove in her van to Congress Street in downtown Boston, near the South Station railroad terminal. After Rick presented identification to the woman behind the window and signed a few pieces of paper, Reed saw the woman hand him "a stack of money."

"I had never seen so much money," Reed said. "(Rick) counted out over one thousand dollars in hundreds and twenties." It was actually two thousand dollars, sent by Rocco Perla, who had inexplicably signed his own name to the transfer. "It's for Sweeney, and some is for me," Kuhn told her.

Kuhn later would have difficulty remembering the exact amount of the money order, but he was sure that he had taken half of it and split the rest between Sweeney and Cobb. Kuhn remembered giving Sweeney his share at Kuhn's apartment, and giving Cobb his at Roberts Center the day before the team left for the West Coast. Cobb later denied receiving any money from Kuhn after the Harvard game, but as Foy would notice during the trip, he was not shy about spending whatever money he had been given.

Another, more sensitive parcel arrived from Rocco at the apartment on Peterborough Street that week. A notice arrived from the post office, and when Barbara and Rick went to pick up the package they found it contained a styrofoam box with a camera in it—filled with cocaine, according to Reed, which she said she had never seen before. Kuhn later denied receiving any cocaine from Rocco, but Joe Beaulieu, who roomed with Kuhn during part of the West Coast trip, testified that one evening when he and Kuhn were sitting around watching a game on television, Kuhn produced some cocaine in a little pill vial that the two players proceeded to share.

The coke almost didn't make it to the West Coast.

"I found small baggies with white powder in my freezer, [in] the ice-cube trays," Reed said at Kuhn's trial. "And when I was dumping them out, Rick came in the kitchen and said, 'Don't do that!'" She remembered Kuhn telling her what it was and that it had been hidden inside the camera sent by Perla. It was not the first time Reed would see illegal drugs in the apartment during the 1978–79 season, nor would it be the last.

Since Sweeney, like the other players, would be spending Christmas several thousand miles away from home, his family had made the trip to Boston for the Harvard game the previous weekend, and they exchanged presents at that time. His father also gave him "three or four hundred dollars" spending money for the trip. This was on top of the five hundred dollars Sweeney received from Kuhn, which actually could have been one thousand. Kuhn had offered Sweeney half of the two thousand dollars, telling his friend, "You've earned it." After initially refusing, Sweeney finally agreed to accept five hundred dollars, which he said he "tacked up" in his locker at school and spent some of it in Hawaii and some later.

Sweeney's actions—first refusing the money, then accepting half of it and diligently putting some aside for later use—are revealing in that they reflect the mix of ambivalence, guilt, and denial that seemed to follow him throughout the whole season, and which has endured to this day. Just as he had done at the November meeting at the Logan Airport Hilton when the scheme was first proposed, his desire not to get his friend Rick in trouble or to "make waves" may have overridden any moral dilemmas he faced over taking the money.

Based on what he told Mayock at the bar after the Harvard game, it was obvious Sweeney still held out the belief that Kuhn's "betting thing" would just disappear, and had already decided that he was going to play as hard as he could for the rest of the season, whatever the psychological cost. At this point, he may even have felt justified in taking the money to keep up appearances to the Perlas and "the man from New York," who had just made a bundle of money from the Harvard game. Whatever the reason, there was no turning back now.

Apparently, neither Kuhn nor Cobb had to go through any such moral gyrations to justify taking the gamblers' money and spreading it around. At least, their girlfriends didn't, regardless of whether or not they understood the source of the windfall. Reed and Laverne went Christmas shopping in the days after the Harvard game, and Reed noticed that Laverne already was wearing a new coat. Laverne also bought Ernie some weights and a new coat, which Reed helped her pick out. Laverne also let Reed buy a pair of boots on her charge card, and Reed gave her a check.

• • •

When Reed drove Kuhn to school Wednesday, December 20, the day the team was scheduled to fly to the West Coast, she offered him half her paycheck for spending money on the trip, which implies that she still may not have fully understood the gravity of what was going on around her. Rick declined her offer, saying, "the team was taking care of his expenses," and besides, he added, his parents had sent him some money.

The trip started inauspiciously with an 81–79 loss to an unheralded St. Mary's team in Los Angeles on Thursday night, which broke Boston College's seven-game win streak. The game ended controversially, with the Gaels awarded two foul shots at the final buzzer on a disputed foul. B.C.'s sports information director, Reid Oslin, remembered an irate Sweeney having to be restrained by his teammates after the game.

Already, Kuhn had called Reed back in Boston, and the two would speak daily for the duration of the trip. Reed remembered Kuhn calling her in the day or two before the UCLA game and giving her the phone numbers of the team's hotel in Los Angeles as well as at the Hawaiian Regency in Honolulu, where the team would be staying once it arrived in Hawaii. Later that night, Tony Perla called Reed and got the two numbers from her, although it is unclear if Perla called Kuhn at the hotel or if Kuhn called Perla in Pittsburgh, since no records of any such calls were ever produced.

Back in New York, Hill was told by either Paul Mazzei or Tony Perla that the players—in other words, Kuhn—had said they wanted to "dump" the game, or lose by more than the hefty point spread, which had UCLA favored by between fifteen and eighteen points. Hill would later claim that he and Burke had gotten down on the UCLA game for "maybe twenty-five or thirty thousand dollars, and it worked out great." (By the time *Wiseguy* was published, the figure had risen to more than fifty thousand dollars, but who was counting?)

How Hill and Burke could have known what really transpired in the hours leading up to the game is a mystery, since there was confusion across the board over who was supposed to do what.

Tony Perla remembered suggesting to Kuhn that B.C. dump the game, and being told by Kuhn that the players didn't want to do that, that they felt they had a chance to win, and that he and Sweeney had agreed to "play to win." Kuhn also wanted five hundred dollars of his own money bet on the game, on Boston College, according to Perla.

"We wouldn't do it, because we felt it was an honor for us to be playing UCLA. It was a big game for us," Kuhn would later say.

One step up the food chain, Mazzei was having trouble figuring out just what to do. He remembered having three conversations with Perla: in the first, Perla said to bet Boston College plus the points, which Mazzei balked at. Fifteen or twenty minutes later, Perla called back and told him they were going to bet on UCLA. Mazzei told him that made more sense . . . but Perla called him back a third time, about fifteeen or twenty minutes after the second call, and told him they were betting on B.C.

"They felt that they could play within the point spread, and they felt they had a shot at beating UCLA," Mazzei said, "which I thought was a joke." Mazzei told Perla, "For my money, I wouldn't bet on Boston College. Just tell them to lay down and lose by a big margin," and everybody would be happy. Ultimately, with all the confusion, Mazzei decided not to bet at all.

On the players' end, Sweeney remembered being approached by Kuhn before the UCLA game, but says that he refused Kuhn's offer to "do business" on the game. Sweeney also denied talking to Cobb about the scheme, during the trip or at any other time during the season.

If Sweeney's latter assertion is to be believed—and it certainly is plausible, particularly since Cobb's words and actions lead to the same conclusion—then this created a situation that would become increasingly muddled as the season progressed. Sweeney knew Kuhn was involved in the scheme and knew—or, at least, thought he knew—that Cobb was involved. Cobb knew Kuhn was involved but was unaware that Sweeney was involved, or that Sweeney suspected that he, Cobb, was involved. To complicate matters further, Kuhn told FBI agents in 1980 that he suspected Cobb may have been contacted separately, by Tony Perla or by persons unknown, to fix other games on his own.

The confusion came to a head during the UCLA game, and may have cost Boston College a chance at a major upset.

• • •

Their impressive won-loss records notwithstanding—UCLA was 5–1, Boston College 7–1 entering the game—there was little similarity between the two schools' basketball résumés. While Boston College had made a name for itself in the still-insular world of Eastern basketball, the Bruins under head coach Gary Cunningham were heirs to a tradition of success unmatched in college basketball history. While the 1978–79 team was not the equal of Bruin teams of years past, it featured a towering front line of future pros David Greenwood and Kiki Vandeweghe as well as seven-footer Gig Sims, and a backcourt composed of highly regarded Brad Holland and Roy Hamilton, the latter player one of Cobb's fiercest rivals dating back to their high school days in Connecticut.

For Cobb, this game meant another opportunity to show what he could do against players from one of the elite programs, and he steeled himself to do his best for the pro scouts who were sure to be in the Pauley Pavilion bleachers that night. That afternoon, he relaxed by spending some time driving around the city before the game with his cousin Gary, who was living in Los Angeles while attending the University of Southern California on a football scholarship.

Boston College coach Tom Davis was nothing if not consistent, and he was not going to tailor his strategy to an opponent, even one as imposing as UCLA. That night, as they had done against Bentley and Stonehill and New Hampshire, and as they would do against every other team that season, the Eagles applied pressure in the backcourt and frontcourt, and Davis ran players in and out of the game freely. The hosts were going to have to win this game themselves, with B.C.'s players in their faces the whole evening. For several stretches during the game, it proved a daunting task.

At one point in the first half, UCLA held a slim, 30–28 lead as Davis's four-man, full-court press disrupted the Bruins' offensive flow. But UCLA went on a 16–4 run and eventually led at halftime, 56–41. The 6-foot-9 Greenwood was manhandling Kuhn, Beaulieu, and the rest of the Eagles' smallish frontcourt players, and by halftime had already accumulated fourteen points, seven rebounds, and five blocked shots.

"We were in over our heads talentwise," B.C. assistant coach Kevin Mackey recalled. "I can still remember, it was like [Greenwood] was out there playing by himself; we couldn't do anything to stop him."

Cobb rose to the challenge, however, and almost single-handedly kept the Eagles in the game with eighteen first-half points, spurring the *Los Angeles Times* to describe him the next day as "a man in perpetual motion with a velvet shooting touch," who "captured the fancy of the crowd with his enthusiastic style."

"We were playing super, super basketball," Cobb remembered. "We were taking it to them, we were scoring baskets, and it was a close first half."

Early in the second half, Boston College cut a 64–45 lead to nine with 14:45 remaining. The gap would have shrunk further had B.C. freshman Vin Caraher not been whistled for traveling on a crucial possession. Still, the visitors had demonstrated that they weren't ready to give in just yet. Soon, they drew even closer.

With Greenwood on the bench with four fouls, B.C. closed to within seven points (78–71) when Michael Bowie culminated a 14–3 run by hitting a fifteen-footer from the baseline with 9:36 left. Suddenly, the game seemed winnable. But just as suddenly, it slipped out of the Eagles' grasp.

B.C. senior Tom Meggers still shakes his head at what happened.

"It was my first time ever being there (in Pauley Pavilion), and it was like, 'Wow,' you're pumped up," Meggers said. "And I just remember because I had a good game. I played well. And we were playing well. And we had a chance to beat them. And I just remember coming into a timeout and looking up (at the scoreboard) and there must have been six, seven minutes left in the game. And the game's close and the momentum's going our way, and I'm thinking, 'We've got a chance here.' Then all of a sudden, the ball goes over someone's head. . . . And Ernie was not the kind of guy that didn't take his shot. He was a guy who could put twenty points on the board every game. Nobody else [on the team] could do that. Then, all of a sudden, he doesn't shoot?"

Cobb has a simple explanation.

"Jim Sweeney wouldn't give me the ball," he says today without prompting, two decades after that night in Los Angeles.

At his 1984 trial, he elaborated: "For some reason I remember that Jim Sweeney was slowing the ball down. He was not looking for me or pushing the ball up the court like he had done in the first half. He changed the game plan. He began walking the ball up very slowly. I was very upset about this because as the leading scorer and in the limelight, it is a delicate situation for me to go up to the player and tell him to pass me the ball. It sounded selfish and I resented that. So I thought it was the coach's responsibility to tell Jim Sweeney to do this."

As Cobb simmered, Sweeney continued to play keepaway. With no one else to step in and take up the scoring slack, the Eagles' momentum faded. Before long, Cobb's emotions boiled over and touched off an ugly scene.

"I kept on playing and I kept my cool," Cobb said, "and about five minutes elapsed without me touching the ball. And I was very upset, and at that time I told Jim Sweeney, 'Pass me the ball.' I yelled at him. And he yelled back at me and we exchanged a few words. And I remember Tom Davis pulled us both out of the game and sat us down for about seven minutes, which felt like an eternity to me."

Chris Foy noticed the same thing, and it was one of the first things he remembered when he was questioned by the FBI two years later.

"There was about five or six minutes left, and we had a shot," Foy recalled. "But there was one instance that just sticks out in my mind. We were bringing the ball upcourt and Cobb is just yelling at the top of his lungs for Sweeney to give him the ball. We'd run certain plays, and Sweeney was bypassing (Cobb)—using the skip pass to get the ball out of the hands of our best scorer.

"I firmly believe that Jimmy felt that we had a chance to win that game, and he knew what was going on between Cobb and Kuhn. And he didn't want those guys getting involved, so he tried to go around Ernie. Ernie was saying, 'Give me the goddamn ball!' and Jimmy's just looking straight ahead. It was just kind of weird."

Why would Sweeney not want Cobb to have the ball? There are two logical explanations: one, Sweeney and Kuhn both are telling the truth when they say there was no fix on in the UCLA game, and Sweeney, thinking that Cobb was trying to shave points, wanted to keep the ball away from him; or, two, Sweeney and Kuhn were indeed shaving points and decided to keep the ball out of Cobb's hands because he was having a good game and could not be relied upon to keep Boston College's score down.

Statements by both Sweeney and Kuhn support the first theory, but the second theory later gained some credence when Barbara Reed said that in February 1979 she remembered hearing Kuhn and Sweeney talking about having Sweeney keep the ball away from Cobb, because he shot all the time. "Basically, they said Ernie was a ball-hog and that he never passed the ball off," Reed said. "That he went right for the basket every time he got it, so they would keep the ball away from him. He couldn't be trusted if you gave him the ball, that he'd pass it back."

The argument between Cobb and Sweeney spilled over into a timeout, and Davis pulled both players. By the time he put them back in with about two minutes left, it was too late, as Greenwood had reentered the game and led a procession of Bruins to the foul line. The final score was 103–81, which hardly did justice to B.C.'s valiant performance. They had played on equal terms with UCLA for thirty minutes, but had been outscored 25–10 in the final 9:36.

Holland (twenty-five points on 10-of-12 shooting) and Hamilton (twenty points, thirteen assists) led the Bruins, while Vin Caraher had his best varsity game so far with sixteen points and six rebounds. Kuhn played solidly and finished with six points and seven rebounds. Cobb, meanwhile, finished with twenty points, but just two in the second half.

Davis, still unaware of the fix despite the Cobb-Sweeney blowup, told reporters, "UCLA is incredible. I thought we worked as hard as we could. I was happy with our effort, but obviously it was not enough."

Years later, when UCLA's Holland was head coach at San Diego State University, he used the game as a cautionary tale for his players about the evils of gambling.

"When I heard about them shaving points, I went back and looked at the tape," Holland told the *Tampa Tribune* in 1997. "You could pick some stuff up. A guy bouncing the ball off his leg . . . making some ridiculous fouls away from the ball."

• • •

Their chance at an upset of UCLA gone, the team traveled to Honolulu for the Rainbow Classic. Boston College had played in the inaugural Rainbow

Classic in 1964, along with five other teams from the mainland plus the host school and two local military teams. From those modest beginnings, the Classic quickly became a coveted destination for college teams looking to escape the dreary winter weather and pick up a few wins that might come in handy at NCAA Tournament selection time.

Sweeney roomed with Kuhn in Hawaii and recalled him having several conversations with Tony Perla, specifically about the Purdue game on December 28, the team's opening game in the tournament. Kuhn would say later that despite his bad advice on the UCLA game, he again convinced Perla to bet on the Eagles against Purdue, as a four-point underdog, and requested that Perla bet five hundred dollars for him as before.

Hill said no business was done during the Rainbow Classic because of the difficulties posed by the time difference and because "the players felt they had a shot to make the NCAA Tournament" and would want to stockpile as many wins as possible. However, Las Vegas oddsmaker Zach Franzi would testify that the point spread on the B.C.–Purdue game dropped on the day of the game—indicating, oddly, that money was being bet on Boston College, if Franzi's memory was accurate.

A bet on Purdue would have come back a winner, though, as the Boilermakers, a team that featured future NBA center Joe Barry Carroll, trounced the Eagles, 82–54. Similar to the UCLA game, Cobb was unstoppable in the first half, scoring B.C.'s first thirteen points and seventeen of their first nineteen. But he cooled off and eventually finished with twenty-three. Kuhn and Perla were losers again, and the insult was magnified for Kuhn when he had his nose broken by an elbow from Carroll. He would play part of the rest of the season wearing a plastic face mask that had been fashioned out of a goalie's mask borrowed from the B.C. hockey team.

In an interesting twist, Boston College had traveled several thousand miles from Boston yet ended up playing its crosstown rival, Harvard, in the next game. The Crimson no doubt were feeling the effects of an overtime loss to Arizona State the night before, but still put forth a good effort in losing to Boston College by five, 83–78. The final score is intriguing: in a game in which there was no point-shaving, B.C. had defeated Harvard by only two points more than they had two weeks earlier, when points allegedly were being shaved.

As he had done in Boston two weeks earlier in the team's previous meeting, Sweeney was more active than usual on the offensive end, as he scored ten of the Eagles' final eighteen points of the game and sealed the win with two free throws with sixteen seconds remaining. The junior guard also set a tournament record with six steals in the game. "We feel if we can beat Tennessee, there's no question we can beat the New England teams we have ahead of us," Sweeney told the *Boston Globe*'s Joe Concannon after the game.

Meanwhile, Kuhn continue to spread the wealth, and later would tell Reed that he had "blown about $650 just going out" with the guys during the trip.

"We were thinking, 'Wow, these guys must have been really working hard [last] summer saving money up for this trip,'" Foy naïvely thought. "It wasn't obscene, but it was just really peculiar that they're totally chowing down at the best restaurants, and we're like, 'What are we doing wrong?'"

B.C. beat Tennessee the next night, December 30, to finish in fifth place in the tournament. The Eagles rallied from a seven-point deficit in the second half, and Cobb sank two free throws with two seconds left in the 74–72 win. His twenty-nine points helped earn him the tournament's Most Valuable Player award. In the locker room after the game, the players popped champagne corks and sprayed the bubbly liquid over everyone in sight, including Davis.

"The key to it all was running," Cobb told Concannon. "When I can get free one-on-one, it's hard to stop me. Today we ran and created things."

The trip had begun with three losses and ended with two wins, and the team headed back to Boston on January 2, filled with optimism.

• • •

If not all of Kuhn's teammates had been able to benefit from his generosity during the trip, Reed received the opposite treatment. After the team arrived back in Boston on January 2, Rick presented his girlfriend with a "whole bag of things," and told her to reach in and pick something out. Reed was overwhelmed. "I expected a T-shirt, you know?" she said. "I got a T-shirt, too."

The bag contained, among other things, earrings made of black and gold coral and a matching black coral ring with two small diamonds on it; a pair of jade earrings and a necklace; a bikini; a "really pretty" black silk kimono that Kuhn told Reed he had bought in San Francisco; plus other trinkets like ashtrays and little gifts he had picked up in the hotels. There also was a teddy bear.

Reed noticed Sweeney's girlfriend, Maura Haggerty, wearing a coral ring like the one Rick had given her.

The spending spree continued for the next few weeks, as Kuhn and Reed went to Sears-Roebuck at the Natick Mall and bought a large color television for about $400, paid for in cash by Kuhn, and a queen-size brass bed at Ruderman's Furniture for about $350, also paid in cash. Later in the month, Rick and Joe Beaulieu showed up at the apartment one night carrying six or eight boxes up the stairs. They contained a complete stereo system—cassette deck, amplifier, headphones, and speakers—that Rick had purchased at Tech Hi-Fi in Cambridge for about $1,500.

• • •

The Eagles returned to the court on Saturday, January 6, and improved their record to 10–3 with an 80–68 win over city rival Northeastern. But plans were already being made for the next game, on the following Wednesday against New England powerhouse Rhode Island.

Reed overheard Kuhn on the phone one night that week telling someone that the game would be "too tough to call," and that Rhode Island was a strong team and he didn't think B.C. would be able to win—and that he wasn't sure if the Eagles would even be able to stay with the Rams. Also, the game was being played on the road during winter break, and few B.C. students would be making the trip to Kingston, Rhode Island, to show their support.

After he hung up the phone, Reed asked Kuhn if he was talking to Tony Perla about betting on the Rhode Island game. An argument ensued as Kuhn became upset that Reed had listened to his phone call. "I told them that I doubted they should bet on it because I didn't think B.C. would win," he told her, and repeated the reasons he had cited on the phone.

Reed drove to Kingston for the game, where she saw B.C. lose, 91–78, a final tally that was not nearly indicative of Rhode Island's domination of the game. The Rams built an 80–53 lead in the second half before B.C.'s press yielded some late points in garbage time. Six-foot-eight forward Sylvester "Sly" Williams, considered by many the best player in New England, scorched B.C. for twenty-five points, many coming at the expense of the sophomore Foy. The Rams were bigger than the Eagles and just as quick, and had no trouble with Davis's pressing defenses as they won their fourteenth consecutive game at home.

The Eagles fell behind early and had to scramble to get back in the game. "It made it sort of a helter-skelter game," Cobb remembered. "It made it more disorganized. You take the first available shot and try to come back quickly."

Cobb lost the individual battle against Williams, but finished with nineteen points to lead B.C. Kuhn played all of two minutes.

"Rhode Island is obviously a really good basketball team. They drove a wedge into everything we tried to do," Davis told reporters after the game. "We could beat a team like Rhode Island, but not tonight. And not on any night we didn't put everything, and I mean everything, together."

Foy describes the game in blunter terms.

"They kicked our ass," he said. "They were ten times better than us. We weren't in that game. They had us from the opening tap. That was Davis's trademark, he'd keep pressing the shit out of you if you were down by thirty-five, hoping to get a respectable score."

Kuhn contended that Cobb and Sweeney were both shaving points, and that both were upset when Kuhn relayed the word from Tony Perla that since most of the bets had been "pushes," or bets where the point spread matched the game's final margin and no money was won or lost, they would not be getting paid for the game. Cobb and Sweeney continue to deny this charge.

Were Kuhn telling the truth, the gamblers would have had Vin Caraher to blame for blowing their bets. The freshman went on a tear near the end of the game, scoring a nearly unfathomable fifteen consecutive points in the waning minutes as B.C. cut a 91–63 deficit to 91–78 at the buzzer.

Hill, meanwhile, had driven to Florida with his daughter, Gail, and one of her friends, and said initially that he was told by Burke when he arrived that the bets were winners. But he told *Sports Illustrated*'s Doug Looney in 1981 that he had gotten most of his money down on Rhode Island as a fifteen-point favorite, which meant Caraher's garbage-time heroics cost him thousands of dollars.

On the other hand, it is almost less plausible to believe that points were being shaved than it is to believe that the Rams, New England's top team in 1978–79, simply were too good on this particular night. Any team that uses the press as much as Boston College did under Davis is bound to get burned by it once in a while; like a tennis player who plays a serve-and-volley style, the potential exists to look great on one point and awful on the next. Perhaps Rhode Island just made the Eagles look awful early on and, playing in front of a large (over five thousand) and boisterous home crowd, poured it on until the final minutes when Caraher began to light it up.

Meanwhile, a few thousand dollars bet on a basketball game pales in comparison to Hill's reason for driving to Florida in the first place: he was carrying thirty-two pounds of cocaine that was to be returned to a man named Richard Eaton, who had sold it to Burke. This fact was never brought out during any of the coverage of the Boston College case, but serves as a reminder of the type of character with whom the three B.C. players had now cast their lot.

• • •

Despite Caraher's scoring outburst at the end of the URI game, as far as Hill knew, a large part of the problem was Cobb, who was proving to be unreliable. The scheme would not work with just Kuhn, or even with Kuhn and Sweeney in concert; Cobb's scoring ability and penchant for shooting at will—a habit supported by Davis and tolerated by the other players—made him indispensable to the gamblers' plan.

Two days after the Rhode Island game, on Tuesday, January 8, Kuhn received his second money order from Rocco Perla, in the amount of two thousand dollars. When he went to pick it up, Reed remembered Kuhn telling her that he would take half and the other half would be for Sweeney. Cobb's name was not mentioned.

Tony Perla was in Miami getting ready to watch his hometown Pittsburgh Steelers play against Dallas in Super Bowl XIII when he found out about the Rhode Island game, and he passed the word to Kuhn that no one would be getting paid from that contest. By this time, though, Perla had heard from Hill that other adjustments were going to have to be made.

While in Florida, Hill claimed to have had a conversation with Burke and a man named Dave Iacovetti, whom Hill knew to be a major bookmaker in Florida. Iacovetti allegedly told Burke that the linesmakers in Las Vegas were getting wise to the scheme and were adjusting the point spreads on B.C. games to reflect what they suspected was a fix in progress.

Iacovetti told Burke and Hill that they needed to bet on B.C. to win a game to balance things out and deflect any suspicions.

Eventually it was agreed that they would use the Connecticut game on January 17, the following Wednesday. UConn, under coach Dom Perno, was then a second-level team in New England, though freshmen Cornelius Thompson and Mike McKay would soon raise the Huskies' profile by the time they joined the Big East the next season.

The Eagles, playing at Roberts Center, were a small favorite, perhaps two or three points, and they won 90–80. B.C.'s won-loss record now stood at 13–3—the Eagles had defeated the University of Maryland–Baltimore and St. Anselm's, Mackey's alma mater, in the week before playing UConn—and the Eagles had won six games in a row.

Perla would would later say that both Kuhn and Sweeney bet on their own team that night, and that both won in the neighborhood of four or five hundred dollars. This flatly contradicted Sweeney's claim that the only money he took was the five hundred dollars Rick had given him before the trip to Hawaii.

A third money order came Kuhn's way on January 19, two days after the win over UConn. Mazzei had sent it and signed Kuhn's father's name, Fred Kuhn, on the receipt. By the time it arrived in Boston, there was a snafu in collecting it that caused another argument between Kuhn and Reed.

After practice that night, Reed told Joe Beaulieu and his girlfriend that they could have a ride home in her van. This angered Kuhn, because he was planning to go to Western Union to pick up the money order and did not want any company for the trip. Reed remembered Kuhn saying he "didn't want Beaulieu to see how much money" he was getting because "I'm giving different amounts to Ernie than I'm giving to Joe, and I'm giving different amounts to Joe than I'm giving to Sweeney."

If Reed's memory was accurate, it means that a) Sweeney and Cobb were both still receiving money for shaving points, something they deny to this day; and b) Beaulieu was involved in some way in the scheme. Kuhn would testify that he divided the money between Sweeney and himself, a claim Sweeney denies, and Beaulieu testified that he rebuffed Kuhn's approach to him before the Harvard game and did not take any money for doing anything.

• • •

The next game was on January 20 against Holy Cross, B.C.'s bitter rival from Worcester, an hour west of the city. The two schools had a lengthy history on the basketball court that stretched back to 1905, the second year Boston College fielded a basketball team. In recent years Holy Cross had held the upper hand in the series, with six straight wins dating back to the 1974–75 season.

The resentments ran deep. Holy Cross star Ronnie Perry's Catholic Memorial High team—then coached by his father, Ron Perry Sr., who later became athletic director at Holy Cross—had staged some epic Boston schoolboy wars with Don Bosco Tech teams starring future B.C. players Beaulieu and Dwan Chandler and coached by B.C. assistant Kevin Mackey, who did not hide his general dislike for the elder Perry.

"It was an unbelievable rivalry," George Blaney, the Holy Cross coach at the time, recalls. "You could play tiddlywinks between Boston and Holy Cross and it would be competitive."

In the two days before the Holy Cross game, Reed overheard Kuhn on the phone, talking about the game and whether or not B.C. would win. She became upset and pointed out to him that of all the games to try and predict, this one would be difficult because of the intense rivalry and the emotions involved. Kuhn repeated this to the person on the other end of the phone, whom Reed assumed to be Tony or Rocco Perla. When Kuhn hung up, all he would say was that a bet was being placed for him on the game.

The game was played at Roberts Center in front of a capacity crowd of forty-two hundred. Cobb was on fire, and everything he launched up seemed to find the bottom of the net. But he missed an off-balance twenty-footer at the end of regulation that would have won the game, and the Eagles needed two free throws by Michael Bowie with two seconds remaining in the second overtime to eke out an 89–87 victory. The win capped a comeback in which B.C. rallied from a 74–68 deficit with 1:19 left in regulation. Cobb, hardly playing like a man being paid to keep his team's score down, made two key free throws, then stole an inbounds pass, was fouled, and made two more to tie the game at 74 in the final minute. A backcourt violation by Holy Cross set up Cobb's miss at the buzzer.

Kuhn, at least, appeared to be trying to do his part. Late in the second overtime, he committed what the *Boston Globe* referred to the next day as a "thoughtless" play by fouling Gary Witts with thirteen seconds remaining after Witts grabbed a rebound of Dwan Chandler's missed foul shot. Witts's two free throws tied the game at 87, but Bowie drove the middle and was fouled on B.C.'s next possession. After his shots gave B.C. the lead, Peter Beckenbach missed on a sixteen-footer at the buzzer for the Crusaders.

The point spread for the game showed Boston College favored by five points, but, according to Hill, some bookies dropped the line to two points by game time, which meant that some of his bets might have fallen right on the point spread. Kuhn may have been the biggest winner of all, if he indeed had been able to have money bet for him in Pittsburgh or New York, and his "thoughtless" play near the end of the game may have been anything but that.

Cobb continued to be an issue that needed to be resolved, however. In the days after the Holy Cross game, Hill allegedly told Tony Perla, "At all costs, talk to" Cobb. Hill later claimed that he was led to believe that Cobb was "all set," but that he wanted another twenty-five hundred for his share; in reality, by this time Kuhn probably was skimming Cobb's share by telling the Perlas and Hill that Cobb was participating in the fix when he actually was not.

Tony Perla returned to Pittsburgh on January 23, three days after the

Holy Cross game, and sent two cashier's checks to Kuhn, in the amounts of four hundred and five hundred dollars, purportedly the amounts that Kuhn had won betting on the game that B.C. had won against UConn a week earlier.

• • •

An 83–75 win over Villanova prepped the team for the Colonial Classic on the weekend of January 26 and 27, a tournament held at Boston Garden and featuring an all-New England lineup of Holy Cross, UConn, UMass, and Boston College. Holy Cross had won the tournament in its first two years, but the upstart Eagles, with their 15–3 record and the win over the Cru-saders a week earlier, were now considered on equal footing with their hated foe.

Ironically, the teams did not end up playing each other. Connecticut defeated Holy Cross in overtime, 109-102, in the second game of Friday night's doubleheader, knocking the Crusaders out of the tournament despite forty-six points by Ronnie Perry.

In the opener, Boston College qualified for Saturday night's final with an 82–70 win over UMass in a game marred by shoddy refereeing that ben-efited B.C. After a poorly played first half in which Boston College made just thirteen of thirty-four shots from the field and Massachusetts commit-ted eleven turnovers, the action gradually heated up. With 7:18 remaining in the game, Minutemen center Mark Haymore, a transfer from Indiana, threw down a dunk to cut B.C.'s lead to five points, but the goal was negated as teammate Brad Johnson picked up his fifth foul. Sweeney sank both free throws to boost the lead to nine, and the Eagles held on to the advantage. Cobb, averaging 22.4 points per game, scored nineteen to lead the Eagles, followed by Bowie with seventeen. Haymore led the Minute-men with twenty.

The team stayed downtown that night at the Parker House, a hotel not far from Boston Garden. The next afternoon, before the Eagles went to the Garden for warmups for the championship game that evening, Kuhn approached Sweeney and asked him if he was interested in shaving points against Connecticut. Sweeney says he again refused, and nothing more was mentioned of the matter.

On Saturday night, January 27, college basketball ruled Boston, as a large crowd piled into the Garden to watch B.C. and UConn square off under the championship banners of the building's more famous tenants, the Celtics and Bruins. The game was featured prominently on the front page of the *Globe*'s sports section the next morning with an accompanying photo. And few in the crowd of 12,653 left the ancient building feeling they had not gotten their money's worth.

Playing for the second time in ten days against the school whose advances he had spurned four years earlier as a high-schooler, Cobb shook off the Huskies' defense to put on a show with eleven first-half points com-plemented by five assists. Boston College, meanwhile, held Corny Thompson to just three points and led by 42–35 at intermission after a late spurt.

UConn closed to within two points early in the second half, and led by five points with 4:37 left in the game, but Sweeney cut the lead to one with 4:01 left when he grabbed a rebound, dribbled downcourt, and sank a jumper from the top of the key. Later, with the Huskies focusing their attention on Cobb, Bowie made an open jumper from the right wing, then followed that with a drive over Thompson that gave Boston College a 72–69 lead with 1:46 left. The Eagles held on through the final, frantic minute and emerged with a 78–77 victory that ended with the players rushing onto the court in celebration.

Bowie finished with eighteen points, Cobb led B.C. with nineteen, Beaulieu scored twelve and Caraher contributed eleven. "We did a good job of stopping Beaulieu low, but that damn Bowie hit his jumpers," Connecticut coach Dom Perno said after the game. Cobb was named the tournament's outstanding player for his performance in the two games, though Holy Cross's Perry received the MVP award after his thirty-one points helped the Crusaders outlast UMass, 78–74, in the consolation game.

After the game, the celebration continued in the locker room, and the boisterous B.C. players threw Davis into the showers. "I don't know what more we could have done in this game," Davis told reporters. "It looked like we might have been out of it, just like against Holy Cross last week, but we hung in."

The next day, the *Globe*'s Sunday sports section featured a picture of a jubilant Beaulieu lifting Sweeney off the floor, the 5-foot-11 guard and the 6-foot-8 center locked in a sweaty embrace with Sweeney pumping one fist in the air and Beaulieu with his left arm extended, his index finger pointed upward.

Neither the players nor Davis could have known that this was to be the high point of their season, and that in the following months and years even this accomplishment would be reduced to little more than a footnote.

CHAPTER EIGHT

Point-Shaving 101

T he terms that describe the act of willfully manipulating the score of an athletic event at the behest of gambling interests are straight out of a hack sportswriter's imagination: "shaving points," "dumping," "tanking," "on the take," "the fix is in." The words bring to mind images of men in trenchcoats with cigar-stained smiles and pinky rings lurking in the shadowy corridors of musty arenas, beckoning the fuzzy-cheeked innocents in short pants with promises of easy cash.

Yet behind the colorful jargon lies the cold truth that virtually any basketball game can be influenced—and perhaps many more have been affected than the ticket-buying public would like to believe—with no one the wiser save the conspirators; and that, like date rape, the proffer is less likely to come from a menacing stranger than from a friend of the player, possibly even a roommate or relative.

The conundrum for the authorities is that point-shaving is a crime that is largely undetectable in its commission and exceedingly difficult to prove after the fact. The smallest misstep, whether an errant pass or missed shot, can blend seamlessly into the back-and-forth action of a game and can be enough to turn a losing bet into a winner, or vice versa. In the majority of cases, there are no obvious clues to be extracted from the games themselves; even game films, the kind of evidence that is rarely available in any criminal trial, can be inconclusive.

This fact partly explains the shock and dismay that inevitably accompany the announcement of the latest point-shaving allegations. Even (or especially) devoted supporters of the team in question find themselves unable to recall any moments when their heroes appeared to be putting forth less than their best effort, and certainly not willfully.

Once the news is out, the reactions follow an established pattern. Fans express outrage that any player would compromise his own principles and prostitute himself for a quick buck. Newspaper columnists lament the continuing erosion of morality in big-time sports, and demand either for players to be given a piece of college basketball's bulging financial pie or for a wholesale return to "true" amateurism in college athletics—conveniently forgetting the widespread gambling scandals of the early 1950s that occurred long before college basketball became the money machine it is today. The affected school then issues a statement assigning blame to a few rotten apples who fell prey to "outside influences," and assures anyone who will listen that the institution had no prior knowledge of the investigation. Finally, the sound and fury fades to the background, replaced by the burning question of who will win tonight's game, and tomorrow's.

Less ephemeral is the black mark affixed to the school's name. Witness point-shaving's Murderers Row from the last twenty years: Boston College, Tulane, Arizona State, Northwestern. Four and five decades ago, the names would have been City College of New York, Long Island University, Seton Hall, Kentucky, Bradley, and a few dozen more. These institutions will forever be associated with scandal—yet what they share is not so much that their basketball players were shaving points, but that they were caught doing it.

And that may put them in the minority.

"There have been cover-ups," one former Division I coach said in 1998, not long after the news broke that two Northwestern players had admitted to shaving points in games played during the 1994–95 season. "When you think about it, could B.C. have been the only place? It's a big country, there are lot of schools, a lot of games. To think that schools like B.C., Northwestern, and Tulane are the only ones is just naïve. I've felt for a long time that the biggest problem for colleges was betting, and people getting to the players. Because it's everywhere: on TV, now on the Internet. It's out there, big-time."

Former Holy Cross and Seton Hall coach George Blaney recalled that in the 1970s, when there were no nationally publicized cases of point-shaving, plenty of rumors circulated among coaches around the country. "There was more stuff that went on in those years," he said. "Almost each year you could go back and find another scandal. It doesn't stop."

It is difficult to imagine gambling being more ingrained in the culture of American sports than it was during the college basketball fixing scandals in the late 1940s and early 1950s, when point-shaving was common knowledge among fans well before the national media finally got off its collective duff and began to write about it. But it has become evident that we live in an age when permissiveness often is surpassed only by naïveté.

Consider the results of a University of Michigan study released in early 1999 that found that 35 percent of *college athletes* had gambled on sports since entering college. Perhaps more surprising was the revelation that nearly 5 percent said they had provided inside information for gambling purposes or had bet on a game in which they participated.

• • •

Betting on athletic contests has its roots at least as far back as ancient Rome, when chariot races and gladiator fights drew heavy wagering from all strata of society and offered slaves a chance to gain their freedom by winning large sums for their patrons. The emperor Caligula was said to have been found playing dice on the day of his sister's funeral, and Claudius had a gaming table installed in his carriage so he could play while traveling.

In their book, *Winning Is the Only Thing: Sports in America Since 1945*, Randy Roberts and James S. Olson date the birth of modern point-shaving to the early 1940s, when a man named Charles McNeil introduced the point spread into sports gambling and changed college basketball forever. Before McNeil's innovation, wagering on college basketball was done using odds; for example, if Kentucky was a 4–1 favorite over Alabama, you could wager one hundred dollars to make a four-hundred-dollar profit on Alabama—but if you wanted to bet on Kentucky to win, you would have to risk four hundred dollars to make one hundred dollars' profit.

With the point spread, however, you would only have to wager $110 to make the same $100 profit. The extra $10 was the bookmaker's commission, or "vigorish," referred to as "the vig," or "the juice."

The crucial difference was that under odds betting, underdog Alabama would actually have to win the game for its backers to win their bets; with the advent of the point spread, they could lose by fewer points than the number posted by the oddsmakers and still make money for their backers. Conversely, Kentucky could win for the gamblers by "beating" the point spread—winning by more than the posted number.

The impact of this development cannot be overestimated. The point spread evened out mismatches between teams of vastly different abilities by giving the better team a handicap. This served to heighten interest among the betting public, which now focused less on the winner of the game and more on the actual final score. It was inevitable that before long, players could be influenced to hold the score down, particularly players on elite teams—like Kentucky—that typically were heavy favorites. A generation of ballplayers now was able to rationalize accepting money to influence their play by saying, in essence: What was the big deal if the point spread was twenty and you won by fifteen? You still were winning the game; this way, you were making the gamblers happy as well as the fans. What was so wrong about that?

It was a disaster waiting to happen, and in the late 1940s and early 1950s point-shaving spread from New York to the South and Midwest, tainting scores of games involving dozens of players. By the time the full extent of the mess had been laid bare to a still-disbelieving public, individual reputations had been ruined, basketball programs discontinued, and the sport itself was under attack from all sides. It was college basketball's darkest hour, and surely would not be repeated—or would it?

Ten years after the revelations about widespread point-shaving in college basketball that nearly killed the sport, the fixers were at it again. George Blaney, who coached Holy Cross from 1972 to 1994, was a senior at the school in 1960–61 on a team that finished third in the National Invitation Tournament. He remembers beating Seton Hall and Tennessee that season, and finding out later that both teams had used players that were shaving points. In the latter game, he recalls sarcastically, "Tennessee dumped against us in a game that we were so bad, we wound up winning the game by one, but they should have investigated us after the game."

It eventually came out that the Seton Hall players Art Hicks and Hank Gunther had been receiving fifteen hundred dollars per game, but were turning around and betting their shares, and doubling and tripling their money. By the time the dust settled in 1962, thirty-seven players from twenty-two schools had been implicated, including future pro stars Roger Brown and Connie Hawkins, and St. Joseph's University of Philadelphia was ordered to vacate its third-place finish in the NCAA Tournament because three of its players, Frank Majewski, Vince Kempton, and John Egan, had allegedly been shaving points. The news hit especially close to home for Blaney since one of the players alleged to be a ringleader in the scheme was a close friend named Lou Brown, a bench-warmer at North Carolina who acted as a middleman between players and gamblers.

Blaney says he was never approached by Brown to shave points, but that he can see how other players might have been unable to resist an offer that sounded too good to be true.

"I understand how easy it is to convince somebody that (point-shaving) is almost not wrong to do," he says. "It's kind of a double-edged sword. It's easy to say what you would do if someone came up to you and offered you a certain amount of money. But I don't think you really know unless you're actually presented with the case.

"And then the other thing that happens is, those guys get their hooks in you different ways. Sometimes they have something on you, or in some cases they've already given you things. That's pretty much how the agents work these days. They start with tickets, taking care of your girlfriend going to a game; then it's a dinner or two, then the next thing you know it's some jewelry. That's how the gamblers did it, too."

If the gamblers had the above inducements—not to mention human nature—on their side, by the mid-1960s law enforcement authorities had added some potent weapons of their own. What the '50s point-shaving scandals did, besides kill college basketball at Madison Square Garden for the better part of three decades and leave an ugly blemish on the sport, was to demonstrate the need for more effective enforcement measures.

The first of these arrived in 1961, when Congress passed Section 1084 of Title 18 of the U.S. Criminal Code, which made it illegal to use wire communications—in essence, phones—across state lines to place, or assist in placing, bets on sporting events. Now, the simple act of placing a phone call was not merely evidence to be used to gain an indictment; it could be prosecuted as a separate crime. Three years later, on June 6, 1964, the legislative body signed Section 224 into law, making it a crime to conspire to influence, *in any way*, by bribery any sporting contest (italics added).

By 1970, sports bribery effectively came under the Racketeer Influenced and Corrupt Organizations Act, which established laws commonly referred to as the RICO statutes. More than anything, RICO enabled the government to prosecute criminals for their associations with organized crime families, rather than having to catch them in any specific criminal conduct. The statutes also meant that the government now could prosecute point-shaving schemes—provided that the gamblers or players made long-distance phone calls or traveled across state lines—using the same weapons they used against other racketeering crimes such as mail or wire fraud, counterfeiting, kidnapping, or murder.

• • •

Every professional and major-college sporting event is made up of two games. One is played between the white lines and is written about in the newspapers the next day and rehashed endlessly on sports-talk radio. The other pits bookie against bettor in a battle for information, for an edge, for a way to predict the behavior of that most unpredictable of animals, the human being.

The focus of all this attention is the point spread, which, contrary to the opinions of the nonbetting public, is not meant solely as a reflection of the strengths and weaknesses of the two teams in question. The best linesmakers, whether they operate legally out of one of Las Vegas's numerous sports books or under the radar of the law from their brother-in-law's kitchen, are guided by a dispassionate interest in dividing the bets evenly between the two teams involved in any game. Achieving this guarantees them a profit, since bettors risk 10 percent more than they can win back on any single bet.

For example, if a bookie accepts $1,000 in bets on an NBA game between the Celtics and Pistons, and $500 is bet on each team, he will have to pay out $500 to winning bettors but will receive $550 from losing bettors—the extra $50 being the bookie's 10 percent commission, or "vigorish."

It sounds straightforward, but it is deceptively difficult. Bookmakers speak of setting a point spread as if it is an art form, and it may not be far from that. While the line by necessity will reflect the statistical tendencies of the two teams—a poor team obviously will never be favored against an elite team—much of the linesmaker's job revolves around predicting how the public will bet on a specific team or game. Arriving at this determination frequently is a matter of intuition, or "feel," which often comes only with experience.

High-profile teams, such as the San Francisco 49ers during the early to mid-1990s or the Chicago Bulls during the same period, tend to draw a disproportionate share of action from bettors, and linesmakers adjust the point spreads higher in an attempt to draw more bets on the underdog and "even out" the betting. The flip side is that this provides an opportunity for the astute bettor. For example, anyone who bet against the 49ers in games against the Los Angeles Rams through most of the '90s would have realized a profit, since the bookies habitually made San Francisco close to a two-touchdown favorite—a reflection of the team's stature among fans and bettors, but a heavier load to bear for the 49ers once the game begins.

Bookmakers possess other advantages over bettors, however. In the above example, if the 49ers were favored by 13½ points against the Rams and one bookie was receiving only bets on the 49ers, he could adjust the point spread up a half-point, making the 49ers a 14-point favorite. This would effectively give pause to bettors who had envisioned a two-touchdown victory by the 49ers bringing home the money, and might even cause some to switch to the Rams as a 14-point underdog.

If the bookie's ledger is unbalanced, bets can be "laid off" to even out the action. Going back to the 49ers-Rams example, if one bookie is holding ten thousand dollars in bets and seven thousand was bet on the 49ers, he would attempt to, in essence, trade bets with another bookie who might be holding more bets on the Rams than on the 49ers.

Other factors can have a more dramatic effect on the point spread. An injury to a key player can sometimes lead to a game being "taken off the board," which means no more bets are accepted on the game. A game might also be taken off the board if inordinately heavy betting is focusing on one team—so-called "unnatural money"—a development that could signify a fix. During the FBI's investigation of point-shaving at Arizona State during the 1993–94 season, it was reported that at least $250,000 was bet in Las Vegas on underdog Washington to cover the spread against Arizona State in a game in March 1994. The huge influx of money caused the point spread to drop from ten points to three, and ultimately prompted the casinos to suspend betting on the game.

• • •

If it appears the odds in the sports gambling equation are stacked against the gambler, it is only because they are. Add to this the fact that, unlike casino gambling, which still can be pursued only in select locations of the country, sports are ubiquitous and attract the kind of followers whose objectivity frequently is clouded by their allegiance to their hometown team. It is no surprise that most gamblers wind up on the losing end at the end of each season.

For this reason, inside information is the holy grail for most gamblers. Any little tidbit of knowledge, passed on from a team trainer, publicist, or even a cheerleader, can cut into the bookie's advantage if it can help predict what may happen in an upcoming game.

Inside information was the source of an unparalleled winning streak that Henry Hill claims to have ridden during the 1970–71 college basketball season. In concert with Ralph Atlas, a powerful New York City bookmaker who also was one of the bookies used in 1978–79 during the Boston College scheme, Hill and James Burke hooked up with two retired schoolteachers—Hill remembers only that one of them was nicknamed "Soda"—who were providing inside information on college teams.

"They had people at every school in the country," Hill remembers. "We were getting the hot games. We knew when the center and the leading scorer from UConn were out drunk the night before, you know? I went to this guy's house with Jimmy, and the guy had charts and everything. . . . It was like a business. I'd never seen anything like it. They did unbelievable, and we caught the last part of the season, from the middle to the end. These guys would be picking fifteen out of seventeen winners a day. And it did not stop. We destroyed more bookmakers that season . . . "

• • •

One of the secrets to Hill's and Burke's success in 1970–71 also applied eight years later during the Boston College scheme; specifically, both scenarios demonstrated the importance of developing a reliable network of bookmakers who were in on the plan and could lay off bets around the country without arousing suspicion.

Once that was established, the bookies who knew what was going on would ask Hill and Burke to call them as early as possible on nights when they had a hot game, so that they could lay their own bets before the point spread began to change and potentially move to a less desirable number.

• • •

As the National Collegiate Athletic Association's director of agent and gambling activities, William Saum is the public face of the war being waged against sports gambling on college campuses. Saum's position was created in 1996 as a response to the growing number of incidents that were being uncovered at colleges and universities around the country during the late '80s and early to mid-'90s, most of which involved students and student-athletes making illegal wagers.

Saum's office has been instrumental in raising consciousness about the perils of gambling on college campuses, an effort that has included seminars for administrators and coaches as well as FBI agents, testimony before a Senate Judiciary Committee subcommittee on Internet gambling, and the creation of a video that is shown to student-athletes across the country at the beginning of each season.

Partly due to these efforts, two separate pieces of legislation were scheduled to be debated in Congress in the summer of 2000: one that would ban sports gambling on the Internet and another that would ban all gambling on college sports in the state of Nevada, the only state where sports gambling can be done legally.

In the winter of 1978–79, David Cawood had considerably fewer resources at his disposal. Cawood, now a senior vice president of Host Communications, which handles broadcast rights for the NCAA basketball tournament, was then the NCAA's assistant executive director. He remembers how the job of gambling enforcement essentially became his by default.

"We were a small staff back then at the NCAA, and I don't really recall how that fell on my shoulders to do, but I imagine it was because (NCAA executive director) Walter Byers told me he wanted me to do it," Cawood recalls.

What Cawood shared with Saum, however, was a reliance on the very element with which the NCAA would seem least likely to want to align itself. It is one of the ironies of modern college sports that possibly the only people more interested than the NCAA in keeping the games free from taint are the bookies themselves. This has made for some pretty strange bedfellows over the years, as Cawood realized immediately upon assuming his new responsibilities.

"At that particular time, a source had contacted me who was involved in the bookmaking business," Cawood recalls, "and he was concerned about what the NCAA's position would be in regard to gambling. Because in order for him to be successful at what he was doing, he had to make sure it was a clean game. Once I convinced him we would be most interested in receiving information and would act on it when we could, he was very helpful.

"It's a strange way to put it, but if there was something going on and he didn't know anything about it, he couldn't do his job very well."

No bookie exists in a vacuum; even the guy operating out of his brother-in-law's kitchen is part of a network that leads upward and usually comes to rest in the lap of organized crime. Consequently, the two thousand dollars wagered on a "hot" game and laid off by one bookie at the bottom of the food chain can snowball as it moves along, until tens of thousands of dollars are changing hands at the top levels—all based on the original information. Through his informants who populated these different rungs on the illegal gambling ladder, Cawood was able to keep tabs on any suspicious betting activity going on around the country.

"Any time there was a large amount of money bet on a game anywhere in the country, the guys who needed to know that would know it within fifteen minutes, in Las Vegas, primarily," Cawood said his informants told him. "And during the time that I worked with those informants, they always had accurate information. When a lot of money was being bet on a game, or when the line changed significantly, most of the time they could tell me why it had changed significantly. Sometimes it was because a lot of money was bet; sometimes they said the opening line was just set incorrectly. The line doesn't always change because of a gambling influence. But certainly there were times when it did change because of a gambling influence."

Sometimes, Cawood would hear something from one informant and call another to confirm the information. Other times, a fan would call to say he had heard such-and-such about a particular team or player, and Cawood would feel compelled to follow up on the lead, lest he find out later that he had ignored a potential violation in progress. Always, he would check with his one, most trusted source, who invariably would already have heard the rumor and could confirm or refute it.

In the winter of 1978–79, the word was out that something suspicious was going on involving Boston College games.

"We had confidential informants both inside and outside of law enforcement, and some of those informants had indicated that they didn't know anything for sure, but that there were some rumors about that situation up there," Cawood recalls.

Cawood says he reported the rumors to Boston College, and that athletic director William Flynn and other school officials "made every attempt to determine if there was any fact to those rumors," but could find no proof to substantiate them.

"The reason that I remembered Boston College so vividly was because I had made the calls to the university to tell them what I'd heard," Cawood said. "And they had called me and told me about their investigation."

Boston College coach Tom Davis also had heard rumors that some linesmakers were refusing to take action on the Eagles' games, and he told the *New York Times*'s Jane Gross in 1981 that he brought his concerns to Flynn during the 1978–79 season. But Flynn, a former FBI agent who died in 1997, denied talking to Davis about possible point-shaving.

"To the best of my knowledge, there was never any question of point-shaving during the season of 1978–79," Flynn told the *Boston Globe* the day after Gross's story ran. "We were just as conscious that year of gambling as we always are, but I positively, emphatically say that there was no suspicion on my part."

Cawood, too, assumed that if anybody had the background to investigate this kind of situation, Flynn did.

"I was convinced there was nothing going on at Boston College, [partly] because I figured that Bill (Flynn) would have had more experience and more resources available than a typical athletic director would have had. At the end of the day, I was surprised."

While the various warning signs thus were being ignored or, at best, not acted upon, the Eagles prepared for a make-or-break stretch of games at the beginning of February. Meanwhile, in New York and Pittsburgh, other preparations were being made to ensure those games yielded more than just new entries in the win column.

CHAPTER NINE

"If We Lose, We Win"

Since opening the season with seven consecutive victories, Boston College had won ten of its last fourteen games through the end of January and owned quality wins over Tennessee, Connecticut (twice), Holy Cross, Villanova, and Massachusetts. The Eagles already could lay claim to being the second-best team in New England, behind only Rhode Island. Throwing out the back-to-back debacles against UCLA and Purdue, they were scoring more than eighty-six points per game and winning by an average margin of ten points.

By any objective standard, then, the season had surpassed the expectations of all but the most optimistic fans and followers, and only figured to get better as February wore on and the ECAC playoffs approached. Following upcoming games against Fordham, St. John's, and Holy Cross were winnable contests against Dartmouth, Merrimack, Boston University, and Fairfield, mixed in with a game against Georgetown in Washington, D.C., on February 17. Clearly, B.C. was in an excellent position to make it to the postseason for the first time in four years.

For the gamblers, however, all was far from well. So far, the scheme had produced one clear win, in the Harvard game; one clear loss, in the Providence game, and two games that yielded mixed results: the UCLA game, in which Henry Hill and Jimmy Burke allegedly won their bets but Tony Perla and Rick Kuhn, betting on B.C., lost; and the Rhode Island game, in which Vin Caraher's late-game scoring burst shrunk the final margin close enough to the point spread so that most of the bets lost.

Hill and Kuhn both later claimed that they won money by betting on Boston College to cover the point spread against UConn on January 17, but there is no independent corroboration for their statements.

It seemed that everyone, from Hill and Burke at the upper levels of the scheme to Mike Mayock sitting in the bleachers watching his friend Jim Sweeney play point guard, knew that the only logical way to influence Boston College games was to get to Ernie Cobb. The problem was, Cobb had been evasive so far, and no one, particularly Kuhn and Sweeney, seemed comfortable approaching the star shooting guard.

Partly for that reason Rocco Perla, who had made the initial approach to Cobb before the Harvard game in December, traveled to Boston again on the weekend of February 2–3, 1979, to watch Boston College play the Fordham Rams. He had already planned to make the trip with his girlfriend, Georgeanne, but before he left, his brother, Tony, asked him to talk to the players—Sweeney, Kuhn, and Cobb—to make sure everything was all set for the Fordham game on Saturday night. Rick had already told Tony Perla that Sweeney and Cobb had agreed to shave points in the game; however, the experience of being burned in previous games made Perla want to be just a little more sure of everyone's state of mind before he placed his faith—and his money—in them.

• • •

Barbara Reed's normal routine was to pick Rick up after practice at Roberts Center and drive back downtown to the apartment. Rick had told her that Rocco and Georgeanne would be in town for the weekend and would be arriving on Friday, February 2, which suited her fine since she and Georgeanne had grown close during the time Barbara had been seeing Rick.

When Reed arrived at Roberts Center, she saw Rick and Rocco together with Jim Sweeney. On the way out to the car, the three of them were laughing heartily, and she was able to discern from their conversation that Jim and Rick were giving Rocco a recap of some of the highlights from previous Boston College games—except what they were bragging about was their mistakes, not their great plays.

It was an odd conversation, to say the least.

Reed overheard them telling Rocco about how Rick "tripped over his own feet and threw the ball into the crowd when no one was around him." In his own defense, Kuhn looked at Sweeney and said, "What about the foul shots you took that didn't hit the rim?"

"Rick would tell Rocco a story about something Sweeney had done, and Sweeney would tell Rocco a story about something Rick had done," Reed said. She also remembered them touching on the subject of Cobb, and how he was unreliable. Rocco then said he would talk to Cobb himself.

Later that evening at Rick and Barbara's apartment, Cobb was again a central topic of conversation. Rocco repeated to Rick that "the men from New York" wanted Cobb involved since Rick did not play that much and Cobb was the team's leading scorer.

Kuhn had his own reservations about Cobb. First, he felt that Cobb "was too into his own game" to cooperate. There also was Ernie's general ambivalence about the scheme. And there was something else that was bothering Rick.

"He hangs out with a lot of weird-looking people," Kuhn told Rocco, and described a group of people that had been coming to the games lately with Ernie who looked older, and said he did not trust these men.

Before the night was over, Reed recalled, Cobb showed up at the apartment with another man, possibly two, whom she did not recognize. When she complained and told Rick that it was late, he told her to go to sleep and he sat down with Rocco, Cobb, and Cobb's friends. When Reed came out of her room sometime later to get something in the kitchen, she remembered seeing the men sitting in a circle, smoking marijuana.

After everyone left, Kuhn explained that Cobb had come to talk to Rocco because the men from New York wanted Cobb involved in "the betting thing." Rick added that although he was skeptical about whether or not Cobb could be trusted, he was feeling pressure from the New York faction, and would try to speak to people down there later in the week when Boston College traveled to New York to play against St. John's.

• • •

On Saturday afternoon, February 3, the day of the Fordham game, Jim Sweeney was sitting in his dorm room watching television with his roommates when Rick and Rocco suddenly appeared at his door. They got him to go into a separate room, out of earshot of his roommates, and told him that the line for that night's game had come out, and Boston College was favored by ten points. Since Fordham liked to play a slow-paced style under coach Tom Penders, they reasoned, "no one would be surprised" if B.C. did not cover the point spread.

Was Sweeney in?

Sweeney, who later would say he felt "locked in" and too deeply involved in the scheme to make a clean break now, agreed to go along.

• • •

Before the Fordham game, Hill and Burke agreed that they would be able to get a favorable point spread since the Rams were a New York team, and local bettors who were familiar with the team but unaware of the point-shaving scheme would probably drive up the betting line.

That's exactly what happened. Boston College was favored by at least ten points at most of the places they or their bookie network called. Hill and Burke got down for about thirty-five thousand dollars on the game.

• • •

In Pittsburgh, Tony Perla and Paul Mazzei, the buddies who booked fifty-dollar football bets and sold dime bags of marijuana to augment their modest legitimate incomes, were preparing to make a single score that would dwarf anything they had ever done.

During the days leading up to the Fordham game, they had managed to raise close to twenty-five thousand dollars, some of it from Hill in New York, for Mazzei to take to Las Vegas and bet against Boston College at the legal sports books. This approach would be cleaner than betting with the numerous bookies in Pittsburgh and New York, some of whom were in on the scheme and some who were not. The challenge would be to spread the money around at several casinos so that suspicion would not be aroused.

Those worries seemed needless after Mazzei, accompanied by George Yensch and Kevin Gurney, two friends from Pittsburgh, arrived in Vegas on February 2. As the three men went up and down the Strip looking at the various sports books to decide which ones to make their bets in the next day, Mazzei ran into a friend from Pittsburgh in the Aladdin Hotel, a book-maker named George, whom Mazzei knew as "Bucky," or "the German."

"Man, I'm glad I found you out here," Mazzei told Bucky. "You're going to save me a lot of problems."

Mazzei explained what they were trying to do, and that they wanted Bucky to make the bets for them. Bucky said he would be able to do it.

The only thing left now was to make sure the players were on board, check the point spreads and get the bets down. A conversation between Tony Perla and Rick Kuhn established the first condition, and Perla called Mazzei in Vegas to tell him everything was set. After the sports books put up the opening college basketball lines at noon on Saturday, Mazzei called Perla and told him that the number on Boston College had gone from twelve down to as low as nine, evidence that money was being bet on Ford-ham but still a hefty enough point spread that B.C. could easily win and stay under the number.

The third task would prove to be more of a challenge.

• • •

True to form, Fordham, which entered the game with a 6–13 record, played at the type of grind-it-out pace favored by coach Tom Penders, and the strategy enabled the Rams to take the lead midway through the first half and hold it until midway through the second half. But Boston College, which committed ten turnovers in the first half, went on a 14–2 run in the second half, led by Cobb and Michael Bowie, that turned a 49–48 deficit into a 62–51 lead.

The 71–64 final score apparently satisfied everyone: the fans, who got to see the Eagles improve their won-lost record to 18–4, and the gamblers, who had bet that B.C. would beat the Rams by less than nine points . . . or ten, eleven, or twelve points, depending on what number the oddsmakers were quoting when the bet was made.

If the meeting at Rick's apartment the night before had persuaded Cobb to shave points against Fordham, he certainly went about it in an odd way. Cobb had one of his best games of the season against the Rams, making seven of his ten shots from the field, all four free throws, and adding seven assists and just one turnover.

It was a late miss of a free throw by Sweeney, however, that helped ensure the visitors would cover the point spread. Sweeney, who made about 80 percent of his free throws over the course of his career, testified in 1981 that he did this unintentionally. But a comment he made to Rocco Perla after the game that never came out at the trial casts some doubt on that statement.

After the game, the Boston College Blue Chips, a booster organization, held a reception in the basement of Roberts Center. While Barbara Reed and Rocco Perla's girlfriend, Georgeanne, talked to Mike Kruczek, a former B.C. quarterback who was now playing for the Pittsburgh Steelers, Sweeney went down to the reception and ran into Rocco, who congratulated him on helping the gamblers win another bet.

Rocco remembered Sweeney talking about the foul shot he had missed, and making a comment that may have been in jest but which could have been construed as evidence that Sweeney knew exactly what he was doing.

"He joked to me later," Perla said. "He said, 'I looked up at that rim and saw a pair of cement shoes. I figured I'd better miss.'"

Rick and Rocco decided to go downtown to the Colonnade, the hotel where Rocco and Georgeanne were staying, and call Tony Perla in Pittsburgh, who was sure to be jubilant over B.C.'s performance. Barbara's shift at the hospital started at 11 o'clock, so they dropped her off in Dorchester on the way to the hotel.

They would soon find out that while they had been taking care of things on the court, three time zones away their fellow conspirators had fumbled the ball out of bounds.

• • •

Out in Las Vegas Saturday afternoon, things had begun to fall apart as the Fordham–B.C. tipoff approached on the East Coast. Bucky had told Mazzei to get to the Aladdin at least thirty minutes before the game started with the twenty-five thousand dollars, and that he would take care of placing the bets.

After going back to the hotel and grabbing all the cash he could, Mazzei found Yensch and Gurney, who were at another casino looking at the early lines. According to Mazzei, the three men jumped in a cab and headed toward the Aladdin, only to encounter a large traffic jam en route to the casino.

Frantically, Mazzei implored the driver to get to the Aladdin as quickly as possible, even telling him to drive on the sidewalk. The driver obliged, no doubt having seen this type of behavior before, and no doubt motivated by a fifty-dollar bill from Mazzei.

But the delay proved costly. Mazzei and his buddies arrived at the Aladdin about ten minutes before tipoff, and when they finally found Bucky, he said it was too late to get all the money down before the game started.

Mazzei made sure to call Tony Perla in Pittsburgh before the game ended to tell him the bad news, and to cover himself in case Perla thought he was skimming the money himself. People were known to have lost their lives after trying that scam—laying a winning bet and then claiming not to have been able to get to the window in time.

Perla didn't believe Mazzei at first, and implied that if Mazzei had been able to call him with the point spread before the game, he should have been able to get the bets down. Perla then told Mazzei to stay in Vegas because he was coming out to meet him. In the meantime, Perla would have to explain to the players that there was no money.

Hill, meanwhile, did not believe Mazzei's story, and feels that Mazzei's only saving grace may have been the fact that he was not carrying Jimmy Burke's money at the time.

"He said he never got down, the little prick," Hill says. "I didn't believe him. Are you serious? Believe me, it wasn't Jimmy's money or he would have come up with it. Or (Jimmy) would have chopped him up."

• • •

When Tony Perla called Kuhn to tell him about the Vegas fiasco, Rick immediately suspected that his Pittsburgh buddies were holding out on him, and that they actually had been betting money and lying to the players. Kuhn later said that at this point Cobb and Sweeney each told him separately that they were done with the scheme—a statement that contradicts the contentions of both men that they were not actively involved in the scheme at any point.

Kuhn's ire was soothed somewhat by the arrival of two cashier's checks from Pittsburgh, totaling nine hundred dollars, that arrived a few days after the Fordham game. He asked Sweeney to cash them for him, and then offered Sweeney half, using the same expression he'd used after the Harvard game, when he gave Sweeney five hundred dollars before the West Coast trip: "you've earned it." But Sweeney says he refused this time, and Kuhn took the money and instead used it to buy a new stereo. The stereo would not be the only extravagant purchase Kuhn made that winter. Sweeney remembered that his friend bought, among other things, a color television and a brass bed.

• • •

Several factors were motivating Ernie Cobb as Boston College headed to New York City for a game against St. John's on Tuesday, February 6. There was the chance to play in New York, which was always a special occasion for any college basketball player. There was the fact that the game was against the Redmen, who were perennially one of the elite teams on the East Coast. And there was the presence of Reggie Carter, a New York schoolboy star who had transferred from the University of Hawaii to St. John's, and who would offer Ernie another opportunity to prove himself against a "name" player from a "name" school in front of the pro scouts who were sure to be in the stands at Alumni Hall.

But this game would be extra special because Cobb's parents, James and Hattie, were going to be in attendance, accompanying Herman Alswanger and his family. It was just the kind of atmosphere in which Cobb thrived, and he was determined to put on a memorable show.

What his parents and Alswanger did not know, what Carter did not know, what all of his teammates with the possible exception of Jim

Sweeney did not know, was that Ernie had already been approached by Rick Kuhn about shaving points in the St. John's game. Kuhn's selling point to Cobb was this: the Redmen were probably going to beat Boston College anyway; they were playing at home and were one of the best teams in the East that season. Why not just lose the game by more than the point spread and take home the money? Besides, according to Cobb, Rocco owed him two thousand dollars from earlier in the season; he could let it ride on the St. John's game and end up with four thousand dollars if everything went according to plan.

"Absolutely not," Cobb claimed he said, adding that his family and friends would be at the game, not to mention pro scouts. He said he again refused when Kuhn came up to him during warmups and repeated the offer, even though Kuhn told him that Rocco Perla had already bet the two thousand dollars that Cobb was owed.

Kuhn would later contend that he never talked to Cobb before the St. John's game, and that he told Rocco to bet with Boston College because they would be playing to win. This account is so contrary to the testimonies of Cobb and Sweeney that it is difficult to take seriously.

Kuhn talked to Sweeney at the team hotel in New York on the night before the game, in the hotel lobby after a team meal. Rick apparently gave the same rationale he had given Cobb, that B.C. would probably lose the game anyway, and that losing by more than the point spread would not be such a big deal. Sweeney ignored the offer and did not even respond when Kuhn posed it to him. Similarly, he rebuffed Kuhn again when Rick approached him on the court during warmups before the game.

As far as Henry Hill knew, however, the players were involved in the fix for the St. John's game. This highlighted the major underlying flaws of the whole scheme, and of any point-shaving scheme: namely, the tendency for the players' natural competitiveness to take over, regardless of what they might have agreed to before the game, and the ease with which communications can break down and throw the whole operation into disarray. These problems were revealed time and again during the 1978–79 season: even though Sweeney and Cobb were reluctant participants at best, Kuhn continued to tell Perla and Mazzei in Pittsburgh that all three players, or at least he and Sweeney, were shaving points.

Throw in the odd occasions when Kuhn or Perla allegedly bet with the Eagles instead of against them—the UCLA and Purdue games, and possibly the St. John's game—and it becomes clear that by the time word trickled down to New York, to the people who were ostensibly charged with the financial end of the operation, no one was quite sure who was agreeing to do what.

• • •

Boston College never led in the game, losing 85–76 to St. John's on Tuesday, February 6, 1979. Michael Bowie had a career night with twenty-seven points, but no other B.C. player managed to hit double figures. Gordy

Thomas (nineteen points) and Reggie Carter (sixteen) led St. John's, which won its fifth straight game and snapped the Eagles' win streak at eight.

Though Hill offered different versions of how the gamblers fared on the game, there is no satisfactory evidence that the point spread dropped below nine points. Clearly the best result would have been a "push" on the bets they had gotten down on St. John's as a nine-point favorite. Anything bet on St. John's at a higher number would have been a loser.

In front of his family and friends and whoever else he was trying to impress on this night, Cobb had a disastrous game. He made just one field goal and four free throws for six points, less than one-third of his normal output. The Wednesday morning papers in New York carried stories that described how the Redmen's defensive scheme held B.C.'s high-scoring guard well below his scoring average.

Alswanger, sitting in the stands with his wife and son and Cobb's parents, saw something else unfold.

"I kept saying, 'Why aren't they passing to him? He never gets the ball,'" Alswanger recalls. "Even at the end of the game, he almost took the ball out of bounds himself and took it downcourt. (It seemed like) there were no set plays for him. He had wanted to beat St. John's so bad."

After the game, Cobb was despondent. Given a chance to test his mettle against one of the elite players in one of the elite programs, he had failed miserably. But, as usual, he placed the blame on his teammates and their inability to get him the ball. He even tried to enlist Alswanger's aid in pleading his case.

"You have to speak to Coach (Davis)," Cobb implored Alswanger when he saw him after the game. "You see how I don't get the ball. It's not that guy holding me."

Cobb also said that Kuhn came up to him after the game and said, "I told you so, Ernie. You could have made a lot of money if you would have just listened to me and lost the game like we did anyway."

But as he was prone to do, Cobb seemed to care less about losing the game than about losing an opportunity to make an impression against a quality team like St. John's and a quality player like Carter.

"I wasn't getting the ball in the game, and I felt it was the coach's responsibility to tell the players, and not my responsibility, to tell the players to get me the ball," Cobb said. "So I was upset at the coach for that reason. My family and friends had come to see me play. I was very upset about it."

• • •

The team returned by bus to Boston that night, but Kuhn did not immediately go to sleep when he got back. Instead, at around four in the morning he showed up at the house where Reed was working in Dorchester and unburdened himself to her.

He told her how upset he was with the way Sweeney had played, and said that Sweeney was "playing too good" and "thought he was Ronnie Perry."

When Barbara told him she had to go back to work and couldn't talk, Rick went home. Later that morning at the apartment, he again talked about the pressure he was being put under by "the people in New York" to get other players involved, particularly Cobb and Joe Beaulieu, who at this time was getting much more playing time than Rick at the center position.

Just how much pressure was being applied became readily apparent a day or two after the game when Hill called Kuhn at the apartment, to find out what had happened in the St. John's game and to see where everyone stood.

"(Kuhn) said it wasn't his fault," Hill said. "He gave me 201 excuses why the game fell that way. And he said, 'We will make it up on the next game.'

"I told him if they wanted to stop this conspiracy . . . stop the syndicate, or whatever, if they didn't want to do any more business, it's fine. If they did, to let me know and we will stop it. Otherwise, I told them that if you are still going to take our money and, you know, not win the games for us, you can't play basketball with broken fingers."

A larger question arises here, however; namely, why did the gamblers continue to fund this point-shaving scheme that was causing them more *agita* than anything else?

After the St. John's game, Hill wondered the same thing. But, he says, Burke was adamant. Even though Burke was still sitting on the proceeds of the biggest robbery in U.S. history, his gambler's mentality would not let him go out on a losing note with the hoops scheme.

"Jimmy was the guy that pushed it more and more," Hill recalls. "As much money as he had . . . that's what I just couldn't understand about those guys. The amount of greed that was there. The junk business, the coke business. . . . I mean, the money was coming in every which way. But he had to have more."

Burke was aiming at the Holy Cross game on Saturday, February 10—the final game that had been circled on the schedule at the Logan Airport Hilton the previous November. It was a rematch of the first game between the two teams that had been won by B.C. This game would be in Worcester, in front of a hysterical crowd, a perfect opportunity for the lads to play their hearts out but fall just short—and bring home the money for the gamblers. As a bonus, the game was also being featured as NBC's regional telecast of the week, so Burke and Hill could sit in the comfort of Burke's living room and watch their cash multiply.

• • •

Burke and Hill were not the only ones hoping to make a killing on the Holy Cross game. Kuhn, too, saw it as the scheme's grand finale, and his chance to cash in. He knew the gamblers would be betting heavily on the game, and he was planning on telling them to take his share and bet it for him.

He needed to make sure Sweeney was going along, though, so he confronted him in the days leading up to the game. Kuhn asked Sweeney to come over to his apartment because Tony Perla, obviously taking no chances this time, would be calling from Pittsburgh. Rick talked up the game to Sweeney, and referred to it as their chance to make "the big kill."

Sweeney, who said later he was still frightened of the Perlas and Hill and the mysterious "man from New York," went to Kuhn's after practice on either Thursday night, February 8, or Friday, February 9. Perla called and told Sweeney that this would be the last game they would need him on, that there would be heavy betting on the game, and that the players could receive as much as ten thousand dollars each if the point-shaving was successful. Sweeney said he offered no response.

After the conversation, Kuhn told him, "Look, these people are betting a lot of money. We're not dealing with petty thieves. You're dealing with some people that are very powerful. Make certain when it comes time to shave points, you're not running around pulling any Ronnie Perry moves."

• • •

Back at the apartment, Kuhn was on the phone frequently in the three days leading up to the Holy Cross game. Barbara Reed remembered overhearing one of Rick's conversations, in which he was telling someone—Tony or Rocco, she assumed—that it would be tough to say who would win Saturday's game since Boston College–Holy Cross games were "always pretty tight."

Reed interrupted the conversation.

"Are you talking about betting on the Holy Cross game?" she asked. "Tell them there is no way, you can't bet on that game."

She went on to say how the rivalry was too emotional, and how "everybody who went to Boston College wanted to kill Holy Cross," and vice versa.

"Besides, it's being played at Holy Cross. It's on TV. Everyone is going to be a nervous wreck," she said.

Kuhn said into the phone, "That's just Barb," and repeated what she had said about the rivalry.

When he got off the phone, Rick angrily told her to stop listening to his phone calls and stop asking him so many questions, which led to another argument. Rick had already told Barbara that he might be able to win five or ten thousand dollars on the game, which made her angry. How was he going to get his hands on that kind of money? How would they be able to pay that much off if he lost?

Rick explained that he had told the men to bet his money for him, the money they were holding that was due him. It was "like his show of good faith to these men," Reed remembered thinking.

Kuhn then told her they weren't actually going to try to lose the game, and uttered his second immortal line: "If we win, we win; and if we lose, we win."

• • •

Sometime in the three days before the Holy Cross game, the Boston College athletic ticket office received a phone call from an anonymous caller who said Ernie Cobb's life would be in danger if he played against Holy Cross Saturday. The caller has never been identified, but people involved in the case have theorized that it may have been an irate bookie who took a beating on either the St. John's or Fordham game.

The B.C. athletic department did not notify members of the team, but quietly set up a security detail for Saturday afternoon's game in Worcester.

• • •

On Thursday, February 8, Tony Perla flew to Las Vegas and checked in at the MGM Grand Hotel. He immediately sought out Mazzei and his two Pittsburgh friends, and told them that he would bet the money himself at the sports books so the fiasco of the Fordham game would not be repeated. Perla was planning to bet "as much as we could" on the B.C.–Holy Cross game. The players, he had been told, were going to dump the game.

On Saturday at noon, when the line came out, Holy Cross was a two-point favorite. Soon, the line jumped to seven, indicating that virtually all of the money coming in was being bet on the Crusaders. Boston College would now have to lose by more than seven points if the gamblers were to win their bets. But there appeared to be another snag. That morning, Perla had talked to Kuhn again, and Rick had repeated what he had said earlier on the phone, that he was not sure if the other players would go along with dumping the game against their biggest rival.

Tony left it that Kuhn would call him before the game to get the line. Since Rick would be traveling with the team, he wouldn't be able to make the call. But Perla said he was adamant that they weren't going to bet the game unless they were sure that points were indeed going to be shaved.

• • •

Along with many other Boston College fans, Barbara Reed had made plans to drive to Worcester Saturday for the game. Before Rick left to catch the team bus on Saturday morning, he gave her instructions:

"Kid," he said, "on your way to the game I want you to stop and make a phone call from a phone booth."

He then gave her a piece of paper that had a phone number as well as two other numbers—1514 or 1512, Reed remembered. Rick told her Tony Perla would answer the phone, and that she was to ask him for a number and then hang up.

On the way from Boston to Worcester, which is only about an hour's drive, Reed and a few friends she was bringing with her stopped for gas, which gave her a chance to try the phone number from a pay phone. But there was no answer.

Farther down the Massachusetts Turnpike, they stopped at a Howard Johnson's for breakfast, and she tried the number again. Still no answer. Reed "didn't think anything of it," and got back in her van and drove with her friends to the game.

When they got to the Hart Center, Barbara saw the Boston College players warming up at one end of the court, and she went down near the side of the court. Rick saw her and came over.

"What did Tony say?" he asked her.

"Nobody answered the phone," Reed said.

"Wait a minute. Go right out into the lobby and call him again," Kuhn said.

This time, somebody answered the phone. After she identified herself by saying why she was calling, the voice on the other end of the line said, "Seven." Reed recognized it as Tony Perla's voice. She went back down to the court and told Rick.

"Beautiful," he said, and he kissed her on the cheek.

Rick went back out to the court, and at some point before the start of the game approached Cobb and told him that a great deal of money had been bet on Holy Cross and that he should, as Cobb remembered it, "lay down." But with Ronnie Perry on the other bench, not to mention a packed house and a regional television audience, there was a better chance of Cobb wearing his shorts inside out than of him compromising his performance.

• • •

The Boston College–Holy Cross game of February 10, 1979, was a classic, even by the standards set over the years in the series between the two schools. Emotions ran high and eventually spilled over into a minibrawl midway through the second half that involved players and fans. It started with some extracurricular jostling after the whistle blew.

"I think it was between (Dwan) Chandler and one of their players, maybe Gary Witts," Boston College forward Chris Foy recalled. "It was wild. Mike Vicens, who had played for Holy Cross the year before, was sitting in the stands holding a baby, and he put the baby aside and just jumped onto the court and took a couple of shots. And security didn't do anything. He just went back and sat down."

Early in the game, NBC announcer Marv Albert commented on how Cobb was "forcing shots" and playing "out of control." What he also may have noticed, but what he certainly could not have explained, was that Jim Sweeney was accumulating personal fouls at an alarming rate, at least by his standards. Early in the second half, Sweeney picked up his fifth foul and was relegated to the bench for the rest of the game.

Two and a half years later, Sweeney would testify that the strain of being involved in the scheme, not to mention Rick's incessant reminders about the powerful people behind it, had become too much to bear, and that he had fouled out intentionally to spare himself any more anguish.

Whatever his motives, it is clear that Sweeney's actions were uncharacteristic.

"When you look back on it, I mean, Sweeney fouled out in twenty-one minutes," George Blaney, then coach of Holy Cross, said recently. "Which is really unusual."

With 1:25 left in the game, Holy Cross led by eight points, 93–85. But Boston College mounted a furious rally, led by Cobb, and pulled to within two points in the final seconds. Cobb took the last shot, which rimmed out with :02 remaining and sealed B.C.'s 98–96 defeat.

Ronnie Perry led all scorers with twenty-eight points, eighteen of which he'd scored in the first half. Teammate Bob Kelly, a flashy freshman point guard, scored seventeen. Cobb, despite shooting 8-for-25 from the floor, had twenty-one points to lead B.C., followed by Joe Beaulieu with twenty. Sweeney managed just four points, and Kuhn, who was given the starting nod at center by Tom Davis, was scoreless.

"We weren't doing that well on the perimeter with the guards, so we couldn't get the ball inside," Davis said after the game. "And then we had trouble in the beginning. But what can I say? This was a great Holy Cross team. We're too mature to let this game affect us for the rest of the season."

In the locker room after the game, the B.C. players learned about the death threat against Cobb, and that they were going to be escorted out of the arena.

"It wasn't like you wanted to be standing next to Ernie when we were walking out to the bus," Foy recalled with a chuckle.

• • •

Henry Hill had gone over to Jimmy Burke's house in Howard Beach that Saturday afternoon to watch the game and take a look at the brick work Burke was having done in his kitchen. When Holy Cross took its eight-point lead late in the game, the two men were prepared to celebrate. When their fortunes turned, though, and the game slipped away, Burke went into a rage and put his foot through his own television set after the game, according to Hill.

What Hill discovered that afternoon was that Burke had been using his connections with Ralph Atlas and playing for higher stakes all along, and had lost close to fifty thousand dollars on the Holy Cross game. Hill claimed he dropped another ten or fifteen thousand dollars himself. Of course, fifty thousand dollars was chump change compared to the loot from the Lufthansa heist—"confetti," Hill called it—but that hardly mattered to Burke, who toyed with the idea of having Hill personally convey his displeasure to them.

"Jimmy was outraged," Hill remembered. "He wanted me to fly up to Boston. Ultimately, nothing happened. We lost our bets and that was it. (Jimmy) said he was finished. He didn't want to be bothered with these kids anymore."

• • •

In Las Vegas, Tony Perla had bet between twenty and twenty-five thousand dollars, most of which was money he had gotten from Hill. Mazzei, who was already on a plane headed to Chicago when the game ended, had bet eight thousand dollars himself. The only bets that were not losers were the ones made with Holy Cross favored by two points, and even those were pushes. Basically, everyone had taken a bath.

Considering the circumstances, Mazzei remembered Hill being relatively calm when he talked to him on the phone the next day. Still, the conversation between the two men seemed to have an air of resignation to it.

"What do you think happened?" Hill asked Mazzei.

"I don't know," was all Mazzei could respond. "What do you think has been happening all along?"

• • •

Tony Perla wanted answers. He called Rick Kuhn and told him, "There's no way in the world this should have happened. You can kiss the dream goodbye," no doubt using earthier language to express his displeasure.

Kuhn claimed that there had been a misunderstanding, that someone was supposed to call and tell Perla not to bet on the game. He also said the players still wanted money for the Fordham game.

At the apartment that night, Barbara Reed overheard Rick talking to Tony Perla and saying he "didn't understand what happened," and that he "didn't know what Cobb was thinking of." She also heard Rick pleading with him to let the players "make it up on the Georgetown game" in another week.

When Rick got off the phone, Barbara asked him why he was so upset. After all, he had told her that if B.C. won, they won, and if they lost, they won. They had lost the game—what other options were there?

"You don't understand," he told her. "A lot of shit went down in Las Vegas and New York, and there are a lot of people on Tony's back and Tony is on my back. . . . Sweeney and Beaulieu and Cobb don't understand how serious this is. They are all going to be on our backs."

A few days after the game, Rick told Sweeney that Tony Perla was "irate," and that "an extraordinary amount of money" was bet on the game. He said one of the results of the heavy losses incurred by the gamblers was that Rocco Perla's car had been repossessed. He said the bettors also had talked about breaking Joe Beaulieu's thumbs.

Nevertheless, he assured Sweeney, "Don't worry, nothing will happen to you."

Kuhn was right on that account—at least for the time being.

• • •

The loss to Holy Cross left Boston College with an 18–6 record and five games remaining in the regular season. Over the next week and a half, they won three of those games, all at home, against Dartmouth (66–56), Merrimack (105–73), and Boston University (99–84). They lost both road games, at future Big East opponent Georgetown (84–81), and against New England rival Fairfield (93–81) in the regular-season finale on February 24.

Though four of its last seven games of the regular season had been losses, Boston College still had finished with a 21–8 record, which was good enough to convince the ECAC selection committee to name the Eagles as one of the four teams to participate in the New England Regionals at the Providence Civic Center. Boston College would play Connecticut in one semifinal on Thursday night, March 1, and the winner would play on Saturday afternoon against either Rhode Island or Holy Cross. At stake was a trip to the NCAA Tournament, which had expanded its field to 40 teams from 32 the year before.

• • •

Rick Kuhn spent the week leading up to the UConn game playing host to a variety of out-of-town friends. First, Rocco Perla and Georgeanne came to town for the weekend of February 24 and 25, and the two couples went sightseeing and went to dinner at Anthony's Pier 4, a popular seafood restaurant.

Two days later, Rick and Barbara went to Logan Airport and picked up another friend of Rick's from Pittsburgh, named John. When they got back to the apartment, John handed Rick a plastic bag filled with pills, about two hundred in all. They were quaaludes, which Rick told Barbara he would be able to sell on campus and make several hundred dollars.

Like the point-shaving scheme, this get-rich-quick scheme fell flat, too. John took most of the quaaludes himself over the next few weeks that he stayed at the apartment, and Rick took the rest. Barbara even admitted to taking some.

Despite his statement to Sweeney that the Holy Cross game was to be "the big kill," and the grand finale of the point-shaving scheme, Kuhn continued to push his friend as the UConn game approached. He told Sweeney in the days before the game that the gamblers had lost a lot of money on the Holy Cross game and wanted to win it back. Sweeney said he wanted no part of it anymore.

Hill, meanwhile, claimed in *Sports Illustrated* that "the players talked us into one more game"—meaning that points were shaved in the UConn game—then changed his story in front of the grand jury in June 1981, saying that the game was not fixed. Kuhn told FBI agents in 1980 that when he talked to Tony Perla about the game, Perla told him they wanted B.C. to beat Connecticut.

• • •

Whether or not any points were being shaved, Boston College played perhaps its worst game of the season in its most important game of the season against UConn. In front of 11,800 spectators in Providence, the Eagles had no answers for a team that they had already beaten twice earlier in the season.

For all intents and purposes, the game was over by the time the teams went to the locker room at halftime with the Huskies leading, 47–26. They had used a diamond-and-one defense to neutralize Cobb in the first twenty minutes, and their inside game, shut down by the Eagles in B.C.'s victory in the Colonial Classic a month earlier, operated at full efficiency as forward Jeff Carr scored fifteen first-half points.

Boston College, meanwhile, played one of its worst halves of basketball of the season, reflected in eighteen turnovers and 31 percent shooting. The Eagles were able to cut the gap to ten with 14:09 left in the game, but even that spurt only served to make the 91–74 final score seem a little more respectable.

Beaulieu led B.C. with thirteen points, followed by Chris Foy with ten. Cobb, playing in his last varsity game, was held without a field goal until 7:03 remained in the game, and shot the ball only nine times overall, a curious statistic for a player who averaged nearly twice that many attempts over the course of his career.

• • •

A few weeks after the season ended, Rick Kuhn and Barbara Reed went to Rick's parents' house in Swissvale for Easter. While there, Barbara remembered, Rick spent some time with Rocco and Tony Perla, and the subject of the Holy Cross game came up. When they returned to Boston, Rick was still upset about the game and told her for the umpteenth time how "a lot of people lost an awful lot of money."

Yet another argument ensued, and Barbara finally asked point-blank: "What if the police ask me any questions?"

At that, Rick became enraged and put his whole hand around Barbara's neck and picked her up off the floor.

"You don't know anything," he hissed, "and if you ever tell anyone, I'll kill you."

Shaken by this sudden outburst, Reed did not tell anyone. Neither did anyone else who had been involved in the scheme or had heard about it from someone who was involved.

What had seemed like such a good idea during the dog days of the previous summer, the simple plan that Hill saw as a "sure thing" had been plagued by miscommunication, errors in judgment, poor execution, and simple greed. A lot of money had been won, but nearly as much had been lost, and some people had lost considerably more than they had won.

Before long, the money would seem trivial next to the other possibilities that presented themselves when word of the plot leaked out.

CHAPTER TEN

Loose Lips

The day of the 1979 NBA draft must have seemed like the longest of Ernie Cobb's life. The league was still drafting ten rounds back then, but for Cobb, it must have seemed like ten years as all his fears were realized.

It was not merely the fact that Cobb was not chosen until the sixth round, or that 108 players were selected ahead of him. It was the slow, steady list of guards who went before him. Some, like top pick Earvin "Magic" Johnson of Michigan State or Sydney Moncrief of Arkansas, were expected. But it was watching the players get selected whom Cobb considered mid-level at best, but who had played for the big-time programs, that must have eaten away at him.

Brad Holland of UCLA, fourteenth pick in the first round, to the Lakers. Kyle Macy of Kentucky, twenty-second pick in the first round, to Phoenix. Jim Spanarkel of Duke, sixteenth pick in the first round, to Philly. Jerry Sichting of Missouri, in the fourth round to Golden State.

Reggie Carter of St. John's, who had won their duel in early February in New York, in the game in which Cobb hardly got to touch the ball, was selected in the second round by the Knicks. Then, in the ultimate insult, two New England guards from small-time programs, Fairfield's Joe DeSantis and Tom Channel of Boston University—B.U., for heaven's sake!—were off the board before the Utah Jazz finally selected Cobb with the first pick in the sixth round.

Apparently, the NBA was not quite ready for a 5-foot-11 shooting guard whom scouts graded as a below-average defender and passer.

"He was a shooter, and I think the question was on the other things, defense, rebounding," former Boston College coach Tom Davis says. "That's normally what it comes down to. That's how the NBA works: they're going to draft the best guy, no matter where he's been, what he's been doing. A lot of times young guys think all it is is statistics, how many points you score. But it's a lot more than that."

Cobb's fellow rookies on the Jazz included non-household names like

Larry Knight, Tico Brown, Arvid Kramer, and Greg Deane. But he was dealt a devastating blow when the Jazz, who would go on to finish 24–58 in its first year in Utah, cut him during training camp. But Cobb picked himself up and headed to Scranton, Pennsylvania, and the Continental Basketball League, and later would hook up with the Harlem Wizards, an ersatz Harlem Globetrotters troupe based in Groton, Connecticut. By September 1980 and the opening of NBA training camps, he had managed to land a tryout with the New Jersey Nets.

• • •

While Ernie Cobb was being cast adrift by Utah, Boston College was being welcomed as a charter member into a conference whose formation and development ultimately would change the way college basketball was packaged, marketed, and televised. But B.C. was far from a lock to be the New England representative among the seven teams that would begin play in the Big East Conference in the fall of 1979.

That honor appeared destined to be bestowed on Holy Cross, which was the school Big East architect David Gavitt coveted for the slot—except that the Crusaders were hesitating.

Tom Davis remembers feeling it was Boston College's time to make a play, and he shared that sentiment with athletic director Bill Flynn.

"Bill Flynn came to me and said, 'Look, this is the deal: We've got a chance to go into this conference, but we've got to come up with twenty-five thousand dollars to go in,'" Davis says. "And he said, 'I don't know where I'm going to get it.' This is how bad it was. So I said, 'Mr. Flynn, I recognize that it might be a problem, but if you look at it the other way, if we don't go in, I think we're dead in the water.'"

Truer words may never have been uttered. Entry into the Big East in the summer of 1980 gave a boost not only to B.C.'s basketball program, but to all of its athletic teams. The New England schools that were left behind—Holy Cross, UMass, and Rhode Island, chiefly—still have not caught up.

"It was a big decision for Bill Flynn to make, and I'm sure he did have trouble coming up with the twenty-five thousand dollars," Davis says. "But within a year or two, they were drawing back a million just from the Big East Tournament alone."

• • •

In the inaugural season of the Big East in 1979–80, Boston College took its lumps, winning only three games and losing in the first round of the conference tournament in Providence, Rhode Island. But one of the league victories was a thrilling 75–74 overtime win over seventeenth-ranked Georgetown in the ECAC Holiday Festival at Madison Square Garden at Christmas. Vin Caraher sank the game-winning shot with :02 left, from a pass by Jim Sweeney.

The Eagles reached the second round of the NIT, where they lost to a Virginia team led by 7-foot-4 center Ralph Sampson, 57–55.

Though there is no mention of it in the Boston College basketball media guide, Jim Sweeney had a remarkable year on and off the court. His play earned him the Frances Pomeroy Naismith Award, given annually to the nation's best college player under six feet tall. The ceremony was held at the Basketball Hall of Fame in Springfield, Massachusetts, the sport's birthplace, where sportscaster Curt Gowdy presented Sweeney with the award.

Sweeney's classroom excellence resulted in his being named an Academic All-American, and he was a finalist for a Rhodes Scholarship, the most prestigious award given to student-athletes.

• • •

Back in New York in April 1980, Henry Hill was enjoying the cause-and-effect relationship between heroin and large amounts of cash, and he was up to his eyeballs in both. It was a lucrative pastime: Hill and partner Bobby Germaine were raking in close to thirty thousand dollars a week by Hill's estimate, with no end in sight. Yet, unbeknownst to the pair, Nassau County authorities had been conducting surveillance on Hill for several weeks, tailing him with cars and helicopters and bugging his phone at home, even bugging the pay phones he used at Robert's Lounge.

Hill had been drawn into the heroin trade by Jimmy Burke way back in early February 1979, during the height of the point-shaving scheme. When he was over at Burke's one day, Burke had tossed him a bag of powder and said, "See what you can do with it. It's pure." Using some of the contacts he'd made at Lewisburg, Hill set up a network and soon was running a profitable business, though he remembers wondering why Burke, who had never been involved in the junk business before the Lufthansa robbery, suddenly was plunging in with both feet.

Hill also was yielding to temptation. Even though he wore a mask when he cut the heroin with quinine, Hill soon began snorting the stuff, and before long was mixing a daily concoction of cocaine and heroin known as a speedball. Henry Hill's life was a high-speed car wreck waiting to happen, and the crash finally came on Sunday, April 27, 1980. Nassau County authorities, who had assembled a mountain of evidence against him, Germaine, Burke, Peter Vario, and others, arrested him and charged him with six Class B felonies, all drug-related conspiracy charges.

Even in such dire circumstances, Hill's luck seemed to hold: earlier that day he had picked up a half-pound of heroin at Germaine's apartment, but by the time of his arrest he was holding only one quaalude.

Still, things looked exceedingly bleak. Hill still owed about five years' parole on his 1972 extortion conviction, and as a result now faced twenty-five years in prison on each of the drug counts. Soon it would become obvious to him that Jimmy Burke, no doubt realizing the extent of Hill's knowledge of the wide range of criminal activities the two men had been involved in, wanted him dead, which was a position no person on earth wanted to be in. His drug habit had become so bad that when he was sitting in the Nassau County jail after his arrest, his wife and mother-in-law wanted to keep him there until he purged the junk from his system.

Two days after his arrest, salvation appeared to Henry Hill at the Nassau County jail in the person of James Fox, Hill's parole officer. When Hill told Fox that he could provide information on numerous crimes, including the Lufthansa robbery, Fox set in motion a series of events that would put Hill at the center of a bitter turf war between the federal government and the Nassau County District Attorney's office—and would lead to his divulging of the Boston College point-shaving scheme nearly two years after the fact.

• • •

As early as Hill's arraignment the day after his arrest, intimations were coming from Nassau County that Hill could walk if he cooperated on the drug case. The trouble was, these originated not with District Attorney Dennis Dillon but with William Broder, an assistant district attorney who would later deny making any such promises.

By Friday, May 2, after a meeting at the U.S. Attorney's office in Brooklyn between Hill, Fox, Organized Crime Strike Force attorney Edward McDonald, a tentative agreement had been made under which Hill would receive immunity if 1) he cooperated fully with the Lufthansa investigation; 2) he cooperated fully in the Nassau County drug case; and 3) Nassau County District Attorney Dennis Dillon was given credit in the media— "scratch," in the jargon of the day—when the investigations were made public. The last condition would come back to haunt Dillon's office when details of the negotiations became public a year later.

An unspoken condition from the Nassau contingent was that they badly wanted a case against Jimmy Burke and would be relying on Hill to get it.

Later on May 2, Fox told Hill that the drug charges had been dropped, and that evening the FBI attempted to remove Hill from the Nassau County jail in order to put him in the Witness Protection Program. But Hill refused to go—fearing for his safety, according to the official version of events.

Hill had another agenda.

"I had a lot of money on the street, a couple hundred thousand owed to me," Hill said. "I did not want the feds to pull me out of there at that point. I wanted some time to go and collect this money that was owed to me."

The drama took another twist when Hill bailed himself out of jail— unbeknownst to the feds—on Friday, May 16. He went to a nephew's bar mitzvah, then met with Burke at a diner on Sunday. When Burke told him he wanted to see him Wednesday at a bar where members of the "Pizza Connection" heroin ring hung out, Hill knew his days were numbered. By Wednesday, May 21, he was back in protective custody and the tug-of-war between Nassau County and the U.S. government had resumed.

Hill took advantage of one last chance to thumb his nose at the authorities, though. On the previous Friday, the day he bailed himself out, Strike Force special prosecutor Douglas Behm had arranged a search warrant for the FBI to search Hill's home in Rockville Centre for guns. But the order was not carried out until Monday—and in the meantime, Hill had gotten rid of any incriminating evidence.

"When we were debriefing Henry later on, he said, 'You fucks, I got the guns out of there that weekend,'" Behm recalled.

• • •

The call came to Robert Simels on Friday afternoon, May 23, just as thousands of New Yorkers were hitting the road for the Memorial Day weekend holiday. It was a federal judge asking him to "witness somebody signing an agreement."

"He said, 'You're the only lawyer left in New York City, and I need you to come over to the Eastern District,'" Simels recalls.

Simels was in private practice in the spring of 1980. He had been a prosecutor in the Manhattan District Attorney's office and had also worked in the special state prosecutor's office for corruption in New York City. He would play a key role in securing Henry Hill's freedom from prosecution—and would be indirectly responsible for Hill's divulging of the point-shaving scheme to the feds. For now, all he knew was that he was being asked to represent a client who was signing a piece of paper.

When Simels arrived at McDonald's office at around 3:30, he met with Broder and McDonald, and then met with Hill. During a ninety-minute conversation with Hill, Simels realized that the nervous, strung-out wiseguy sitting in front of him was sitting on information that went far beyond the scope of just the Lufthansa robbery. So he went back and told Broder that no deal could be signed unless all the Nassau indictments were dismissed, and told McDonald basically the same thing regarding any future prosecution by the government.

"I told them, 'The deal is no good; we want a wash on everything he's ever done, other than obviously homicides that he actually committed,'" Simels said. "And they agreed to that. They were sort of buying a pig in a poke, because they only knew he had information about Burke and about Lufthansa, and they wanted that. It was clearly understood by everybody that the Nassau County case had to be dismissed."

Simels then had to convince Karen Hill's parents to go along with having their daughter enter the Witness Protection Program. (In *Goodfellas*, McDonald had a bit part as a lawyer telling Henry and Karen Hill about the Witness Protection Program, a task Simels performed in real life.)

"The mother was screaming at me," Simels recalled. "They didn't want it to happen. But I was being told that Henry had to leave right then, that the marshals were ready to take him away."

According to Simels, Broder called his boss, Nassau County DA Dennis

Dillon, and got approval on the deal that would let Hill walk on the drug charges. The agreement was executed, Hill was taken away by the U.S. Marshals, and Simels assumed his role in the story was over.

He found out differently the next Tuesday, May 27, when McDonald called and told him that Nassau County had decided to go forward with the prosecution of Henry Hill, and would he like to stay involved with Henry and represent him?

It would be another year before the dispute would be settled. By then, the Boston College point-shaving scheme had been splashed across the national headlines, Paul Mazzei and Jimmy Burke were in jail on unrelated charges, and several former B.C. basketball players were fearing for their futures.

• • •

The stormy relationship between Rick Kuhn and Barbara Reed was about to come to an end as the summer of 1980 wound down. The two had talked about getting married on several occasions, but no concrete action had been taken by either of them to advance that end. Rick had scuttled the original plan by leaving the country to play ball in South America after the school year ended in 1979. In the spring of 1980 he told Reed he wanted to get married that fall, but by this time Barbara had decided she wanted to wait until the following spring.

As their relationship was spiraling downward, Rocco Perla and Georgeanne, his longtime girlfriend, were busy planning their own wedding for August 6. Reed, who was to be a bridesmaid in the ceremony, spent two weeks in Swissvale during that period and talked to Rick about ending their relationship. The two appeared in the wedding together, but both knew it was over.

Reed remembered Rick saying at one point, "You came here to break up with me." Then, the hulking former basketball star, who had once threatened to kill her if she breathed a word about the point-shaving scheme, started to cry.

Still, they agreed to keep seeing each other, and when Reed went back home to Syracuse a week after Rocco and Georgeanne's wedding she expected to see Rick a few days later on August 17, which was her birthday. But he left a phone message that said he was not coming.

The next time Barbara Reed saw Rick Kuhn was over a year later, in federal court in Brooklyn, under drastically different circumstances.

• • •

While Hill told his questioners where the bodies of the participants in the Lufthansa robbery were buried, the battle over who would control his fate continued. Nassau County authorities were insisting on prosecuting Hill on the drug charges, and promising "heavy time" if he was convicted.

The dispute seemed to have been ironed out on Thursday, May 29, when Ed McDonald and Douglas Behm, representing the U.S. Attorney's office, met with Nassau County ADAs Robert Del Grosso and Broder, as well as FBI special agents Steve Carbone and Thomas Sweeney and Nassau County Detective Daniel Mann. Though the parties dispute what happened at the meeting, it appears that the Nassau authorities agreed that Hill would not be prosecuted on the drug charges if he cooperated fully with both sides and if Dillon was given "appropriate credit" in the press if and when the Lufthansa case was solved.

The table was set once again for Hill to begin offering up his former cohorts, including Burke, the prize catch—or so it seemed. Dillon now said that there had been a misunderstanding, and that the deal was essentially off. Behm and McDonald cried foul, but to no avail. Hill eventually was indicted on the drug charges in August, the result of testimony given in May by his paramour and drug partner, Judy Wicks, who had gone in front of a grand jury under the assumption that her testimony would not be used against Hill.

The feds still had Hill, though. And a month before his arraignment, during one of his endless debriefings with Behm and McDonald, he let slip a piece of information that was about to change the lives of everyone with any connection to the 1978–79 Boston College basketball team, and shake the sport of college basketball to its foundations.

• • •

Jim Sweeney's college basketball career was over by the summer of 1980, but his love for the game was undiminished. So, he lined up a roster spot on a team in the Swedish professional league for August. Originally, he had hoped to bring along Rick Kuhn, but details could not be worked out, so Sweeney went alone. His plan was to come back from Sweden and enroll in law school the following fall.

"He had always talked about going to law school, but I think he had an itch like the rest of us, to play a pro sport, and he was going to play that out," says Sweeney's former roommate Mike Mayock. "He didn't come from a lot of money, and this was a way he could have financed it, if it had worked out for him."

The plan went awry, not for money, but for love, according to Sweeney. Not wanting to lose Maura, he came back from Sweden after less than two months.

"I recognized that if I didn't come back I might not have an opportunity to marry her," he says. "I spoke with her regularly when I was in Europe, and I could tell that I would have lost her if I didn't come back."

• • •

Henry Hill was only one of a number of people the feds were trying to get to cooperate in the Lufthansa case. A parade of wiseguys came through the Strike Force's offices in Brooklyn, though as the investigation dragged on their number began to shrink.

"One of them I remember very distinctly was Fat Louie Cafora," special prosecutor Douglas Behm recalled. "He came in and sat down, and Ed (McDonald) and one of the FBI agents said to him, 'Look, we've got good information that you're next. Everybody's getting killed who was involved in this robbery, and you ought to cooperate with us.' And he said, 'Fuck you,' and walked out. A couple of weeks later, his body parts were washing up."

Hill underwent intensive questioning on every aspect of the Lufthansa robbery and its aftermath. During the many hours, the fast-talking ex-con developed a certain rapport with his interrogators: Behm, McDonald, FBI agents Edmundo Guevara and Steven Carbone. The jocular nature of the relationship, combined with Hill's penchant for embellishing his stories, nearly conspired to keep the Boston College point-shaving scheme buried for eternity.

Hill already had mentioned the B.C. scam to Robert Simels, his attorney, during one of their many conversations. But the feds had no clue and did not seem likely to ask anything that would elicit any statements about it from Hill. So Simels, who was in a room next door to where Hill was being interrogated, dropped a hint with Thomas Puccio, then the head of the Strike Force, that McDonald should ask Hill what he was doing in the days just before and just after the robbery.

"I kept mentioning that I was in Boston that week," Hill recalls. "I mentioned it two or three times. So finally Ed asked me, 'So what the fuck were you doing in Boston?' And I said I was fixing some college basketball games, with Boston College.

"He almost jumped over the desk and grabbed me by the fucking throat. He says, 'Who put you up to that? That's my fucking school. I played for them.' I had no idea that he went to that school."

When McDonald's initial anger subsided, he immediately assumed Hill was just trying to get his goat, and that one of the FBI agents had put him up to it as a joke. Soon, he realized that Hill was telling the truth. And he was going to do something about it.

Hill, meanwhile, did not grasp the significance of his admission. What could the government possibly care about some basketball players shaving points a year and a half earlier, when so much else was at stake?

"I didn't even consider it a crime worth talking about while they were debriefing me," Hill recalls. "I mean, what the fuck is the big deal, you know? They shaved a few points. And he went ballistic on me. He took it really personal. He really did. Then he had the feds start to debrief me, when he knew it wasn't a prank.

"I didn't even think he was going to make a case about it at the time. Here you've got Burke, Paulie, the wiseguys. . . . What do you want to fuck with these kids for?"

But McDonald's shrewd prosecutor's mind must have been working overtime at this point. Whatever personal animus he might have borne toward Hill resulting from his own wounded pride, he was shrewd enough to know, though perhaps not at that moment, that this was a case that could not only help him snag the lowlifes who had tarnished his school and the sport he loved, but could give him a leg up in his climb to the top of the mob ladder to Jimmy Burke and Paul Vario, his ultimate targets.

For the next year and a half, the Boston College point-shaving case became McDonald's personal obsession.

"My personal opinion? He took it real personally," Hill says. "That was his school, you know? How dare I, or anybody else, go up there and fuck with those games, that he used to fly up to Boston to go and watch? He's the one who pursued it. I don't even think the people in Washington (cared) in the beginning. They cared about Lufthansa, and that's all they wanted. And that was the deal they made with me."

Once the cat was out of the bag, Hill gave up everybody: Paul Mazzei, the Perlas, the players. The tough-talking wiseguy—who had warned Jim Sweeney at the Logan Airport Hilton eighteen months earlier not to tell a soul about the scheme because of the "powerful people in New York" who were backing it—now spilled his guts without remorse in order to save his own skin.

To this day, Hill insists that he had no personal grudge against anyone involved in the scheme, and that the only reason he blew the whistle was because he was bound by the terms of his agreement with the government to answer all questions truthfully and completely.

"There was no agenda," he says. "I knew (the point-shaving) was illegal, but the stuff that they were after was so much more serious than that shit. I thought it was just going to get swept under the carpet. They catch you with one fucking lie, the contract is null and void. There was no bull-shitting. There were bodies buried all over the fucking place. I knew I wasn't going to play any games with them."

• • •

Fred Kuhn woke his son out of a sound sleep early on the morning of September 8, 1980. Two FBI agents were at the front door and wanted to speak to Rick about "a serious matter." Within a few minutes, Rick appeared at the door wearing pajamas. After the agents talked to him briefly in the living room, they suggested that he might prefer talking to them in their car, which was parked across the street. Kuhn then went back to his bedroom to change, and he emerged wearing a pair of shorts.

Kuhn then got in the back seat of the unmarked Ford while the agents, James Byron and Thomas Sweeney (no relation to Jim), climbed in the front seat. Byron, who was from Boston, engaged Rick in small talk about the city and about Boston College, and then began to ask him questions as Sweeney took notes.

"Someone" had brought allegations about point-shaving involving the 1978–79 Boston College basketball team that he had played on, Byron said. Did he know anything about this?

Kuhn's response was summarized from Agent Sweeney's notes in an FBI report. The report described how Kuhn had been approached by Tony

Perla in the summer of 1978, and how he had met with Paul Mazzei some-time after that; how he had attended the meeting at the Logan Airport Hilton in which he and Jim Sweeney agreed to go along with the scheme.

The report also said Kuhn mentioned three games that involved the gamblers: the Harvard game, which included a description of how he was wired money after the Harvard game which he split between himself, Sweeney, and Ernie Cobb; the January 17, 1979, Connecticut game, in which Boston College won and covered the point spread; and the Holy Cross game of February 10, in which the gamblers lost their shirts. He also mentioned the final game of the season against UConn, but said he had told the gamblers that he could not guarantee a Boston College win by "at least five points."

At one point during the thirty-minute interview, Kuhn asked if he was required to talk to the agents. Byron responded that he was not. Byron would admit later that he didn't tell Kuhn either that his statement could be used against him at a later date, or that he should talk to a lawyer before he talked to the agents.

When Byron and Sweeney produced photographs of Sweeney, Cobb, Mazzei, and Henry Hill, Rick identified them immediately.

Several miles away in Braddock Hills, Tony Perla denied everything to the FBI agents who showed up at his door that morning, and he said he wouldn't speak to them until he had talked to a lawyer.

• • •

That same morning, a man asking for Ernie Cobb was seen in Stamford and Bridgeport, Connecticut. John Bowe, an FBI special agent for seven years who specialized in thefts and hijackings at New York's Kennedy Airport, had been given addresses where Cobb could be found in his hometown and nearby, but Ernie was at neither place. At one of Bowe's stops, though, someone told him that Cobb was at a gym in northern New Jersey trying out for the New Jersey Nets. So, Bowe got back in his car and headed back down I-95.

When Bowe arrived at the gym, practice had ended, but a spectator told him where he could find out where the players were staying. He finally managed to extract the information that Cobb was staying at the Holiday Inn in North Bergen. Once there, Bowe got Cobb's room number from the desk clerk and went up to the room, but found no one there. So he went back down to the lobby and eventually was joined by another FBI agent, Gary Kirby.

The agents waited for about an hour, then saw Cobb walk through the lobby with several other people and take an elevator upstairs. After waiting a few minutes to give time for the group to disperse and for Cobb to go to his room, Bowe and Kirby went upstairs and knocked on Cobb's door. Cobb let them in after they identified themselves and their purpose for being there. They then had what Bowe termed a relaxed conversation, with Bowe sitting on one bed and Cobb on the other, and Kirby propping himself up on the dresser and taking notes as the two men talked. Bowe remembered someone coming into the room about five or ten minutes into the interview, and Cobb telling him that Bowe and Kirby "were his friends"(!).

Cobb was anything but relaxed, though. He immediately saw his NBA career being derailed again, despite the fact that he had impressed Coach Kevin Loughery enough to crack the Nets' starting unit in scrimmages.

"At that time I was very, very nervous because I thought that for them to get permission to ask me questions they had to go through management of the team," Cobb said. "I felt my chances to make the team were already ruined."

Bowe remembered Cobb saying at one point, "You guys would have to come now; you couldn't come before I had a chance to make the Nets."

Cobb initially denied everything, according to Bowe: being involved in point-shaving, being aware of any point-shaving going on, or being approached by anybody during the 1978–79 season. Bowe then showed Cobb photographs of Henry Hill, Nick Botta, Jimmy Burke, Marty Krugman, Paul Mazzei, John Savino, and Peter Vario, none of whom he said he recognized, although he said the picture of Hill looked "vaguely familiar." He also said he did not know Tony Perla.

At this point Bowe advised Cobb of his rights and gave him an Interrogation Advice of Rights form, also known as an FG-395 form, which they read to him and which he signed at 2:38 P.M.

After Cobb filled out the form, Bowe recalled, the substance of his responses changed dramatically. Suddenly, he began talking about point-shaving going on, and about being approached by someone he knew as "Rocco," who "told him that there was a lot of money, cars, anything, to be made off of basketball games." Cobb went on to say that Kuhn had told him that Rocco was from Pittsburgh and that he, Kuhn, had received gifts, like a pink Cadillac.

During the course of the hour-long interview, Cobb also described a sequence of events that threw a different slant on things. His basic contention was that, yes, he had accepted the one thousand dollars from Rocco Perla at Boston Garden after the Harvard game, but that it had been for covering the spread in Boston College's earlier game against Bentley College. He also claimed that Perla offered him two thousand dollars to make sure B.C. covered the spread in the Stonehill game, which followed Bentley on the schedule.

Not once during the interview did Cobb admit to shaving points himself. He said that Perla later tried to get him to shave points in a third game, which he refused to do. Cobb claimed the third game was the Colonial Classic final against UConn at Boston Garden on January 27, 1979.

At the conclusion of the interview, Bowe handed Cobb a subpoena for a grand jury, which was convening within a week or so.

It was not long before Cobb called Herman Alswanger, his high school coach from Stamford.

"There's trouble," Ernie told him. When Alswanger asked him if he was involved, Cobb replied, "No. I know what I did and what I didn't do."

As far as Cobb was concerned, even though he had taken money from the gamblers, he had earned it by playing his best. The game was the thing, and his performances had been pure.

When the story broke four months later, Alswanger would again stand by Cobb, just as he had done nearly a decade earlier, when Ernie had showed up as an eighth-grader trying to make the basketball team at Stamford High.

"I said, 'Now look, if you're in trouble we'll help you,'" Alswanger remembers. "He said, 'Coach, I'd never do this. Believe me.' During the season, I don't think he believed it was going on. They told him he could earn a lot of money, ten thousand dollars, whatever it was. And he said 'That sounds like losing. That's not in my vocabulary.'

"He only thought it was (Kuhn). He couldn't picture Sweeney doing it, because Sweeney came from a nice background, always looked nice, had nice clothes."

Two and a half weeks after the FBI's visit to New Jersey, Ernie Cobb was cut by the New Jersey Nets along with forward Steve Sheppard and guard Robert Smith. One of the players who made the team was rookie guard Rory Sparrow of Villanova, a player about whom Cobb still says today, "I had him in my hip pocket."

• • •

Sticking to policy, FBI agents knocked on Jim Sweeney's parents' door in Trenton at 6 A.M. on September 8, 1980. This initial meeting lasted about twenty minutes. It continued that same day for another hour or so at the local FBI office, where Sweeney was interviewed by special agent Edmundo Guevara and two other FBI agents.

Not unlike Cobb in his interview with the feds, Sweeney first denied any knowledge of the point-shaving scheme to the agents. But when he was advised of his right to have an attorney present and that anything he said could be used against him in court, he changed his tune and admitted that he actually did know something about it. During this interview, Sweeney mentioned only the Providence game and the meeting at the Logan Airport Hilton, which he misstated as the Boston Sheraton.

Sweeney would later testify that the reason he told the agents what he knew was not because he was afraid of being prosecuted; rather, he still felt that he had done nothing wrong and thus had nothing to fear. When the agents showed him photographs of Henry Hill, Jimmy Burke, Paul Mazzei, and Peter Vario, he denied knowing any of the men.

Though Sweeney remembers being shaken up by the interview, he was not caught too far off-guard.

"I think I always knew that there would come a day when someone would be calling or knocking on the door," he said. "I just sensed that. I knew that. I was not surprised."

Sweeney was genuinely surprised, however, when he visited McDonald in Brooklyn the next summer to discuss testifying for the government. He walked in just as McDonald was finishing up with another visitor.

"They kind of messed up—they're supposed to keep people separate, whatever the procedure is—and I walked into the room and Ed McDonald, I could tell, was tense," Sweeney remembers. "And this guy was sitting there, and I said, 'My name's Jim Sweeney.' And he said, 'I know who you are.'"

The man was Henry Hill, whom Sweeney had not seen since the night of the Harvard game at Boston Garden nearly two years earlier. Sweeney remembers McDonald acting surprised that the two men were not better acquainted, obviously based on Hill's account.

"It was really brief; then they escorted him out of the room," Sweeney said. "In terms of Ed's investigation, I thought that that really spoke volumes, because I didn't even know who the guy was. His countenance had changed, his look had changed."

• • •

Barbara Reed was working at a hospital in Syracuse on September 23 and was attending to a patient in labor when two FBI agents came calling. After speaking to her in the hospital personnel office for fifteen minutes, they agreed that they would pay a visit to her house when she got off work. She spoke to the agents for a total of about ninety minutes.

"They had a lot of things written down that they told me Mr. Kuhn had told agents in Pittsburgh and that he had given them my name and said, you know, we know you know about this," she said. "They mentioned some players' names. They mentioned some hotels in Boston. And they mentioned some basketball games."

The agents asked her about the call she made to Las Vegas on the day of the Holy Cross game, and asked whether she had ever bet on anything before. Reed remembered being "pretty shook up" by the interview. When her father, John, arrived home at a little after 5 o'clock, he told her not to make any more statements until she spoke to a lawyer.

• • •

In Boston, Mike Mayock was preparing along with the rest of the Boston College football team for a nationally televised season opener against Pitt and quarterback Dan Marino in early September 1980. Mayock had gotten his undergraduate degree in the spring along with Sweeney and his other four suitemates, but had decided to stay on an extra year to take some graduate courses and use up his final year of football eligibility.

Even though Mayock was one of the few people who knew about the scheme, he remembers being caught off-guard when Boston College athletic director Bill Flynn approached him on the field with someone from the FBI who wanted to see him "right away."

"I remember my reaction to Mr. Flynn, kind of kidding with him, was, 'Hey, I know I cheated on that test last week, but the FBI—you've got to be kidding me,'" Mayock says. "They literally took me right off the field, wouldn't let me change, and took me right into an office, and for a couple of hours they grilled me. They tried to get my story to change, and I retold it a bunch of times. I was as honest as I could be. They basically said, 'Listen, here's what's going on: We know what happened, and Jim Sweeney has agreed to turn state's evidence. He told us that he confided in you and Dan Conway, and we have to investigate both of you regarding corroborating Jim's story.'"

Mayock admits that he left out one detail of the story Sweeney had told him back in December 1978, after the Harvard game.

"I told them everything I knew except for the money," he says. "They didn't ask me about it, and I wasn't going to volunteer. He was my roommate and friend."

• • •

Head coach Tom Davis had heard about gambling and point-spread fluctuations on Boston College games since the end of the 1979 season, but had not noticed anything amiss during the season and could not really pinpoint anything in retrospect, either.

A visit from the FBI in September 1980 drove home the point that something had, indeed, been amiss. Davis was stunned at first.

"I didn't believe it," he says. "I just didn't believe it could have been true. You liked the guys, you liked them as people, and they gave a great effort. They were giving everything they had."

Davis later went over game films, trying to pick out instances where one of his players might have made any mistakes that could be deemed suspicious. He still came up empty-handed.

Assistant coach Kevin Mackey remembers hearing that the FBI was asking questions around his neighborhood, perhaps to ascertain whether the scheme had any Boston connections outside of the college. When he was interviewed by the FBI, Mackey couldn't resist having some fun with the agents.

"I said to them: 'Why are you picking on us?' They said, 'What do you mean?' I said, 'You know what I mean. Do you want the big guy from Cambridge to go to Georgetown?'" Mackey says with a laugh, referring to B.C.'s ultimately futile efforts to recruit local schoolboy star Patrick Ewing.

Mackey also let them know that he had heard a rumor that there was a similar investigation being conducted at St. John's, which ultimately was never publicized.

• • •

Joe Beaulieu, Rick Kuhn's counterpart at center for B.C. during the 1978–79 season, denied being approached by Kuhn before the Harvard game when he was interviewed by FBI agents at Flynn's office on September 23. He claimed that he and Kuhn were not close because of "a dispute over a girl." The second half of that statement, at least, may have been true: one teammate remembers Beaulieu having a thing for Barbara Reed, Kuhn's girlfriend.

After telling head coach Davis about the late-night discussion at Kuhn's apartment when Kuhn asked him to join the scheme, Beaulieu finally told FBI agents the truth six weeks later.

Chris Foy, who would be named captain by Davis for the 1980–81 season, was interviewed once during the fall and then again the following summer at his parents' house in Philadelphia after his graduation from B.C.

"One day I happened to be home, and a call came from (Tom) Davis and he said the FBI wanted to ask me some more questions. I said okay. So they called up the house a half-hour later and asked when was a good time, and I told them to stop by around 8 in the morning."

By the next morning, when two agents showed up at the door, Foy had forgotten all about the interview and was sitting at the kitchen table, eating Cheerios.

"My mother answers the door and comes back in the kitchen almost in tears, saying, 'Christopher, it's the FBI—what have you done?'" Foy says with a laugh. "'Thanks for the vote of confidence, Mom.'"

The agents wanted to know about the trip to Hawaii and how much money Kuhn, Cobb, and Sweeney were spending; the agents also wanted to hear about the dispute between Sweeney and Cobb during the UCLA game. Foy did not hesitate to tell them all he knew.

"I didn't feel any obligation to protect those three guys," he says today. "I knew if I didn't tell the truth and they found out through somebody else that I was painting a story, it was my balls on the line. That was made painfully clear to me."

●　●　●

As 1980 drew to a close, it was becoming clear that despite providing information on drug trafficking in Nassau County that the District Attorney's office had used to initiate numerous investigations; testifying at a parole hearing that sent Jimmy Burke back to jail for associating with, among other people, him; and testifying at a drug trial at which Paul Mazzei was convicted and sentenced to eighteen months, Henry Hill was not going to be able to provide Nassau County DA Dennis Dillon with a prosecutable drug case against Burke on his own, since Hill was an accomplice of Burke's in the commission of the crimes.

For similar reasons, the Lufthansa investigation had stalled again, as Hill had become a witness in desperate need of corroboration. "There were only about two people alive who could have corroborated on Burke regarding Lufthansa," Robert Simels remembers. "Everybody was dead except for Paul Vario, who was not going to be a witness, and Henry."

The only thing that saved Hill from being charged by Nassau County was the federal government, which had become his lifeline. The very authorities that he once held in such sneering contempt were now his saviors, an irony that was not lost on Hill.

"In the beginning I was very skeptical," he says. "I walked on real thin ice because I didn't know what to expect. Coming from the life that I came from and seeing what people did to friends. . . . I could never believe in a million years that Paulie and Jimmy would turn against me. For no fucking reason. And it was hard for me to accept (the feds) as my lord and savior at that point. I was really skeptical.

"But basically, I put my trust in them. I had no other choice at the time. I knew in my heart . . . we had never reached an FBI agent, so I trusted them completely, with myself and with my family. The more I lived with them, the more confident I felt."

CHAPTER ELEVEN

Eye of the Storm

Dan Lauck had been a reporter for long enough to know that he was sitting on a dynamite story at the close of 1980, one he knew he had to get in print before someone else stumbled onto it and beat him to the punch. But time was working against him. He had already given his notice and was leaving *Newsday*, the biggest newspaper on Long Island, when he learned of an investigation into possible point-shaving at Boston College in the 1978–79 season. His new assignment was at the *New York Daily News*, where editor Clay Felker was inaugurating a new section, dubbed "Tonight," which would feature Lauck and other prominent writers.

Lauck, now an investigative reporter for KHOU-TV in Houston, remembers the reception he got when he arrived at the *Daily News* and proposed the story.

"They said, 'That's great, but can you get us a story on Dave Jennings?' who was the Giants' new punter," Lauck recalled. It was a sign that this was not to be a match made in journalistic heaven, so within a few weeks Lauck left the *Daily News* and accepted a job at the *Washington Post*, which had been interested in hiring him when he left *Newsday*. Bob Woodward, then an editor at the *Post*, immediately gave Lauck the go-ahead to pursue the story.

Before Lauck even started at the *Post*, however, someone at the paper had heard from a source at Georgetown University that a reporter had been snooping around asking questions about an investigation into possible point-shaving involving a college basketball team. Suspecting that the *New York Times* had caught wind of the story, Lauck sprang into action.

On Thursday, January 15, 1981, he drove to Connecticut and waited at the Stamford YMCA where, he had been told, Cobb played every afternoon. Lauck waited and waited, but Cobb failed to show up.

Suddenly, Lauck realized that if he didn't call Ed McDonald, who was heading the investigation under the auspices of the Organized Crime Strike Force of the Eastern District of New York, McDonald might leave work and go home for the evening. So, he called McDonald's office and left a message spelling out what he needed to talk to him about, and jumped in his car and sped back down I-95 to Brooklyn.

Unbeknownst to Lauck, while he was in transit his scoop was exposed. An assistant in McDonald's office had seen Lauck's phone message on a secretary's desk and immediately called a friend at the *New York Post*. By the time Lauck arrived in Brooklyn and went in to see McDonald and confirm the details of the story, the *Post* was already hot on the trail.

Lauck left McDonald's office and hightailed it to a friend's apartment in Manhattan, where he pounded out his story and transmitted it to Washington. His story ran in the *Washington Post* the next morning, Friday, January 16, with the byline shared by Joe Pichirallo, a *Post* staffer who had rewritten Lauck's copy in *Post* style since Lauck hadn't even written a story for the paper yet.

But the *New York Post* was working behind the scenes, and in a maneuver straight out of the city tabloid wars, snagged the story.

Lauck says that a friend of his at the *New York Post* told him later that a pressman from the *Washington Post* called New York when the first edition came off the presses Thursday night and read the story over the phone. The story appeared in the *New York Post* the next morning as an exclusive—naturally with no mention of Lauck's story.

But the truly amazing part of the story was yet to come. While back-checking some of his facts and sources, Lauck eventually figured out that the person who the source at Georgetown had referred to, the unnamed reporter who had persuaded Lauck's editors to kick-start Lauck's pursuit of the story . . . was none other than Lauck himself. In effect, he had been chasing his own tail—and in the process, Lauck had inadvertently tipped off a competitor.

● ● ●

Boston College was again surpassing expectations in its second year in the Big East Conference. Picked to finish sixth in the eight-team league, on Wednesday, January 14, 1981, the Eagles defeated conference foe UConn, 58–57, to raise their record to 9–2.

The basketball team's won-lost record was the furthest thing from Bill Flynn's mind, however. For more than four months, since the day the FBI first visited the B.C. campus and notified him that the school was under investigation for point-shaving, Boston College's athletic director knew that eventually the story would go public and that the school would be held up in the national spotlight as another example of the evils of big-time college sports. It would be a devastating blow to a school that had always prided itself on resisting the temptations that had toppled so many other Division I programs.

Flynn was in Miami to officially conclude his two-year term as president of the NCAA at the organization's annual convention. As Michael Madden reported in the *Boston Globe*, Flynn had no sooner returned to his hotel room at the Fontainebleau Thursday night than the phone rang. It was someone at the school telling him that the story was going to be in Friday morning's papers.

As predicted, the *Boston Globe*, citing Lauck's story in the *Washington Post*, ran a short item atop its sports page that mentioned the point-shaving investigation but did not name any players or games believed to have been influenced. Flynn told the paper, "If you watched a Tom Davis team, you'd feel it was impossible to fix a game. He uses all ten players. We won all fifteen home games that year, and the games we lost we should have lost. . . . This is devastating. It looks awful. . . . We never thought it would happen, not the way we play the game."

As details began to filter down through the various news outlets over the next few weeks, the story began to take shape. The distancing from the players by the school and the denials by all alleged to be involved predictably followed. In the middle was the forlorn figure of Davis. The coach is usually the last to know when his players are shaving points, and this case only reinforced that axiom.

"I am extremely disturbed by the allegations," Davis told the *Boston Globe*. "When the Justice Department first talked to us about it, I thought back as to whether there were any games, to my knowledge, where a player gave less than his best effort. I could think of none."

"The only thing, if I look back on it, was (the) death threat when we were playing up at Holy Cross," Davis said in a 2000 interview. "They brought that to my attention prior to the game. But you wrote that off, you never gave any thought as to any kind of wrongdoing."

Today, Davis still is pained by the memories of the day when he was notified of the allegations. They were his players—players he had not recruited, true, but players he had come to know and like. His sense of betrayal was mitigated in part by the school's swift response to the charges.

"Boston College was terrific," Davis recalls. "They were outstanding in terms of helping me sort my way through it, to make sense of it all. And I really appreciated that."

Senior captain Chris Foy was as stunned as the rest of the team. Foy shared a bond with teammates Vin Caraher and Chris Chase, both of whom had been members of the 1978-79 team. The rest had either graduated or left the program.

"We had just beaten Connecticut, and Connecticut had a great team," Foy recalled. "We were coming up from the rear in the Big East that year, and we were having a good year. It was a great game, and the next morning it was in the paper. I got a call from Coach Davis [at my dorm], and he said, 'You may be contacted by people. I suggest you don't say anything until we have a team meeting. The authorities are going to want to talk to you.'"

The next day, Flynn met the team and made a brief speech. He stressed that the players were at liberty to talk to the authorities, and that if any of them needed assistance the school would provide it. Above all, Flynn said, if any of the players knew anything, they should come forward now.

That same day, Saturday, January 17, the *Globe* carried a story that identified Ernie Cobb, Rick Kuhn, and Michael Bowie as the players under investigation, and speculated on the effect the scandal might have on the attempts to recruit 7-foot center Patrick Ewing, then attending high school in Cambridge. (B.C. was never really in the Ewing race, one source close to the situation says, claiming that Georgetown already had a lock on him by virtue of the relationship between Cambridge Rindge and Latin coach Mike Jarvis, Hoyas coach John Thompson, and Celtics general manager Red Auerbach.) The Fordham and St. John's games were mentioned, with Cobb's lackluster performance in the latter game recounted.

Kuhn was quoted by the *Globe* as telling the *Washington Post*—which somehow was able to contact him while the *Globe* was not—that he did not know Henry Hill and that, "Nothing like that ever went on while I was there. This is all pretty crazy."

The *New York Times* hinted in its story at the involvement of Richard Perry without naming him, and ran a quote from Cobb's mother, Hattie, saying, "That is something he is denying. He says it's not true. That's all that I know."

When Cobb was finally reached through his attorney in Stamford, Franklin Melzer, on Monday, January 19, he told the Associated Press, "I have not been involved in point-shaving in any way." Since being released by the Nets the previous September, Cobb had been playing for the Harlem Wizards, a touring team based in Groton, Connecticut, for one hundred dollars per game plus expenses. He reportedly learned about the point-shaving investigation from some of his teammates on the Wizards.

Melzer added that he was "shocked by the unfounded accusations," which were "personally damaging and a flagrant affront to legal and ethical proceedings. . . . Mr. Cobb categorically denies any involvement in point-shaving. This present attack on everything he has worked to achieve is ill-founded."

Howard Davis, the Wizards' owner, also was taken aback by the allegations. "If this kid is guilty, I'll be amazed, unhappy, and very disappointed," he told *Times* columnist Dave Anderson a few weeks after the story broke. "He's the kind of kid you'd want for a son."

Jim Sweeney's name first appeared in connection with the investigation in a *New York Times* story written by Leslie Maitland on January 20. The story also mentioned Richard Perry's name for the first time, and established Paul Mazzei as the connection between Henry Hill and Rick Kuhn. The *Globe*'s Lesley Visser had quoted Sweeney in a story two days earlier but had not linked him to the investigation.

Former Boston College head coach Bob Zuffelato, who had recruited Kuhn, Cobb, and Sweeney, heard the news at Marshall University in West Virginia.

"I was totally shocked," he remembers. "Are you kidding? Actually, upset would be more accurate. I was really, really upset, and shocked too.

Ernie Cobb in action for Stamford High School in 1975, the year he was selected to the All-America team.

Courtesy of Stamford High School

Henry Hill (second from right) at Lewisburg Federal Penitentiary in the mid-1970s. It was at Lewisburg that Hill met Pittsburgh drug dealer Paul Mazzei, who provided the link to Boston College center Rick Kuhn in the summer of 1978.

Courtesy of Henry Hill

Paul Vario Sr., reputed capo in New York's Lucchese crime family and the model for the "Paul Cicero" character in *Goodfellas*. Vario reportedly gave his OK to Henry Hill and James Burke to proceed with the point-shaving scheme in the fall of 1978.

AP/Wide World

Dr. Tom Davis at the February 17, 1977, press conference announcing his appointment as head coach at Boston College, replacing Bob Zuffelato.

AP/Wide World

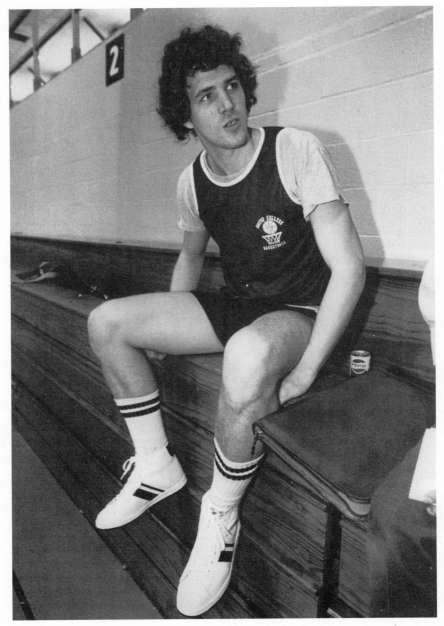

Former Boston schoolboy star Joe Beaulieu testified that he rejected teammate Rick Kuhn's offer to shave points in the December 16, 1978, Harvard game.

AP/Wide World

Jim Sweeney dribbles against Connecticut's
Randy LaVigne at Boston Garden on January
27, 1979. Boston College, a five-point favorite,
defeated the Huskies, 78–77, to win the Colonial Classic.

AP/Wide World

Chris Foy (wearing #44) played on the 1978–79 Boston College team as a freshman and was captain of the 1980–81 team when news of the point-shaving investigation broke.
AP/Wide World

The cover of *Sports Illustrated*, February 16, 1981, the issue in which Hill told his version of events to reporter Douglas Looney.
Sports Illustrated

Former Boston College center Rick Kuhn at U.S. District Court in Brooklyn, October 1981.
AP/Wide World

Henry Hill in the new millennium.
Courtesy of Henry Hill

Disappointed, not that I had recruited those kids, because when I had recruited them I had thought they were a perfect fit for our program and would be good citizens."

On the Boston College campus, the shock was dulled somewhat by the excitement over the current team's successes.

"People looked at it and said they couldn't believe it had happened," says John Feudo, a communications major who later worked as a broadcaster, "but there was also an attitude of, 'It happened, (the players are) gone, let's move on.' Because at that time we were really good."

They certainly were good, and against all odds the team was able to maintain their focus through the intense scrutiny that fell on them. At each visiting arena they were met with signs and derisive chants referring to the investigation.

"People would hold up dollar signs, or throw Monopoly money on the floor," former Boston College sports information director Reid Oslin remembers. "The kids at Holy Cross played the Gillette song and put shaving cream on their faces. It got pretty nasty a couple of times."

But the extra attention merely served to draw the B.C. players closer and strengthen their collective purpose.

"When I look back on it, yeah, it should have been a distraction, but we were on a roll," Foy says. "We were undefeated at home that year. . . . It's not that it was water off my back, but things were just going so well. It was not a nonevent, but in the big picture it was, 'Hey, maybe that did happen, maybe it didn't, but you know what? We're 24 and 6 and we're beating Georgetown, we're beating St. John's, we're beating Connecticut. Things are going great. The stuff was in the paper every day, but I didn't do anything wrong, so let's move through it.'"

Only a few players remained from the 1978–79 team; to the rest of the team, it was a lot of sound and fury that had little to do with them. It was a much bigger crisis for a school that for decades had prided itself on doing things the right way when it came to intercollegiate athletics.

"It was not the kind of thing that happened to our program," Oslin says. "You had heard about the previous (scandals) in the '50s, but . . . the hardest thing was that this would happen to Bill Flynn. For Bill Flynn, who was a pillar of what is good in college athletics, it was staggering. I know it hurt him very badly.

"It wasn't that everything (at B.C.) was perfect, but it was in perspective. It was run the way a college athletic program is supposed to be run. That's why it was a stunning revelation when it came out."

• • •

More details dribbled out as January wore on, and it often seemed that each successive B.C. win on the court was accompanied by more seamy revelations in the newspapers.

A day before the Eagles beat Syracuse, 66–63, Paul Mazzei—who by then had been publicly connected to the conspiracy—surrendered to authorities in New York on a charge of conspiracy to distribute heroin. A 72–68 overtime win over Seton Hall was preceded by the news that the school had been notified by the NCAA of irregular betting on Boston College games during the 1978–79 season and that Davis allegedly voiced his own suspicions to Flynn but could find no proof of anything underhanded.

By the time Boston College dispatched Villanova, 73–60, on January 26, to improve its record to 13–2, the *Globe* had reported details of a meeting at Boston Garden between Cobb, Laverne Mosley, Rocco Perla, and Kuhn at which Cobb was offered money—though the story incorrectly placed the meeting in late January 1979.

On January 24, one week and a day after the story first appeared in print, NBC devoted five minutes of its halftime show during the Notre Dame–Maryland game to the investigation. The segment featured footage of Cobb missing shots against Holy Cross in the fateful February 10, 1979, game in which the gamblers lost tens of thousands of dollars. Cobb also appeared on camera and nervously read a prepared statement denying any wrongdoing.

By the end of January, a grand jury had been impaneled in the Eastern District of New York to hear testimony on the point-shaving case. It had been a tumultuous month for Boston College and for college basketball. But the worst was yet to come, and soon.

• • •

By early February 1981, Robert Simels began to see that his decision to trade out some of his legal expertise in exchange for the rights to Henry Hill's story had been a stroke of genius. The first suitor to come knocking was *Sports Illustrated* magazine, which offered Hill ten thousand dollars to do a first-person account of the point-shaving scheme.

A short meeting was arranged at the U.S. Attorney's office (in Brooklyn) between Hill, Simels, *SI* writer Douglas Looney, and *SI* editor Larry Keith. After that, a routine was set up under which Simels would have Hill and Looney call him at his office and then connect the two via conference call.

Before the magazine hit the newsstands, *Sports Illustrated* already was called to task when it was divulged that the magazine had paid Hill for the interview. The *Globe* was particularly critical, and columnist Ray Fitzgerald mocked "Henry Hill: literary giant" as a "first-class thief, dope peddler and all-around sleaze who also has a way with words."

Sports Illustrated's Keith defended the paying of Hill, telling the *Globe*, "We paid Henry Hill just as we would any other writer. In this case, Hill, with Douglas Looney, brought more than information to the story. Hill brought expertise, understanding, and authority through his byline. . . . We think Henry Hill's story has news value, and we reached out as far as we could to get the story. We didn't want to restate what had already been written by the *Boston Globe*, *New York Times* and *Washington Post*."

• • •

Reached by the *Globe*, Kuhn commented bravely, "I ain't got nothing to say about it. I'm not afraid of anything. I'm not talking to anybody. I'm just not payin' attention to none of it."

The week before the article ran, NBC's *Sports Journal* aired a segment hosted by Edwin Newman in which Simels confirmed Hill's version of events but stopped short of identifying which players were being investigated.

Ernie Cobb, meanwhile, continued to appear at high school gyms with the Harlem Wizards. His specialty was a dribbling act he performed at halftime that featured kids chosen from the audience. Cobb remained mum about the investigation, and anyone who asked about the 1978–79 season or the subject of point-shaving went away disappointed.

• • •

The picture on the cover of the February 16, 1981, edition of *Sports Illustrated* featured a cascade of one-hundred-dollar bills filling up a basketball hoop below the title, "Anatomy of a Scandal." Inside was an article with the headline, "How I Put the Fix In," by Henry Hill with Douglas S. Looney.

"I'm the Boston College basketball fixer," the article began. "It was a day's pay, it was interesting and it gave me a nice feeling. If you're not a gambler, you'll never understand, but it was a rush."

The rest of the seven-page article, which also featured still and action photos of Sweeney, Cobb, and Kuhn, spun a seamy tale of greedy players eager to sell out their school for a few thousand bucks and some drugs. Hill boasted that he and his associates, whom he named as Jimmy Burke, Richard Perry, and Peter Vario, made a quarter of a million dollars off the scheme, and that the players made about ten thousand dollars each.

There was only one problem: Much of what was in the article was exaggerated, embellished, or simply untrue. It would come out at Kuhn's trial later in 1981 that Hill confused names, dates, and numbers, and that he omitted pertinent facts—such as the Providence game, which was the first "test" game in the scheme.

"They wanted it out so quick, and I hadn't discussed the games with Ed (McDonald) at that point," Hill remembers. "I had a card that had all the games on it that Sweeney had circled. And Ed had it. That's why a lot of the inconsistencies were there."

No one would know this for several months, though. For now, the sports world was stunned by Hill's description of the players' cavalier attitude toward gambling and point-shaving. Among other observations, he described Sweeney at the November 1978 Logan Airport Hilton meeting trying to get thirty-five hundred dollars per game out of him before "chewing him down" to twenty-five hundred.

"The main thing is that the players struck me as over-ambitious," Hill wrote. "They couldn't wait.

"See, Sweeney was businessman like me. Birds of a feather . . . Sweeney took out one of those little schedule cards, circled the games he thought they could fool with, and gave the card to me. . . . The thing that got me was that they were familiar with betting, they knew about spreads, they were not dumb kids. They knew how to shave, because when I tried to explain to them, they said, 'Naw, we know all that s—t.' They were the salesmen, not me."

Hill went on to describe winning approximately fifteen thousand dollars on the Harvard game—which he claimed was a test game—then winning another twenty-five or thirty thousand dollars on the UCLA game a week later. He recounted the mini-debacle against Rhode Island, then the first Holy Cross game, the one in which B.C. won and Cobb scored thirty-one points. Hill mentioned the Colonial Classic game against UConn as another game that was fixed—later disputed—plus the Fordham and St. John's games. He finished by detailing the Holy Cross disaster on February 10, and then claimed that the players "talked us into doing one more" in the ECAC playoff game against UConn on March 1.

Hill saved his parting shot for Sweeney.

"Funny thing," he wrote. "I sit around now and I think, 'Ain't that Sweeney something?' He looks like a little choirboy, a legitimate kid. So why did he do it? The money, man, the money. That's why we all did it."

• • •

Jim Sweeney picked up the *Sports Illustrated* article at a newsstand in Morristown, New Jersey, and read it sitting in his father's truck in northern New Jersey. Even today, Sweeney can remember his reaction to seeing himself described in print as a greedy hustler.

The story was "grossly inflated . . . blatantly exaggerated," Sweeney recalls. "Certain things were based on fact, but the way he wrote it wasn't factual. It looked like he wanted to pin the blame on other people."

Mike Mayock, Sweeney's former roommate who had been one of the very few people told about the scheme as it was happening, nevertheless was stunned to read the details provided by Hill. This was not the Jim Sweeney that Mayock remembered living with for three years. Could it be that his friend had another side to which he'd never been given access?

"The thing that blew me away in the article, aside from the fact that *Sports Illustrated* would pay a convict ten thousand dollars to write the article, was that he made Jimmy out to be the ringleader," Mayock said. "And the references at the Airport Hilton where Jimmy was ordering wine and drinking wine . . . anybody that knew Jimmy knew that he drank about once a year. So it just didn't ring true for me from the beginning. And it shook me a little bit."

The part about Sweeney trying to negotiate a higher payoff also struck a wrong note with Mayock.

"It made Jimmy out to be this street-smart con man, and Jimmy was anything but that. Did he come from money? No. But he did come from a loving family, and he was the last guy that you could make those kind of overall indictments about."

Gary Vogler, Sweeney's American Legion baseball coach back in Trenton, was stunned when the local newspapers called him in 1981 after Sweeney's name was linked to the point-shaving investigation.

"I was mad that [people] would even think of him doing something like that," Vogler remembers. "I really defended him. That's what you do when you believe in somebody like that. Even now, it almost makes me cry, as silly as that may seem. Because I had that much faith in him, and we had that kind of relationship."

• • •

In Pittsburgh, Rocco Perla remembers being "absolutely" in shock when the article came out. "We had no inkling that somebody was investigating it or that something was going on," he said. He and his brother Tony had been issued subpoenas the previous September, when the FBI had attempted to interview both of them, but had essentially blown them off.

"We said through an attorney, 'We're sorry, we'll not have anything to say, we won't be interviewed, we'll just take the Fifth on any questions,'" he said.

By far the strongest reaction to the article came, interestingly, from Ed McDonald. The Strike Force attorney had not been notified that Hill had granted an interview with *Sports Illustrated*, and when he found out, he was livid.

"He went berserk," Hill recalls. "He blew his fucking top. Hey, they didn't tell me I couldn't do it. I didn't think there was anything wrong with it."

McDonald knew that Hill had just created a major headache for the prosecution, since the defense could now use the article along with Hill's impending grand jury testimony to expose any inconsistencies in his testimony once he got on the witness stand. There was also the prospect of complications arising from excessive pretrial publicity caused by the article, an opportunity any defense attorney with half a pulse would be foolish to pass up. It was a disaster all the way around.

"Ed was not pleased, the marshals were not pleased, the FBI was not pleased," Simels recalled. "The marshals, because it was a potential breach of security to a person under their control, and Ed because it created fodder for cross-examination—and because we hadn't told him."

• • •

The *Sports Illustrated* article caused a stir in Swissvale, which was hardly surprising since it made prominent mention of three local men. One person who bought the magazine when it hit the newsstands was Christine Siano, formerly Christine Ludwig, who had grown up in town and lived a few blocks away from the Perlas.

Siano had known the Perlas since her youth. One of her younger brothers knew Rocco, and another brother, David Ludwig, had employed Rick Kuhn to do paving work at Tony Perla's house in the summer of 1978, at the time when the subject of point-shaving was first broached. David Ludwig also had been a friend of Tony Perla's, and Christine remembered filling out a football pool sheet and giving it to David, who would give it to Tony.

About two or three days after the article came out, Siano was at her mother's house having lunch, something she did frequently since she worked close to her home. Tony Perla stopped over on this day, and during a forty-five-minute conversation managed to all but confess on a stack of Bibles to everything that Hill described in the magazine article.

First, though, he told Christine, her mother, and her brother, Billy, that the article was "all lies." But eventually, he couldn't help himself.

"So I shaved a few games," he told them. Then, proving his powers of prognostication had not improved since the 1978–79 basketball season, he added, "It's no big deal. They're not going to put me away for this."

Two weeks later, Siano was interviewed by the FBI and recounted the entire conversation.

• • •

On February 14, 1981, Colorado defeated Oklahoma State 85–57 in a Big Eight game. A week later, Missouri beat Nebraska 55–45. On the surface there was nothing extraordinary about the scores, but later it would be revealed that the FBI contacted Big Eight Conference officials because unnaturally high amounts of money had been wagered on the two games. In the latter game, Missouri trailed by one point but held Nebraska scoreless in the final 5:57 to win and cover the eight-point spread. Colorado had been a three-and-a-half point favorite against Oklahoma State.

• • •

Henry Hill's numerous interrogation sessions with state and federal authorities continued to bear fruit as the winter of 1981 turned to spring. Already he had provided information that had sent Jimmy Burke back to jail on a parole violation in the summer of 1980, and he also had given up Paul Mazzei in the Nassau County drug case for which he, Hill, was escaping prosecution. On top of that, Hill had managed to ensnare Mazzei in federal heroin conspiracy charges with one well-placed phone call, and now his former Pittsburgh buddy faced thirty years in prison on that charge alone.

The federal charges highlighted one of the government's more questionable tactics.

"He called Paul up in Pittsburgh from the DEA's office in New York, and Paul was all stoned on whatever he was taking then," Mazzei's lawyer, Leonard Sharon, recalls. "And (Hill) started vaguely discussing getting some heroin, which was a figment of his imagination. They recorded it and they busted Paul for that."

By late February 1981, Mazzei pleaded guilty to fourth-degree conspiracy in the Nassau County drug case from 1980, but decided to fight the federal heroin charges. It was during Mazzei's federal trial that the persona of Henry Hill, star witness, began to take shape. It was the first trial in which he took the witness stand and offered a glimpse into the kind of criminal background that later would transform him from low-level wiseguy into multimedia phenomenon.

The trial was enlivened by the introduction into evidence of a taped phone conversation that caught Mazzei and Hill discussing the quality of their product:

"I don't believe it," Mazzei was heard saying. "I don't eat a quaalude for a week. Then I ate two of them and nothing happened. I ended up eating five. Then I passed out.

Joan had to check my pulse. She thought I was dead."

After repeatedly rebuffing the government's offers to get him to join Hill as an informant, on March 12 Mazzei was convicted in Brooklyn federal court of conspiring with Hill to distribute approximately $160,000 of heroin that had been imported from France. In April, U.S. District Judge Jack Weinstein sentenced him to six years, to run concurrently with the eighteen months he was already serving on the Nassau County charges.

The sentence could have been longer, according to Jerry Bernstein, the government's prosecutor in the case. At the sentencing hearing, Weinstein apparently noticed that Mazzei's wife, Joan, was holding a baby in the courtroom. That was enough to convince Weinstein to shave two years off what would have been an eight-year sentence.

The next domino to fall was Nick "Iron Shoes" Botta, one of the bookmakers in Hill's inner circle during the point-shaving scheme. Information provided by Hill in January had led to the arrest of Botta in Woodside, Queens, on charges of running a gambling operation that local authorities estimated brought in approximately $50 million a year.

While all of this was going on, John Bagley, Martin Clark, Jay Murphy, and the rest of the Eagles continued to win. After an upset first-round loss to Providence in the Big East Tournament, they beat Ball State and Wake Forest in the NCAA Tournament before losing to a St. Joseph's team still soaring after its first-round upset of No. 1–ranked DePaul.

The loss ended B.C.'s season with a 23-7 record, an accomplishment for which few superlatives seem adequate in retrospect. The entire second half of the season had been played under a microscope, and the players had responded by blocking out the distractions and playing above perhaps even their own expectations. Assistant coach Kevin Mackey considers it one of the greatest seasons he has been associated with—greater, even, than the 1978–79 season when a team that had three players allegedly shaving points was able to win twenty-one games.

"They were young, it was their year," Mackey said about the 1980–81 team. "The kids were into themselves. They were nineteen, twenty, twenty-one; they were on a great team at a great school; they had their whole lives in front of them. I was closer to the situation (than in 1978–79) because I'd brought them in, and it amazed me."

CHAPTER TWELVE

Choosing Sides

By the spring of 1981 it had been two and a half years since the Lufthansa robbery, and Jimmy Burke and the rest of the Lucchese crew had hung a string of goose eggs on the government's score-sheet. True, Burke was back in jail for violating parole—courtesy of the testimony of his now ex-friend Henry Hill—and most of the Robert's Lounge crew was either dead or missing and presumed dead. But after thirty months on the case, all the feds had to show was the May 1979 conviction of former Lufthansa cargo supervisor Louis Werner, one of the inside men in the robbery. This was especially galling for Ed McDonald and the rest of the Strike Force team because, as they became fond of repeating over the years, they had been supplied the names of the accomplices in the holdup within hours of the commission of the crime in December 1978.

The investigation had not been without its comical moments. In the summer of 1980, the Queens District Attorney's office had obtained a search warrant to dig underneath Robert's Lounge in hopes of finding the bodies of some of the murdered accomplices, some of the money from the heist, or both. When investigators unearthed what initially were thought to be human remains but later were found to be animal bones, Michael Coiro, a lawyer representing Burke, took full advantage of the opportunity. Coiro, a flamboyant advocate who would defend Burke in the Boston College point-shaving trial in 1981, reportedly hired his own bulldozer and invited reporters and law enforcement authorities to dig up the whole neighborhood. Not surprisingly, there were no takers.

If by the spring of '81 it was beginning to look less and less likely that Burke would ever be banged up for the Lufthansa job, the Boston College point-shaving case seemed to offer the feds a wider net with which to snare the feared mobster. Hill already had fingered Burke as the brains behind the operation, the "boss" from whom he received his daily orders. Tying the two together in court would be a difficult, but not impossible, challenge, certainly not as difficult as pinning Burke down on Lufthansa.

"Lufthansa was a case that couldn't be made," remembers Robert

Simels, Hill's lawyer, "at least in the way that the government would have liked to make the case. . . . B.C. came up as an alternative to make a case against (Burke) that would stick. The only issue was, how do you corroborate Henry?"

There would be more than one answer to that question by the time the trial began in late October. But for now, the government's case seemed to rest on the slender shoulders of former Boston College point guard, Rhodes Scholar candidate, and Frances Pomeroy Naismith Award winner, Jim Sweeney.

It had been several months since Sweeney met with FBI agents in his home in Trenton, when he initially denied knowing anything about the point-shaving scheme. Eventually he told the FBI what he knew, and subsequently met twice with McDonald in September in New York, once for about two hours and a second time for about an hour on September 25, the day of his grand jury testimony. The next time Sweeney would meet with McDonald would be the following August, after the indictments had been handed down—with his name conspicuously absent.

Why Sweeney was not charged, and why he never entered a plea in connection with the Boston College point-shaving case, remains a mystery to all but perhaps McDonald. The Strike Force prosecutor, who denied repeated requests to be interviewed for this book, said publicly that Sweeney was not given immunity in the case, which appears to rule out the only other logical possibility.

Sweeney claims today that, at the time, he was left in the dark. He does not remember exactly when he found out he was not going to be charged, but confirms that he was not granted immunity and was not promised anything by the government.

"I was told nothing. I didn't know what to think," he says. "It was an extremely scary time. It was so overwhelming. I was a witness testifying against organized crime figures. . . . The only way to express it was: it was very confusing."

One belief that has remained constant for Sweeney over the years, though, is that he did not break the law in the winter of 1978–79.

"I didn't think I would be eligible for immunity because that's for somebody who's committed a crime. And I could look you right in the eye and say with assurance and confidence that I didn't commit a crime. I'm not a lawyer, I'm not a judge, I don't really know that much about criminal law, but I know the position I found myself in, and I regret that I never spoke up. But I never had that fear that I was ever going to be charged.

"I felt that (McDonald) was fair. I felt that he was empathetic with my situation."

How was Sweeney able to avoid both prosecution and a plea agreement when he had admitted to meeting with, and accepting money from, the gamblers who were about to stand trial? This is particularly troubling when compared to the plight of Ernie Cobb, Sweeney's former teammate, who also admitted accepting money and also offered to cooperate with the government's investigation—yet who was charged two years later, in 1983, nearly five years to the day after the meeting with Hill and Paul Mazzei at the Logan Airport Hilton . . . a meeting that Cobb did not attend, but Sweeney did.

Lawyer David Golub, who represented Cobb at his trial in 1984, echoes the feelings of many involved in the case who felt that McDonald, who played freshman basketball at Boston College in the mid-1960s, was far too lenient on Sweeney.

"I think there were a lot of decisions that were very questionable," Golub says. "McDonald was a guard on the Boston College basketball team. A lot of people said he identified with Sweeney. I thought it was very inappropriate that a white guard was not prosecuted by a former white guard at Boston College, and a black guard was. I thought it looked very bad.

"I didn't know all the reasons McDonald decided not to prosecute Sweeney, not have him plead to something. You know, maybe have him plead to something and give him probation. But to give him a free ride . . ."

• • •

Before McDonald could devote his full energies to prosecuting the Boston College case, however, he had another, higher-profile case on his plate: From early 1978 through early 1980, FBI agents posing as Saudi Arabian investors had been approaching public officials and offering bribes in exchange for political influence. The case, dubbed Abscam, came to trial in mid-1981 and, through McDonald's prosecutorial efforts, resulted in bribery and conspiracy convictions against Sen. Harrison Williams (D-N.J.) and several congressmen and local officials.

Another issue that refused to die was the festering dispute between the government and the Nassau County District Attorney's office over the status of Henry Hill vis-à-vis the felony drug conspiracy counts he was facing from 1980. The matter finally came down to a hearing in front of Nassau County Judge Edward Baker on April 30, 1981. McDonald and Strike Force special prosecutor Douglas Behm represented the government at the hearing, which Behm recalls as being hostile, as the ill will between the feds and the Nassau County DA's office had not lessened during the year since Hill's arrest.

During the course of testimony, it was revealed that William Broder, who by now had left the Nassau County DA's office, had brought up the issue of Dillon receiving partial credit for solving the Lufthansa robbery if he allowed Hill to slide on the drug charges, and that ADA Del Grosso had later called and said that Dillon would not agree with the deal. Dillon claimed during the hearing that he had never authorized any deal that would have allowed Hill to walk on the charges.

The government's case was enough to persuade Baker, who handed down his decision on July 14 in favor of Hill getting a walk on the Nassau County charges. The judge used as precedent the case of *Chaipis v. State*

Liquor Authority, in which the defendant, a restaurant/club owner, pled guilty to a criminal offense but cooperated with authorities in exchange for the promise made by the local district attorney that his liquor license would not be revoked. A similar situation to Hill's developed when the Authority refused to go along with the DA's promise.

Baker also offered a stinging indictment of the conduct of Dillon's office.

"Whether you call it a 'walk,' 'to skate,' or a 'free ride,' the DA's office, through its representatives, promised it to Henry Hill for his full cooperation," the judge wrote. "The offer of one ADA is to be considered an offer by the office.

"In this case, with dreams of massive headlines of breaking the Lufthansa case floating in the respective heads of the District Attorney's office, their normal calm exterior cracked. In light of the federal offer to Henry Hill for his cooperation, it would only have been natural for Nassau County to have made a similar offer, and they did. The subsequent withdrawal of the offer would appear, from the testimony, (to be) the result of a clash of egos rather than the failure of the defendant to fully cooperate . . ."

Baker also noted that the making of the offer and its subsequent withdrawal did not by itself require dismissal of the drug charges against Hill. But he characterized Hill's testimony so far at Burke's parole hearing, Mazzei's drug trial, and his statements in the Boston College case as "truthful and forthright," which stuck to the letter of the agreement. He also pointed out Hill's cooperation in identifying code words and names of people overheard on surveillance tapes that gave insight into the structure of his former drug operation.

Dillon took exception, and launched his own attack on Baker in the New York tabloids.

"The personal references go beyond judicial responsibility," he told a *New York Daily News* reporter. "I can only say that Judge Baker is even more cracked than usual for him. Around here he has a reputation for being crazy, and this confirms it. He is crazy."

Hill was now totally free from prosecution, so long as he kept feeding the feds the information they needed. But the government now faced another problem: namely, that Hill was now totally free from prosecution. He was all theirs, but he was an ex-con with a lengthy criminal background who had admitted to, among other things, participating in the largest robbery in the history of the country and operating a lucrative drug trade. Now, thanks to the government, there was a good chance that he would never again see the inside of a prison cell. Nor had he done so much as plead to any wrongdoing, a common act in situations where a criminal is putting his coconspirators' heads on the block.

"After the fact, the government realized that the deal they had made with Henry was indefensible, because he got a total walk," Simels, the architect of the original deal, said. "And they were strongly criticized by the defense in all of the prosecution's cases. They were kicking themselves over the deal."

Naturally, Hill has a different take. He contends that he had an even bigger stake in telling the truth, since not doing so would put him in danger of reneging on his agreement. And that would surely land him back in jail.

"I knew that I had to be totally honest. I didn't bullshit them," he says. "I just said, 'If I'm going to do this, I'm going to cooperate one hundred percent, that was the agreement.' These guys did save my ass. I knew I was getting whacked. I had nowhere to go. I was hanging out there. At that point I decided I was not going to hold anything back. And they just kept pumping me and pumping me."

• • •

As the government's star witness in the point-shaving trial, Hill spent the summer of 1981 shuttling back and forth between Brooklyn and his new, undisclosed home in the Midwest. By this time, reports had surfaced that the Lucchese family had put out a one-hundred-thousand-dollar contract on him, so security was of paramount importance.

Hill would follow a prescribed routine whenever he came to New York. He would never fly direct, but would always switch planes somewhere along the route. Two U.S. marshals would put him on the flight where it originated, and two more would meet him when he arrived. He would wait until the last passenger disembarked from the plane, then step into a waiting car with the marshals that would be tailed by another security car from the airport.

He would generally fly in on a Sunday, spend three or four days in New York being debriefed and going over his testimony in the B.C. case, then fly back at the end of the week. Then he'd have a week off, and he would come back the following week for more of the same. The point-shaving scheme certainly was not the only topic discussed; Hill remembers being debriefed by the district attorneys of all five boroughs in New York and what seemed like every other law enforcement agency in the country during this period.

Doug Behm spent the most time with Hill as he prepared for the point-shaving trial, and the Strike Force special prosecutor gradually developed a keen sense of his newfound buddy's often flexible concept of the truth. Behm's challenge was to make a credible trial witness out of someone whose credibility was bound to be bludgeoned by the defense repeatedly throughout the trial.

"Henry was a challenge," Behm recalls. "He had learned that the way he was going to survive was to please whoever he was with at the moment. I don't think he really had a strong sense of right and wrong, truth and untruth. He was driven by expediency. And one of the problems was explaining to him that this was not a process that lives on expediency. This is a process that lives on accurate recollections of what happened, and his accurate recollections were fine. Obviously, they weren't perfect at all times, and obviously he had done some stuff that was going to be challenged, but his accurate recollections were what we were looking for.

"Henry was not socialized the way you and I were. So he had a whole different framework for dealing with a trial and testimony and what happened. Because he had now decided that the power on the street, if you will, was the government, and he was going to work hard to try and please us. And you had to work very hard to make sure that Henry was telling the truth. It took work. When Henry wasn't thinking, when he was just sitting there talking to you, he could tell you what happened. But as soon as he felt he had to figure out a situation, then sometimes he would leave this piece out, or add that piece in. But even with all of that, he was consistent, mostly. It was the stuff around the edges he would miss sometimes."

It would be the role of Sweeney and others to supply the stuff around the edges, as well as corroborate the details at the heart of the scheme.

• • •

On July 12, 1981, two days before Judge Baker's ruling on Hill's status in Nassau County, Zachariah Franzi, an oddsmaker employed by the Barbary Coast Hotel and Casino in Las Vegas, appeared on NBC's *Sports World*. During the segment of the show devoted to the point-shaving investigation, Franzi claimed that point spreads for the Boston College–Harvard and Boston College–UCLA games during the 1978–79 season—two games that the government would allege were fixed—had fluctuated significantly at the Barbary Coast sports book, indicating the possibility that something nefarious was afoot.

Franzi's revelation seemed to buttress what the government had been saying all along, but there was one small problem: the Barbary Coast's sports book did not open for business until after the end of the 1978–79 basketball season.

Franzi later would admit that the reason he went on the show was to gain publicity for the Barbary Coast; nevertheless, he was deemed plausible enough to be used at trial by the prosecution, which called him as an expert witness.

• • •

On July 28, 1981—more than two years after Rick Kuhn's last game in a Boston College uniform, and two years and eight months after Kuhn and Jim Sweeney sat in a hotel room in Boston across from Henry Hill, Tony Perla, and Paul Mazzei and discussed shaving points—a grand jury in the Eastern District of New York handed down indictments containing three counts against each of five defendants in the alleged point-shaving scheme.

The eight-page indictment named James Burke, Paul Mazzei, Tony Perla, Rocco Perla, and Rick Kuhn as codefendants, and charged them with violating the following statutes:

- Title 18, Section 1962. This was the most detailed part of the indictment and the part that would take the most explaining to the jury during the trial. Essentially, the defendants were charged with conspiring to engage in a pattern of racketeering activity, demonstrated in overt acts such as the November 16, 1978, meeting at Robert's Lounge between Burke, Mazzei, and Tony Perla, and the Logan Airport Hilton meeting later that evening with Kuhn and Sweeney. Other overt acts included conversations between Kuhn and Sweeney before games, phone calls between the defendants, trips by Rocco Perla from Pittsburgh to Boston, and the wiring of money by Rocco Perla to Kuhn.
- Title 18, Section 224, the sports bribery statute, which comes under the definition of racketeering activity and which forbids anyone to conspire to "influence in any way, by bribery, any sporting contest."
- Title 18, Section 1952, which prohibits the use of interstate travel or commerce in aid of racketeering enterprises.

Mentioned in the indictment were six games: Providence, Harvard, UCLA, Fordham, St. John's, and the February 10 Holy Cross game. The government would cut that list of games in half when it indicted Ernie Cobb two years later, but for now, this was the official version.

The first count carried a ten-year maximum jail term, while the second and third counts of the indictment each carried a five-year maximum, along with possible fines. Immediately, lawyers representing the Perlas, Burke, and Kuhn filed motions for relief from the indictments, with the Perlas' lawyer pressing in vain for the dismissal of the indictments because of excessive pretrial publicity—the first of many times the defense would try to use Hill's *Sports Illustrated* article to its advantage.

Paul Mazzei and Jimmy Burke were already in jail, Mazzei on the federal heroin conviction in March and Burke on violating his parole from his 1972 extortion conviction in 1980. Bail was set at fifty thousand dollars each for the Perlas and Kuhn. Tony Perla covered his end by putting up the deed to the house he and his wife, Sharon, had owned in Braddock Hills, Pennsylvania, since 1973. Rocco used the deed to the house his parents, Rocco Sr. and Mary Perla, had bought in Swissvale in 1954.

Kuhn did likewise, putting up the house owned by his parents, Frederick and Geraldine Kuhn, on Homestead Street in Swissvale, the house where he had been awakened early one morning the previous September by two FBI agents, who now would be telling a jury how he had confessed to his crimes.

The contrast between the five defendants in *U.S. v. Burke* was embodied by James Burke and Rocco Perla. One was a middle-aged ex-con who was reputed to have been involved in more than a dozen murders and whose criminal exploits were legendary even in New York's organized crime circles; the other was a small-town kid barely out of high school who may have sold an ounce of marijuana here or there.

They had never met, and had never so much as spoken on the phone, yet when a jury would see them sitting next to each other at the defense table as defendants in a conspiracy trial, it would take a leap of faith to view them as distinct individuals. The "birds of a feather" notion would apply to all five men, as it does in every conspiracy trial with multiple defendants.

"I was nineteen or twenty at the time," Rocco Perla recalls. "I had no money. I wasn't a pending gangster or anything like that. Our efforts at the time were (toward) playing ball and making enough money to go to a concert or dinner, things like that. We didn't have any exposure to the underworld."

What the Perlas and Kuhn did have was a sense of loyalty that, however foolhardy it may seem in retrospect, would not allow them to take the path Hill and Sweeney had taken and offer the government incriminating information against each other in exchange for immunity.

"I don't mean to describe myself as a tough guy or standup person either, but nonetheless, if it meant I would have to testify against my brother, I wouldn't have done that anyway," Rocco Perla says. "And I wouldn't have said anything that would have jeopardized (Rick)."

The same could be said of Kuhn. Kuhn's lawyer, Gary Zimmerman, said in a 1998 interview that he believed that Kuhn already had decided not to cooperate with the government before retaining counsel, and that the forces behind this decision probably included a fear for his own life from the Hill-Burke faction in New York and loyalty to his childhood pal.

The government was irritated when Kuhn wouldn't cooperate, Zimmerman added. "When you cooperate, that's what they like, and they help you."

● ● ●

If the defendants made up a cross-section of human experience, the lineup of lawyers offered similar variety. Perhaps the most interesting of the bunch was Leonard Sharon, a lifelong resident of Pittsburgh who had been retained by Paul Mazzei in the spring of 1981 for Mazzei's federal heroin trial. Sharon's bread-and-butter cases ran the gamut of urban vices, from gambling to drugs to massage parlors and the occasional murder, but he had come of age in the 1960s and identified with what was still referred to as the "counterculture."

Sharon was a member of the left-wing National Lawyers Guild that provided legal assistance during the trials from the American Indians' occupation at Wounded Knee in the early '70s. He wore his hair long, below his collar, and at 6-foot-7 was one of the only people in court who could look Rick Kuhn in the eye when both were standing. Sharon had been a basketball player in high school and still followed the sport avidly.

The Perlas' lawyer, James K. O'Malley, went by his middle name, Kerry, and was the most restrained of the group of advocates. The Pittsburgh resident's button-down style often was the only voice of reason during the many contentious sidebar debates during the trial.

In his early forties, O'Malley had had his own practice for ten years before the Boston College trial. He was an expert in wiretapping who testified before Congress on the issue in the mid-'70s during the post-Watergate fallout. He had attended John Carroll University in Cleveland and received his law degree from Georgetown, both Jesuit-influenced schools. At Georgetown he was two years ahead of Ed McDonald, who would be trying the government's case.

McDonald was only thirty-four, but within five years of being admitted to the New York bar in 1972 he had risen to the position of special attorney with the U.S. Department of Justice's Organized Crime Strike Force. A New York native and a standout basketball player for Brooklyn's Xaverian High, he had played freshman basketball briefly at Boston College in the mid-1960s before coming to the realization that his best days on the hardwood were behind him. His foes considered him a tenacious and skilled prosecutor who knew how to effectively use the vast government resources at his disposal.

"I thought he was a terrific lawyer," Sharon says. "But it was really warfare. And the Strike Force lawyers were of a different mind-set than regular prosecutors. Those guys were all about a mission, and he went about it. He had all the investigative resources and all the money. And he was a good lawyer."

Pittsburgh-based Gary Zimmerman was the quintessential big-city defense attorney, a sharp-tongued defender who abhorred snitches and informants and had a perpetual chip on his shoulder over a system that seemed weighted against the kinds of clients he frequently represented. By the time he took on Rick Kuhn's defense in the Boston College point-shaving trial, Zimmerman already had tried dozens of murder cases and boasted of a success rate above 90 percent. A Western Pennsylvanian to the core, he had attended Slippery Rock State College and Duquesne University Law School, and sometimes wore cowboy boots in the courtroom, as did Sharon.

The most controversial choice to represent any of the defendants, though it may not have been evident at the time, was that of Michael Coiro. Coiro, fifty-one, had been a New York City policeman before earning his law degree, and had been practicing law for nearly twenty years by the time of the point-shaving trial—about as long as he had known Henry Hill. Coiro had first represented Jimmy Burke in 1969, and earned his client two hung juries and an acquittal since then before suffering his first loss in 1980 at the parole violation hearing in which Hill testified.

Coiro was known for his grandstanding tactics in the courtroom, but he also was one of the most well-liked lawyers who worked in the Eastern District. His familiarity with Hill and with various other reputed mob figures was a double-edged sword for Burke's defense. At best, it allowed Coiro to speak the language of the street and describe to a jury a slice of life to which most of them had never been exposed. At worst, however, he came off as a camp follower, a wiseguy wannabe who dressed and acted like the people he often sought to discredit on the witness stand. Both of these tendencies would surface at the trial, particularly during the cross-examination of Henry Hill.

For now, Coiro contented himself with sniping at Hill in the newspapers.

"Henry Hill is nothing but a hood with a drug problem who used a vivid imagination to escape prosecution himself," Coiro told *New York Post* reporter Jerry Capeci. In the *New York Daily News* he was quoted as saying, "All Henry Hill knows how to do is tell stories about Jimmy Burke."

No one on the defense team could have been rejoicing after hearing which judge had been assigned to the case. Henry Bramwell was the first African-American judge in the Eastern District, and was a staunch Republican who kept a picture of himself with President Richard Nixon in his chambers. He was known as a jurist who ran—or tried to run—a tight ship in his courtroom and who was not averse to matching attorneys, particularly defense attorneys, barb for barb.

"He had very good instincts," one former prosecutor who tried cases in front of Bramwell recalls. "He didn't always have the most sophisticated way of expressing himself. And I think he was a good judge, though I'm not so sure how I would have felt if I was a defense attorney. Because his instincts were generally progovernment. I think he was a guy who didn't overanalyze situations, and I don't think he spent a lot of time trying to figure out all the legal niceties. He operated a lot on instinct, but I think generally his instincts were good.

"And he had a temper."

Bramwell's temper would boil over several times during the trial, directed far more often than not toward one of the four defense attorneys, usually Sharon, whose left-of-center leanings did little to endear him to the judge. Near the end of the trial, Bramwell saw Sharon looking at the picture of him and Nixon and half-asked, "You hated Nixon, didn't you?" To which Sharon replied, "Well, he wasn't one of my favorites." Bramwell said, "Yeah, I knew that."

There also was a clear demarcation between the big-city lawyers—McDonald, fellow U.S. Attorney Edward Korman, and Coiro—and the out-of-towners, if only due to familiarity with the vagaries of the criminal justice system as applied in the Eastern District of New York, specifically Brooklyn.

The Eastern District is, or certainly was at the time of the trial, made up of "real" New Yorkers. Instead of the transients and wannabe cosmopolites who inhabit Manhattan, which is in New York's Southern District, an Eastern District jury could be made up of Brooklyn or Queens residents, some of whom might be recent immigrants, or conservative suburbanites from the nearby towns of Nassau or Suffolk Counties on Long Island. Any lawyer expecting an upscale, urbane jury pool was likely to be disappointed.

Robert Simels, Henry Hill's lawyer, recalls being in court in the Eastern District during the Abscam trial and watching one of the attorneys whose mannerisms seemed all out of place:

"I remember when he went to the lectern one day, I saw him as he lifted his foot to put it on the (footrest) on the back of the lectern, and pick up his pant leg so the crease was still in place," Simels said. "And as I looked at that and looked at the jury looking at that, I said to myself, 'You know something? This guy's dead right now.' Just the formalistic, Philadelphia–Washington, D.C.-type of attorney is not going to play in Brooklyn."

• • •

By August 1981, Hill and Simels had entered into negotiations with Simon and Schuster for a book on Hill's life in the Mafia. The publisher was reported to have offered an advance of $175,000, with Hill said to be getting a little more than $100,000.

• • •

Within a few weeks of the indictments, Judge Bramwell was hit with a flurry of pretrial motions. In addition to O'Malley's motion for dismissal of the indictments based on excessive pretrial publicity, Coiro moved for dismissal on grounds that the grand jury had not been notified of Hill's criminal background and previous inconsistent statements about the point-shaving case, and should not have been told that Hill and Burke were convicted of extortion together in 1972.

In addition, Kuhn and both Perlas claimed that they had been unfairly prejudiced when Ed McDonald required them to go before a grand jury when he knew that they would be invoking their Fifth Amendment rights. Charles Clayman, another attorney representing Burke, also moved for dismissal of the first count of the indictment, claiming that there was no evidence that interstate commerce was involved in the alleged scheme, and that the defendants could not be charged with engaging in a racketeering enterprise.

To the surprise of no one, Bramwell denied all motions. On the latter, he agreed with McDonald that the facts in *U.S. v. Burke* resembled those in *U.S. v. Errico*, a 1980 case in which a group of jockeys was charged with engaging in a racketeering enterprise for conspiring to hold back their horses in certain races to gain an edge for gamblers.

Three separate issues would take some more wrangling to settle, however. One would be decided before trial, at a separate hearing, but the other two would crop up repeatedly during the trial and would be the cause of considerable debate.

The first was the statement Rick Kuhn made to FBI agents James Byron and Thomas Sweeney in Swissvale almost a year earlier. Zimmerman vigorously claimed that the interrogation had been custodial; that is, that the circumstances—the early hour, the conducting of the interview in a car across the street with Kuhn barely clothed—were designed to make Kuhn feel intimidated or, at least, caused him to feel that his freedom was restricted during the interview. If it was a custodial interrogation, then by law Kuhn should have been read his Miranda rights.

At a pretrial hearing, Agent Byron testified that Kuhn asked twice, once in the house and once when they got into the car, if he had to talk to them, and both times Byron said he didn't. But Agent Sweeney admitted during his testimony that Byron's statement was only made before they told Kuhn about the point-shaving allegations and not after. He also said it was the first time in his five-year career as an agent that he had interviewed a potential suspect at 6:30 in the morning who was wearing only a pair of shorts.

"The facts in this case smack of custodial interrogation, even if the custody was in fact only in a limited way," Zimmerman said in his closing statement. "The time of the interview, rousing Mr. Kuhn out of bed, taking him to a strange environment, which would be the police vehicle, with two officials of the government . . ."

In his reply, McDonald declared, "There is not one shred of evidence offered by the defense . . . that his freedom of movement was impaired in any way. The fact that he was not advised of his Miranda rights is totally irrelevant, and the statement should not be suppressed."

Bramwell agreed, ruling that Kuhn was not technically in custody at the time of the interview and that his Fifth Amendment rights had not been violated. This brought up another thorny issue, though. Kuhn's statement, which now would be admitted into evidence, implicated Rocco and Tony Perla and Paul Mazzei. Citing *U.S. v. Bruton* (1968), O'Malley claimed that admission of Kuhn's statement would deny the Perlas' Sixth Amendment right to confront their accuser, since Kuhn would not be testifying at the trial.

Bramwell resolved this by having a redacted, or censored, version of the statement introduced into evidence that did not mention the Perlas or Mazzei by name.

• • •

From the moment "Anatomy of a Scandal" hit the newsstands in February, Ed McDonald knew he would be in for a protracted fight over not only what was contained in the *Sports Illustrated* article, but the background materials reporter Doug Looney had used to write it. Sure enough, on August 20, Charles Clayman, on behalf of James Burke, served a subpoena *duces tecum* on Looney and *SI* managing editor Larry Keith. A subpoena *duces tecum* means, literally, "under penalty of court you shall bring with you the goods to your court-ordered appearance." The defense wanted Looney to bring his notes, tapes, contracts, page proofs, checker notes, and checks or money orders, with the aim of impeaching Hill's memory on the facts or, possibly, unearthing evidence that could exculpate Burke.

In his motion for a subpoena of Looney's materials on September 18, Clayman noted that Hill already had given conflicting versions of events to the FBI, *Sports Illustrated*, and the grand jury. The most blatant example was that the *SI* article listed nine games as being fixed, compared to the six that Hill detailed in front of the grand jury and that were now included in the government's indictment.

"One awaits with bated breath to hear Mr. Hill's final chapter at the trial of Mr. Burke," Clayman wrote. "One is hard-pressed to imagine a greater set of forces than those at work on Henry Hill. Simply put, Hill was confronted with the choice of extricating himself and those close to him by offering Burke in exchange. Such an overwhelming motivation to lie makes Mr. Hill's testimony inherently suspect."

Like most judges, Bramwell was loathe to trample on the First Amendment and force Looney to hand over his notes, but he gave the defense a glimmer of hope when he said that although the files would not be turned over, the issue would be revisited after Hill's testimony. In the meantime, the defense would be allowed to impeach Hill only on those statements he had made in the article that he later denied making while on the witness stand. This would make for some interesting, if convoluted, cross-examinations once the trial began.

• • •

Conspiracy cases frequently are referred to as "the darling of the government's nursery," and for the defendants in the B.C. case, this was all too accurate. Severance, the splitting up of the defendants to create separate trials, thus became their last, best hope to gain equal footing before the start of the trial.

"We had gotten to know more and more about the people involved that we didn't know at the time, via written articles and grand jury testimony we had reviewed," Rocco Perla said. "We viewed it as extremely bad luck to have done something . . . with people who were involved with so many other things."

The Perlas and Paul Mazzei wanted to be severed from Kuhn because of Kuhn's FBI statement, which, even in redacted form, could allow a jury to make inferences and form prejudice against them. The Perlas, Mazzei, and Kuhn all wanted to sever from Burke, no surprise given Burke's past and the fact that his name was constantly being splashed across the city tabloids as the alleged mastermind of the Lufthansa robbery.

Their chances were negligible at best.

"You don't get severed in conspiracy cases," Zimmerman says, looking back. "I don't ever remember a case that I've ever had in federal court, since 1971, where there was a conspiracy charge and there was a severance. And there have been some of the most egregious dynamics that you could ever imagine, involving personnel with different defendants and different statuses. It doesn't matter."

Ultimately, it was Lufthansa that drove a wedge between the defendants. The lawyers for the Perlas, Mazzei, and Kuhn all petitioned Bramwell for the right to question Henry Hill about the robbery, to impeach Hill's credibility and also to elicit any information that might exonerate them, since the robbery occurred around the same time that the point-shaving scheme became a reality.

The problem was, any mention of Lufthansa would be prejudicial to Burke, their codefendant, and therefore had to be kept out of the trial. This Catch-22 cuts at the heart of any conspiracy defense.

The defense lawyers argued their case in front of Bramwell on Thursday afternoon, October 22, the week before the trial was scheduled to begin. Clayman and Coiro, representing Burke, pointed out that Hill already had made prejudicial statements to newspapers and magazines about Burke's involvement in the robbery, and urged that any mention of Lufthansa be excluded from trial testimony, along with mention of Burke's 1972 extortion conviction.

Sharon, meanwhile, argued that under Rule 609 of the Federal Rules of Criminal Procedure the defense had the right to cross-examine Hill on Lufthansa since Hill had testified about the robbery during Mazzei's drug trial in March.

"That is not part of this case," Bramwell said.

"Wait—" Sharon implored.

"That is not part of this case," Bramwell repeated.

"Certainly not," Sharon said, and was about to explain what he meant when Bramwell cut him off.

"That is what I am going to hold," the judge said, closing the discussion.

The tone of the exchange was a harbinger for the rest of the trial, as the two men wound up battling over every conceivable issue.

"He would do things like, we had four or five defendants and four lawyers wedged in at a table, and I'd go, 'Object!' and he'd say, 'Stand up when you object!' but I couldn't get up in time," Sharon recalls. "So I'd finally get up and he'd say, 'Sit down! Denied!' It was get up, get down, get up . . . like a puppet. He just made me nuts, just got under my skin."

The various motions to sever were denied by Bramwell, and it also was decided that Hill would be instructed not to refer to Lufthansa during his testimony, but instead could be asked whether or not he had ever participated in a robbery or burglary, and whether money or jewelry had been stolen. Hill's immunity agreement could be brought out, but without mentioning Lufthansa.

When McDonald pointed out that a question on cross-examination might leave Hill no choice but to say something that might incriminate Burke on Lufthansa, Coiro replied, "Judge Bramwell, I will be trying the case. My mother didn't raise any stupid children, and I'm not about to ask a question that's going to unload on my client."

Coiro also noted that he would refer to Hill as "Mr. Hill," and that he did not want Hill calling him "Mike."

"Because he is not my friend," Coiro said of the man he had known for almost twenty years, adding, "and never could be."

During an earlier pretrial conference, Coiro had become animated when McDonald mentioned that the prosecution would be calling Zach Franzi, the Barbary Coast Casino oddsmaker who had lied his way onto Brent Musburger's television show in August.

"And we will bring in Jimmy the Greek, who will take odds on the case and move the line back and forth," Coiro cracked.

For all his bluster, though, Coiro had a sharp eye for detail, which he demonstrated at a meeting of counsel two weeks before the trial. McDonald had unveiled a chart depicting telephone calls between the defendants, accompanied by booklets that listed the calls. Coiro immediately claimed the chart would be prejudicial to his client because Burke's name was in the center, and written in larger letters than the other defendants'. McDonald claimed not to have noticed the discrepancy, but Bramwell nevertheless told him he would have to change it.

The booklets, which McDonald had planned to hand out to jurors, also were objected to as being potentially prejudicial, and Bramwell ruled that they could be used, but only for the purpose of following along with testimony.

"The jury will have (the booklets), and then they'll take the chart and say, 'Oh, there he is. Page one says he's right here,'" Bramwell told McDonald. "You see? It might be a little prejudicial."

McDonald argued that he had used similar aids during the Abscam trial, but Bramwell was not swayed. The phone calls would turn into a major source of contention during the trial, as would several other issues.

CHAPTER THIRTEEN

The Trial

The United States District Courthouse in Brooklyn sits at the western edge of the borough, with a clear view of the Brooklyn Bridge and, in the distance to the west, the office buildings of lower Manhattan. In the courthouse's illustrious history it had been the venue for several noteworthy trials in the 1940s and '50s, when it shared a building with the post office, across the street from where it resided in 1981.

One of the most famous was the 1943 trial of Paul Hermann Karl Grohs and Frank Heinrich Wilhelm Grote, who were sentenced to fifteen years in prison for microfilming secret documents for the Germans in a case that was the basis for the Alfred Hitchcock film *Notorious*. Another film, *The House on 92nd Street*, was based on the 1940s trial of the so-called Duquesne spy ring for stealing the plans for a bomb-aiming device. And in 1952, Colonel Rudolph I. Abel, who at one time used an apartment across the park from the courthouse, was sentenced to thirty years for transmitting defense secrets to the Soviet Union, and was later exchanged for U.S. pilot Francis Gary Powers after Powers's U-2 bomber was shot down over Russia.

On Tuesday, October 27, 1981, *U.S. v. Burke*, the point-shaving trial of James Burke, Paul Mazzei, Rick Kuhn, and Tony and Rocco Perla, opened to a swarm of media and spectators. Kuhn and the Perlas would be commuting each day to the courthouse from a hotel in Queens, near JFK Airport, along with their attorneys. Mazzei and Burke would be escorted from nearby jails, Burke from Danbury, Connecticut, and Mazzei from the Arthur Kill state prison on Staten Island.

Every morning, Henry Hill would be driven by U.S. marshals from Manhattan, where he was being housed in a special underground hotel used strictly for government witnesses who required special protection.

Though Hill put on his usual wiseguy front during the trial, his first in the public spotlight as a government witness, inside he was a bundle of nerves. He anesthetized himself with Valium and booze each night back at his hotel, which tried the patience of the FBI agents and U.S. marshals who were responsible for him.

"I tried to put on a façade, but I was scared to death," Hill says. "I was worried they were going to find me, I didn't know what to think. Even driving down the streets in the city with all the protection. . . . I feared maybe they'd blow the courthouse up. I knew how sick Jimmy was. I knew what the man was capable of doing. The feds (probably) didn't worry about it as much as I did."

The twelve jurors and four alternates, who had been culled from a pool of forty-four, also would be commuting to the courtroom each day, thanks to Bramwell's ruling the previous week against having them sequestered. As a precaution, though, it was an anonymous jury: the attorneys were only given the jurors' names, not their occupations or home addresses. And Bramwell ordered the courtroom locked for five minutes at the end of each day while the jury left the room.

The trial would begin with opening statements from each of the attorneys—four in this case, since Kerry O'Malley represented both Perla brothers. McDonald would start by laying out a road map of the prosecution's case, going over what was in the indictment and what the government needed to prove. He would be followed by the defense attorneys, each of whom would remind the jury about their responsibilities and about applying the concept of reasonable doubt when deliberating the defendants' guilt or innocence.

As the crowded courtroom watched, the young prosecutor stepped to the podium and addressed the jury box.

"Good afternoon. As Judge Bramwell told you, my name is Edward McDonald. I am a lawyer with the United States Department of Justice. It is my job to prove the guilt on the part of the defendants in this case."

With that, McDonald launched into a forty-five-minute opening statement that covered the major points of the prosecution's case, focusing on the definition of "conspiracy" and how the defendants engaged in a racketeering enterprise by conspiring to fix six of the games, and that their common goal was to engage in a "pattern of racketeering activity." He explained that the government had to prove that the defendants agreed to fix at least two of the six Boston College games listed in the indictments, and that they had used interstate travel to further the scheme. The latter charge referred to the trips between Pittsburgh, New York, and Boston made by Tony Perla, Paul Mazzei, and Henry Hill.

"We will not necessarily prove that they were successful in fixing the outcomes of every single game," McDonald said, "but we will prove that they agreed that they tried to fix these six games."

The prosecutor then shed his formal demeanor and characterized the case as one of "greed, corruption, disloyalty, carelessness. Remember in particular carelessness, because the evidence will show, ladies and gentlemen, that we are not dealing here with five people [who] are master criminals. . . . The evidence will show that all five defendants here left a trail of evidence a mile wide."

Within minutes, the jury got a taste of what to expect when Coiro sprang up to object loudly about McDonald's mention of Paul Vario, Burke's reputed boss in the Lucchese family and an unindicted coconspirator in the case. In the first of what would be scores of sidebars over the course of the next three weeks, after being told to calm down by Bramwell, Coiro asked for a mistrial—also the first of many such requests—and was denied by the judge.

As McDonald proceeded through the plot from its genesis in the summer of 1978 through the meeting at the Logan Airport Hilton, he paused to tell the jury about Jim Sweeney.

"A brief word at this point about Sweeney," he said. "Sweeney will testify that he told Tony Perla and Paul Mazzei and Henry Hill at the Logan Hilton that he would cooperate. And later during the same season he again told the same thing to Tony Perla. And he told his brother Rocco Perla he was in on the scheme. However, Sweeney will testify that while he said he was cooperating, he never intended to do so. He was too scared to say he wouldn't. And he was too scared to tell the authorities at school. He will admit on one occasion he took five hundred dollars from Kuhn, but he will testify that he never did anything to alter his play or improperly influence the outcome of a Boston College game."

With his star corroborating witness thus absolved of any blame by the government itself, McDonald went on to describe how the scheme played out during the 1978–79 season. Then, he got to Henry Hill and did some advance damage control.

"You will quickly see, ladies and gentlemen, that Henry Hill is no saint. Indeed, a very unsavory character who will admit to an extensive lifetime of crimes." But, McDonald added, "this case will not stand and fall on Henry Hill alone," and he mentioned Sweeney, Barbara Reed, Joe Beaulieu, and others who would corroborate Hill's story, along with physical evidence such as phone and hotel records. He mentioned Rick Kuhn's statement to FBI agents in 1980, and also let it slip that he would produce a witness who would claim that Tony Perla admitted his guilt to her, a statement that brought a motion for mistrial from O'Malley that was denied by Bramwell.

In closing, McDonald appealed to the jury's "common sense, your life's experiences as New Yorkers, which are the most important things which you bring to this case." Coiro would later allege this remark was a veiled invitation for the jurors to consider all they knew as New Yorkers about organized crime activities in the city.

The flamboyant Coiro, his well-coiffed black hair set off against the perpetual suntan he got from spending much of the year in Florida, was up next, and he immediately addressed McDonald's opening statement.

"You just heard Mr. McDonald make an opening statement. And for once and probably the only time in this entire trial, I will agree with him—what he said to you was not evidence. What I'm about to say to you is not evidence. As he so aptly stated, the evidence is going to come from the witnesses that take that stand."

One of those witnesses would be Henry Hill, Coiro reminded the jury before he began his attack on Hill's criminal record, his deal with the government, his "skate" on the drug charges in Nassau County, his shifting versions of the truth, and his overall character. He appealed to the jury to not let Hill "use" them as he already had used the government.

"When Frank Sinatra comes to Carnegie Hall, he wants some accommodations and money," Coiro said. "Henry Hill, when he testifies, he wants money, he wants his liberty, and he wants all of the other benefits that the United States Government has provided for. The irony of it all [is that] twelve, fourteen, sixteen people, and everybody out there in the audience, pays for this man. It's out of our pockets so that he can come here and he's going to do his thing. Believe me, he's going to do it."

O'Malley was due up next, but chose not to make an opening statement. Leonard Sharon then followed with a brief statement in which he implored the jury to assess each defendant's guilt separately. "You can't have guilt by association," he cautioned, and noted that Paul Mazzei could not be connected to the conspiracy by the evidence the government was planning to offer.

Gary Zimmerman went last, and the veteran defense attorney began by reminding the jury not to take McDonald's opening statement as evidence of anything, saying "I suggest to you that you can't believe anything at this particular point because in fact, you don't know anything about this case."

Zimmerman pointed out that Kuhn's limited role on the team made it impossible to affect the outcome of games. He also said that if McDonald were not able to prove the games were actually fixed, the jury would have to tackle a "sophisticated area of the law which we lawyers call conspiracy. Frankly, most lawyers in the United States don't understand it." (Bramwell later issued an instruction to the jury that the government did not have the burden of proving the games were actually fixed.)

It was regarding Kuhn's alleged confession that, in retrospect, Zimmerman may have committed an error in judgment. Saying the jury might get "a little bit of suspense and a little bit of surprise at the end of the case," he hinted that Kuhn might take the stand and refute what was in the FBI report about the confession. This never occured, a damaging fact that McDonald would bring out in his final summation.

• • •

After a short recess, the government called its first witness. It was a man in his mid- to late thirties, about 5-foot-9 with an average build, wearing a conservative suit. This was Henry Hill, and he took the stand at 3:50 P.M. on October 27, cleaned up and looking, as his attorney Robert Simels recalls, like Everyman.

"Henry doesn't really come across as a mobster," Simels said. "(If you met him) I don't think you'd think anything, you'd think he was a normal guy. He wasn't a very polished guy, but he didn't sound thuglike; he sounded normal. He didn't have the look of a mobster; he just looked like a guy."

McDonald started by having Hill go over basic information: his age, marital status, children, and his immunity agreement with the government. The prosecutor then had Hill recite his criminal record dating back to his army court martial in 1962 and finishing with a description of his illegal activities after he was released from prison in 1978.

Then McDonald cut to the chase.

"Now, Mr. Hill, I ask, do you know the defendant James Burke?"

Hill answered, "Yes, I do," and pointed to Burke, who stood up from his seat at the defendants' table. The two men had known each other for nearly thirty years, but it was only now that Hill was seeing Burke's stony gaze from the other side. The two would make eye contact occasionally during Hill's time on the witness stand, though Hill recalls that Burke did not stare at him.

In describing their relationship, Hill termed Burke a "friend, boss, partner," which elicited an objection from Coiro that was overruled by Bramwell. McDonald then asked Hill to identify Mazzei and Tony Perla, which he did, and also Rocco Perla and Kuhn, whom he identified as his "business partner."

Hill then began to describe—guided by McDonald's questions—the entire story, beginning with his first trip to Pittsburgh to meet with Paul Mazzei in the summer of 1978. McDonald had Hill establish that Mazzei and Tony Perla approached him because of his connections to Burke and Vario, and later elicited that Hill had gone to Burke in October 1978 to get his approval for the scheme. Hill went over the meeting at Robert's Lounge between Mazzei, Perla, Peter Vario, and Richard Perry, and described how the scheme would work: who would provide the money, how the bets would be placed.

The trial's first blowup occurred when Hill recited a list of bookies he had used in the scheme. When he reached Martin Krugman, an alleged accomplice in the Lufthansa robbery, he casually mentioned, "Until he got killed . . ." which brought an immediate objection from Coiro. But before Bramwell could stop him Hill had slipped in, "Got murdered, excuse me."

At sidebar, Coiro was furious. "If Your Honor please, I move for a mistrial and the withdrawal of a juror," he sputtered. "There is no proof that Martin Krugman is dead, only a figment of this man's imagination. I ask the government to come forward and show me what documentary evidence they have that Martin Krugman is dead."

"You want to see the body?" Bramwell asked.

Bramwell denied Coiro's motion, but agreed to give a limiting instruction to the jury in which he would tell them that there was no proof that "the party Krugman" was murdered, and that it had nothing to do with this case whatsoever.

• • •

Day Two started with a delay due to a juror's lateness and finished with Coiro and Hill engaging in the kind of skirmishes that would eventually threaten to bring the trial to a standstill.

The floor still belonged to McDonald when juror Jane McCarter finally arrived, and he resumed his questioning by focusing on the Logan Airport Hilton meeting. Hill went over the events of the evening and how the players both seemed eager to "do business" on the upcoming season. At one point, after Hill mentioned that he had taken down Kuhn's phone number in Boston, McDonald attempted to place Hill's address book in evidence. But Coiro noted that introducing the book would be prejudicial . . . chiefly because his own phone number was in it.

"That is bad," Bramwell agreed, and ruled that only the page with Kuhn's number on it would be permitted into evidence.

As Hill continued describing the fiasco of the Providence game, O'Malley began to notice something strange about McDonald. As Hill gave his answers, McDonald would silently form some of the words along with him.

"As the witness is saying the names, Mr. McDonald is saying the names along with him, giving the impression this is what the witness told him previously and reinforcing the credibility of the witness," O'Malley objected.

"I won't do it," McDonald responded.

Coiro chimed in. "You might not know you're doing it, but you are," he said.

"It's a habit my grandmother always had, and it drove me crazy," McDonald admitted. "Maybe I picked it up from her and do it all the time and don't realize it."

"You have to be careful," Bramwell cautioned.

McDonald then took Hill through a chronological review of the scheme, from the first mention of Ernie Cobb after the Providence disaster, to the Harvard game and the payoffs afterward in Boston Garden, to the UCLA game and all the way through the Holy Cross game of February 10, the day Burke put his foot through his own TV set. Some of this testimony, particularly regarding the UCLA and Holy Cross games, would come back to haunt the government two and a half years later during the trial of Ernie Cobb. But for now, it sounded plausible enough.

In a preemptive strike aimed at his own witness, McDonald then asked Hill about inconsistencies between what he was saying in court and what was in the *Sports Illustrated* article. He also had Hill detail how much he was receiving from the government ($1,086 per month plus medical expenses), from the Drug Enforcement Administration for information he had provided them ($1,000), from *Sports Illustrated* ($10,000) and finally, the $101,800 he was scheduled to receive from Simon & Schuster for the rights to his life story.

That concluded McDonald's direct examination of Hill, and after the jurors were excused for lunch, Coiro immediately renewed his motion to subpoena all notes and materials relating to the *Sports Illustrated* story, revisiting the issue Bramwell had left open-ended at the beginning of the trial.

Bramwell just as quickly denied the motion.

"The basic reason [the motion] was put forth was credibility, you know," he began. "Now, with what's come out as to this witness, I mean . . . it couldn't be worse as far as what would show as to a man in his condition. I mean, he's done everything, every type of crime and situation."

But Coiro held firm. "I want to see the notes because as a cross-examiner getting prepared to cross-examine Mr. Hill, I want to see what other inconsistencies are in the notes," he countered.

"The inconsistencies are in the article and . . . you can get them directly from the article," Bramwell said. "Motion denied."

By the time Sharon joined the fray, Bramwell had heard enough. "Mr. Coiro is a pretty good lawyer, and if you are here to bolster him I don't think it is necessary," he said.

As the four lawyers argued back and forth, Bramwell finally stood up and said, "See you later," and left the bench to take his lunch break.

• • •

When the jury and spectators returned after lunch, they were in for an abrupt change of pace. Standing at the podium now was Coiro, who couldn't wait to get his hooks into Hill and show the court what kind of lowlife was sitting before them. Hill's demeanor would change accordingly, and he would match his former acquaintance at every turn.

"I wasn't going to let him rattle me," Hill recalled. "He tried. He used every trick in the book. Actually, I was kind of glad that it wasn't some other attorney, because I knew Mike, I knew his screaming bullshit. I could read the guy."

Coiro began his cross-examination from close to the witness box, and he spoke in loud tones. He questioned Hill on his relationship with Jimmy Burke, and his relationships with the bookmakers he used in the point-shaving scheme.

In no time, Hill was copping an attitude.

"What were some of the other names that you mentioned of these major bookmakers?" Coiro asked.

"You tell me," Hill retorted. "You are cross-examining me, sir."

"Judge, is that remark called for?" Coiro complained to Bramwell.

As Coiro continued with questions about how often Hill was at Burke's house during the time period covered by the point-shaving scheme, McDonald objected to Coiro's standing close to the witness box and "yelling" at Hill. Coiro agreed to step back behind the podium.

"Maybe we can draw a foul line," Sharon offered.

"Well, the foul line is the podium," Bramwell said.

Coiro moved on to the *Sports Illustrated* article, and Hill offered the surprising revelation that he never told author Doug Looney, "I am the Boston College fixer," which is how the story begins.

"[Looney] had his own investigation," Hill said. "I answered some questions and ultimately received ten thousand dollars for it. And we had a few conversations and he put my name on there. He could have put anybody's name [on it]."

During this line of questioning, Coiro handed a copy of the article to Hill to read.

"Did you say that to Mr. Looney?" Coiro demanded, referring to the introduction to the story.

"Part of it," Hill replied.

"What part of it?" Coiro continued as he tried to take the document back from Hill.

"Don't grab it out of my hand," Hill protested.

"Don't grab it out of your hand? I don't even like to touch it after you did," Coiro said with a sarcastic tone, raising an objection from McDonald.

Coiro continued to play up the discrepancies between Hill's direct testimony from the day before and what was in the *SI* article. Then, he shifted gears and took on a bizarre line of questioning that must have surprised even the unflappable Hill.

"When you were in Allenwood, did you enjoy a good reputation in the jail?" Coiro asked.

"Yes."

"Were you known as a punk? A go-fer?" he said tauntingly.

McDonald objected, and just as Hill was about to speak out of turn, Bramwell called an emergency sidebar.

"What is the basis for this?" Bramwell demanded. "Who is going to be brought in to say this man was a go-fer?"

Sharon interjected, "He was a go-fer for Rick Ferry. He lives in Pittsburgh. He was in Lewisburg with Mr. Hill and he would testify that [Hill] . . . carried his tray and butter—"

"If you want to do it, it doesn't make any difference to me, you go right ahead," Bramwell said. "You go right ahead."

"You ask me questions and then you answer them. You're supposed to call balls and strikes, not pitch," Sharon said to Bramwell, trying to be as tactful as possible.

Finally, McDonald raised a question. "If I can make some argument here, I don't see how one being a punk or go-fer has any bearing on his credibility at all. I don't know what a punk is."

"You want me to tell you," Coiro said. "It's a fag. He takes it in the ass."

"I object to that," McDonald said.

"That is not so," Bramwell added.

"That is the term for a punk," Coiro insisted. "That's the terminology," to which O'Malley added his assent.

"Who are you going to bring in, some prisoners?" Bramwell asked, on the verge of incredulity.

"We will have to put an X-rated sign out," Coiro smirked.

"That's right," Bramwell said.

Back in open court, Coiro delved into Hill's drug use, eliciting from Hill that he was using narcotics "every day" in the latter part of 1979, and that some of his friends had nicknamed Hill "The Doctor" for the bag he would carry around that always seemed to be full of drugs. By the end of the day's session he had insinuated that Hill's wife had "given" him Judy Wicks as a Christmas present, a charge Hill denied, though he admitted he had had a physical relationship with the graphic artist from Pittsburgh.

Today, Hill laughs as he recalls how he visited Wicks during the trial in her new home in Virginia Beach—all on the government's nickel.

With Hill back on the stand on the morning of Thursday, October 29, his third day, the defense again was stymied by the constraints unique to a multiple-defendant conspiracy trial. Coiro began questioning Hill about whether he sent Wicks to Germany to bring back a shipment of quaaludes, which brought an objection from McDonald. In actuality, it had been Mazzei who had sent Wicks, but by answering the question, Hill would have prejudiced the jury against Mazzei.

Once again, testimony that might have aided one defendant would have to be left out in order to protect another defendant.

Coiro then began hammering away at the inconsistencies between Hill's various statements to the FBI, the grand jury, *Sports Illustrated*, and his testimony the previous day. Who circled the games on the schedule at the Logan Hilton meeting? Did he go straight to Robert's Lounge when he returned from Boston? Which was the first game in the scheme, Harvard or Providence? Coiro became so animated that Bramwell had to gently remind him to keep his voice down.

During Coiro's questioning, Hill repeatedly glanced over at an enlarged Boston College schedule printed on a board that McDonald had put on an easel, prompting Coiro to ask, "Is there something magical about that board that you use it to refresh your recollection?" to which McDonald objected.

"You feel he shouldn't look at it?" Bramwell queried.

"I thought maybe there were answers written up there," Coiro said.

"Maybe there was a code up there," Hill added.

"You tell me, you're part of the prosecution team," Coiro retorted, which earned another objection from McDonald.

Hill held his own, yet Coiro effectively made the point that Hill had changed his story so many times that it was impossible to differentiate fact from fiction. But was his aggressive style eliciting sympathy for the fallen mobster?

"He got into a Mike-and-Henry routine. It was unbelievable," Robert Simels recalled. "Henry was not the greatest witness at the (B.C.) trial. But to the extent that Coiro got down to his level, and essentially gave credibility by their familiarity, was a good indication that he was the wrong attorney for the job. They got down in the street together."

Coiro's antics were momentarily eclipsed, however, by what happened next. Just as Coiro elicited that, during approximately two hundred hours of questioning by the FBI and Strike Force attorneys, Hill had never mentioned receiving any money from Burke for the scheme, McDonald sprang to his feet.

"I ask defendants' counsel and defendants not to make remarks during the testimony of Mr. Hill," he said.

This instruction brought Sharon and Zimmerman up out of their chairs, and Sharon immediately moved for a mistrial. "There haven't been any remarks," Zimmerman said angrily.

"Quiet! Quiet!" Bramwell shouted above the din.

"Don't yell in my face!" Sharon replied. "And I move for a mistrial, and that you recuse yourself. Don't yell."

"I have been here a half-minute asking you to moderate your tone," Bramwell said. "You refuse. I yelled at that time for you to be quiet. That is what happened."

At sidebar, Bramwell first denied Sharon's application for a mistrial.

"My application for you to recuse yourself?" the lawyer repeated.

"Denied," said Bramwell.

"I move for a mistrial," Sharon insisted. "I don't feel I can effectively defend my client. This man, this judge shouted at me in front of the jury. If you want to testify," he told Bramwell, his sense of tact long gone by now, "take the witness stand. I no longer can provide effective assistance of counsel."

Bramwell tried to explain. "I requested you moderate yourself and you refused," he told Sharon. "I had my hand up."

"What does that mean?" Sharon asked. "You're a judge."

"You're admitting it?" Bramwell shot back.

"You're a judge, your judicial conduct requires you to act with—"

"You don't tell me how to act," Bramwell snapped.

"I am asking you to recuse yourself," Sharon repeated, which Bramwell again denied, as he did Sharon's application to withdraw as Mazzei's counsel.

"I want the record to show I cannot be badgered, and I object to ridiculing in front of the jury," Sharon said.

Zimmerman then added his own motion for mistrial, charging that McDonald inferred that "something sinister" was going on at the defense table. Bramwell denied this motion, too.

McDonald, on the defensive, claimed he "clearly" heard snickers and remarks coming from the defense table.

"That is a lie," Sharon replied.

"That happened throughout yesterday," McDonald continued. "I had my back to them during direct, but during cross I was looking at the two Perlas staring at Mr. Hill."

In a small victory for the defense, Bramwell wound up telling the jury that McDonald's statement was "not consistent" with what was happening in court.

After a lunch break, Coiro finished up his cross-examination by exposing more inconsistencies in Hill's statements, ranging from the amount of the payouts to the players after the Harvard game, to how much Hill received from Richard Perry in New York the day after the game, to who actually gave the players the money at Boston Garden.

Before Coiro started in, though, he had a request for Bramwell.

"Your Honor, set the ground rules about Mr. Hill calling me 'Mike,'" he asked Bramwell. "My name is Mr. Coiro or it is Michael Coiro."

When the session began, Bramwell called Hill around to the far side of the bench with the attorneys.

"Mr. Hill, in front of the jury, you have to call Mr. Coiro 'Mr. Coiro' only, and do not refer to him as 'Mike' or 'Michael.'"

Not wanting to leave the last word for someone else, McDonald interjected, "You know, Judge, these people knew each other prior, and the fact that he slipped only on one occasion is remarkable."

Within five minutes, though, Hill had slipped again. During one exchange, he told Coiro, "I just answered the question, Mike—Mr. Coiro."

"I might have been going at him," Hill recalls. "If he came at me with a dig, I'd go back at him with a dig. McDonald didn't mind. In the courtroom he'd say something, but he'd pat me on the back when we were back at his office."

Coiro continued to catch Hill in contradictions, first concerning his trip to Florida in January 1979 during the B.C.–Rhode Island game, then on details about Tony Perla's and Paul Mazzei's trip to New York in mid-November 1978 to discuss the scheme.

On the Florida trip, Hill contended, "I was ordered to go down there by James Burke."

"You were ordered—listen, I don't want you to leave out Jimmy Burke's name once," Coiro said sarcastically.

"Is that a question?" McDonald said.

"Yes," Coiro retorted.

"It's an offer on Mr. Coiro's part," Bramwell said.

"Maybe it's an offer he won't be able to refuse," McDonald said in an attempt at levity that brought Zimmerman to his feet.

"I move that Mr. McDonald's remark be stricken," the defense attorney said.

"I'm sorry," McDonald said.

"That's all right," Bramwell said.

Hill's recollection of his cohorts' trip to New York was far from rock-solid. On direct testimony, he had said he had picked up both men at the airport, but now told Coiro it was just Mazzei who had arrived. Suddenly, Hill seemed confused.

"Mike, don't try and confuse me," Hill said.

"And the name is 'Mr. Coiro,'" Coiro interjected.

"Well, don't try and confuse me, Mr. Coiro," Hill said. "You are trying to trick me," he added.

"Trick you? You can't trick a trickster," Coiro said.

"You should know," Hill said, not wanting to give up the last word.

Coiro then tried to delve into Hill's fidelity to his wife with questions about Wicks, but Bramwell ruled that any impeachment of Hill's credibility would be cumulative, since he had already been ripped to shreds.

"Anything else is just a waste of time," McDonald remarked.

When Coiro resumed questioning, he began to ask about the Fordham game, but Hill cracked, "You're talking about my love life, or basketball?" Thus challenged, Coiro replied, "I'll stick with your love life. I'll go all the way."

"Please, don't," Bramwell pleaded, but it was too late.

"Did you commit a degenerate act with your sister-in-law when she was eleven years old?" Coiro demanded.

McDonald immediately objected, but Hill and Coiro continued their exchange, with Hill challenging Coiro to produce his sister-in-law and Coiro promising to do just that. By this time Coiro had moved from behind the podium and was practically yelling his questions at Hill, earning him another warning from Bramwell.

Coiro finally finished his cross-examination by getting Hill to admit he had "exaggerated a little bit" when he talked to Looney for the *SI* article. Now, three more crosses awaited.

O'Malley stepped up to the plate next, and though his cross lacked the fireworks or panache of Coiro's, he was able to effectively make his points without resorting to bombast. First, though, he requested to introduce Lufthansa into the questioning, and was again rebuffed by Bramwell.

Zimmerman then contended that a paragraph in Hill's agreement with the government that referred to the consequences if Hill didn't tell the truth would, in essence, vouch for Hill's truthfulness and respectability.

"After hearing this witness for a couple of days, you judge for yourself," Bramwell said. "I mean, for you to say that somehow this gives him an aura of respectability, I don't think so."

O'Malley started by reviewing Hill's criminal record and catalogued all the oaths Hill had broken in his lifetime. Then, in a question about Hill's cooperation with the government, he took a gamble.

"You could help them in the largest hijacking in the history of the country?" he asked.

McDonald immediately asked for a sidebar. "It seems to me we are getting into a delicate area," he said. "When you start talking about the largest hijacking in the country, I think people, jurors, could associate it with the Lufthansa case."

Bramwell ruled the question could not be asked, but that did not stop Coiro from making his umpteenth motion for mistrial on behalf of Burke.

"That is denied," Bramwell replied.

"In the alternative, I ask for a severance," Coiro responded, a request that Bramwell also denied.

O'Malley then began to build the foundation of the Perlas' defense: that Kuhn had merely been providing them with inside information about B.C.'s opponents, rather than shaving points, and that the prosecution's list of phone calls merely represented bettors shopping for the best point spreads.

He also focused on a key inconsistency in Hill's account—namely, that Hill had said in the *SI* article that Cobb had been involved in "the last five games" of the scheme, which would have begun with the Rhode Island game on January 10, 1979. This meant that Cobb could not have been on board for the December 23 UCLA game, which was the second game listed in the article. O'Malley got Hill to agree that if Cobb was indeed not on board for the UCLA game, then the scheme could not have been carried out since the gamblers had agreed that they needed Cobb for it to work.

When O'Malley pressed Hill on the information he had given Looney, Hill again admitted that he "exaggerated a little bit"—but that he was sure Cobb was involved from the Harvard game onward, and that Looney was incorrect when he wrote that Cobb was involved only in the last five games . . . even though Looney was allegedly quoting Hill in the article.

By the time the jury took a break around 4:00 P.M., O'Malley had begun to make further inroads into Hill's credibility without having to resort to the street tactics of his predecessor, Coiro. He elicited more admissions of exaggerations in the *SI* article before he gave way to Sharon.

With the door now wide open, Sharon plunged ahead. He noted that Hill's statement to the FBI in 1980 about the point-shaving scheme had taken up all of one page, and that by the time of his next interview eleven months later he had offered much more information—the implication being that the government had "suggested" various things to him in the interim.

By this point the day was nearly over, but there was still enough time for Sharon and Bramwell to have one last flare-up.

During questioning about point-spread fluctuations before the St. John's game that Hill had mentioned in his grand jury testimony, Sharon began to read a part of one of McDonald's questions when the prosecutor objected and a sidebar ensued. There, Sharon made the mistake of interrupting Bramwell, which raised the judge's ire again.

"If you had Mr. McDonald for a witness for this question, you see, it would mean a lot," the judge said. "But I don't think this in any way shows that this man is saying something different from what it says."

"Let me say something," Sharon said, then thought better of the idea and turned and began to walk away from the bench.

"Yes? What do you want?" Bramwell asked after him. "Come back."

"No, never mind," Sharon said.

"Come back here," Bramwell repeated.

"I can't," Sharon responded.

"You said you wanted to say something. Then you walk away from me," Bramwell said.

"It's obvious," Sharon said.

"I want you to say it," Bramwell said.

"I want for you to recuse and withdraw," Sharon said.

"Denied," Bramwell responded, turning away as he spoke, which bothered Sharon.

"Would you not turn away if I am not allowed to turn away?" he told the judge.

"Listen, I am running this court," Bramwell said.

"It's obvious," Sharon remarked.

"I am going to run it my way."

"That's also obvious."

"After I deny something, I am going to go back to work and I think you should be, too, and that's what I suggest you do," Bramwell admonished. "Listen, when I make a ruling, after I make a ruling, I'm going to move and let the court move. At that point you move, too. I am now ordering you to go out there and continue."

"Yes, sir," Sharon muttered. "I'll go out there and continue."

By the time Sharon resumed his questioning, the day was almost over. Henry Hill would be on the witness stand for a fourth day when court resumed Friday, October 30.

• • •

Before testimony began on Friday, Bramwell heard arguments on motions by Clayman and Coiro to subpoena the *Sports Illustrated* documents. Charles Koeltl, representing *Sports Illustrated*, argued that under the First Amendment, not only should Looney not have to give up his notes, but he should not have to testify about his conversations with Hill.

Bramwell took the middle path, ruling that Looney's notes would not be subpoenaed but that Looney would have to take the stand, with the condition that he would only be questioned about what Hill said vis-à-vis what was in the published article.

"The government witness is almost a crime wave," Koeltl pointed out. "I mean, read the record in the case and wonder what else the defendants need in order to impeach this fellow."

"That is just the way I feel," Bramwell said. "But that is the way it may be properly worked out. He (Looney) is going to have to carry the ball. When you read what he writes you will see where you are."

Coiro rightly pointed out that since Hill had provided the information for the article and also was identified as its author, there was no First Amendment issue of protecting a source, but Bramwell passed over this point without comment.

• • •

With Hill back on the stand on Friday, Sharon continued to poke holes in his various stories. He noted that Hill had not mentioned Mazzei's trip to New York in early November 1978—when Mazzei allegedly met with Hill and Burke to discuss the scheme—until his testimony a few days earlier, again implying that the government was putting words in Hill's mouth.

At this juncture, Hill dropped an aside that brought the trial to a standstill.

"Do you recall going out to a diner not far from the motel with your wife, yourself, and Mr. Mazzei?" Sharon asked. "Do you recall at that time you were driving a 1972 Buick Mr. Mazzei had given you?"

"That's the one he sent the gun with," Hill said, prompting Sharon to immediately ask for a sidebar.

"I make a motion for a mistrial," Zimmerman fumed. "Mr. Hill has gratuitously blurted out something that has nothing to do with Mr. Kuhn. It's one of·the dangers of a joint trial. With a brush effect, [he has] totally prejudiced my client and I move for a mistrial."

McDonald quickly came to Hill's aid. "This is the fourth day of testifying," the prosecutor said. "Under the circumstances, in the extensive and heated cross-examination, he's done very well in not blurting anything out."

Sharon and Coiro each echoed Zimmerman's motion for a mistrial, to which Bramwell responded, "You fellows are well aware of the criminal involvement of Mr. Hill as an individual. . . . It almost seems to me from the criminal involvement that he had, having a gun was not abnormal."

Bramwell offered to make an instruction to the jury, but reconsidered when Zimmerman said that might prejudice his client more than the initial statement.

Focusing on the Harvard game, Sharon elicited that Hill never mentioned Mazzei being in Boston, either in the *Sports Illustrated* article or in his grand jury testimony. He also showed that the dollar figures Hill had mentioned—the three thousand he had given the players at Boston Garden, plus the fifteen hundred, two thousand, or twenty-five hundred he got from Perry in New York the next day—did not add up to seventy-five hundred dollars, or twenty-five hundred per player, that allegedly was agreed upon at the beginning of the scheme.

When Sharon pointed out that Hill told Looney he gave Rocco Perla five thousand dollars but told the grand jury that he'd given Tony Perla three thousand dollars, the following "Who's on First" exchange ensued:

Sharon: "You told [Looney] that you gave Rocco Perla five thousand dollars, is that correct?"

Hill: "Repeat that."

Sharon: "It says that in the article—"

Hill: "That what it says."

Sharon: "That's what it says you said."

Hill: "That's what Mr. Looney says it says."

Sharon: "That's what Mr. Looney says you said."

After such witty repartee, Zimmerman's cross almost couldn't help but be anticlimactic. But Kuhn's attorney still managed to elicit that Hill could not say for certain if Kuhn had ever actually been notified of any point spreads, since Hill was in direct contact with Kuhn only three times: at the Logan Airport Hilton meeting, at Boston Garden after the Harvard game, and in the telephone conversation in which he threatened to break Kuhn's fingers.

It was late Friday afternoon, and Hill had been on the witness stand since Tuesday. But he would have to return on Monday for redirect by McDonald and recross by the defense. Even Bramwell could not believe McDonald had more to ask Hill, saying, "You really want redirect of this guy? You want it?"

When the jurors entered the courtroom on Monday morning, November 2, they must have felt a strong sense of déjà vu. There was Henry Hill on the stand, again. It must have seemed like this trial was going to be about him and nobody else. But this was Ed McDonald's chance to use his redirect examination to apply some liquid cement to Hill's fractured credibility.

The prosecutor began by reading Hill's agreement with the government into evidence, establishing that Hill had great incentive to be truthful in all his statements. Then, he brought out that Hill was not supposed to associate with Burke during the fall of 1978 because he was on parole, an admission that caused Coiro to move again for mistrial since Hill's testimony implied some criminal activity on Burke's part.

Here, McDonald overstepped his boundaries when he said to Bramwell, "First of all, I think it is a balancing test that has to be conducted here—"

"But you can't conduct a balancing," Bramwell said, interrupting him. "That's my job."

"It's for you to do," McDonald said.

"I can't do it after you have already done it," Bramwell pointed out.

"The question is, does the probative value outweigh the prejudicial effect?" McDonald offered.

"That is the balancing test that I use, but that is not for you to use," Bramwell chided. The judge clearly was sending McDonald a message, yet he still denied Coiro's application for a mistrial.

The sharp Zimmerman wasn't through, though. He pointed out that while the defense was not allowed to mention the Lufthansa robbery, McDonald appeared to be trying to sneak it in through the back door. Bramwell agreed to give the jury a limiting instruction on statements about Hill's visits to the Burke house.

McDonald offered the explanation that Hill's memory was, indeed, better now than when he talked to Looney because of the materials he had been able to review with the government, such as hotel records and phone records. Hill then testified that the *SI* article was "basically" true, and that all the statements about Burke were accurate. He admitted that he had exaggerated his role in the scheme and the amounts of money that were bet.

"What about the language that was used?" McDonald asked.

"That's not the way I talk," Hill said.

In painstaking detail, McDonald then went over the basic facts of the *SI* article and had Hill confirm that they were what he told Looney. This exercise provided a preview of what would transpire when Looney took the stand, as McDonald asked Hill first about what Looney wrote, then asked if that was what Hill had told the *SI* writer. One of the questions focused on Paul Mazzei's attempt to fix the B.C.–St. John's game, which was not mentioned in the article, and Bramwell again admonished McDonald at sidebar.

"One thing I will tell you, Mr. McDonald, you have the tendency to, you know, overstep your bounds," he said. "This is not consistent with what you as a prosecutor should be doing. I'm cautioning you. I'm telling you."

By the time Coiro was preparing to do his recross of Hill, McDonald was still troubled by Bramwell's remark, and stammered an apology.

"Don't let it worry you," Bramwell said.

"Don't lose any sleep," Coiro added.

With one last chance to take his shots at Hill, Coiro zeroed in on whether or not Hill had read the *SI* article before it was published. Hill had claimed on Friday that he had approved the article, but now said he had not. Then, during Sharon's recross, he said Looney "had read me the article but I didn't approve it."

Hill's flip-flopping caused another set-to with Coiro:

"Tell me what the truth is, what you testified Friday, or—" Coiro's voice rose.

"You know what the truth is, Mr. Coiro," Hill interrupted.

"I would like Your Honor to come down on him as you do on us when we make a mistake," Coiro said angrily. "This witness is unruly. He's surly. He's nothing but just what he is on the stand."

Hill interrupted again. "I'm telling the truth, Mike," he said, using Coiro's first name again.

"You're telling the truth?" Coiro said sarcastically.

"You know it," Hill retorted.

"You don't even know the word 'truth,'" Coiro sneered.

After a lunch break, Zimmerman wrapped up his recross and Henry Hill was free to go. In his five days on the witness stand he had sat and listened as the four defense attorneys impugned his memory, his morals, his past, present, and future; attacked his credibility and made insinuations about his sexual predilections. If this had been Robert's Lounge, none of them would have lasted two minutes. But Henry Hill was now a representative of the United States government, and he had to sit there with his hands tied, like a common schmuck.

"They tore me a new asshole," Hill said. "Or they tried to. And you have to sit there and take it. I had a terrible record; I wasn't a nice person in that life.

"How much worse could I have looked? They had me up there for a while. It was exhausting. And I made errors. They'd get me so confused sometimes. I'd take a deep breath. . . . I didn't know what the fuck they were talking about, what game. It was nerve-wracking."

• • •

The prosecution spent the rest of Monday afternoon's session presenting evidence that established that there had been interstate travel in connection with the scheme, and that the defendants had been at the places where Hill said they had been—leaving a trail "a mile wide," as McDonald had said in his opening statement.

The evidence included phone records and registration cards from the Logan Airport Hilton and Boston Sheraton, as well as the Sunrise Motor Inn and Rockville Centre Holiday Inn—all places where Mazzei, the Perlas, and Hill were alleged to have stayed—and credit card receipts showing that Rocco Perla flew on Allegheny Airlines from Pittsburgh to Boston on December 16, the day of the Harvard game.

• • •

Over the years, James Burke had earned the nickname "Jimmy the Gent" in part because of his dapper appearance, and to court observers he fit the moniker with his well-tailored suits and stylish wave of silver hair. But his codefendants noticed other signs that bespoke a darker side.

"He had the coldest eyes I've ever seen on a human being," Kerry O'Malley recalled. "They called him 'Gentleman Jimmy Burke,' and he could be a gentleman, but if he got crossed, all the life went out of those eyes. It was scary."

At one point during the trial, Burke introduced Rocco and Tony Perla to his wife, Frances, and she invited them to dinner at the family's house in

Howard Beach (Burke, who was in jail, was unable to attend). There, they met Burke's two sons, whose father had named them Jesse James Burke and Frank James Burke—one latter-day outlaw tipping his hat to two predecessors.

CHAPTER FOURTEEN

The Perfect Front

By the late fall of 1981, Jim Sweeney was moving ahead with his life like any ambitious recent college graduate, albeit one whose day planner for the week of November 2 included a visit to District Court in Brooklyn to testify against organized crime figures in front of a horde of media and onlookers—one of whom would be his former friend, Rick Kuhn.

Three months earlier, Sweeney had married Maura Haggerty, his sweetheart since his sophomore year at Boston College and the reason behind his cutting short his basketball adventure in Sweden a year earlier. He had recently taken a job as an executive recruiter at a company run by one of his cousins in northern New Jersey, and was taking classes toward a master's in business administration at nearby Fairleigh Dickinson University.

In short, Jim Sweeney was everything that Henry Hill was not, and this fact would become more evident as soon as he strode to the witness stand that Monday afternoon wearing a crisp, blue pinstripe suit and exuding an air of purposefulness.

Sweeney began answering Ed McDonald's questions about his career at Boston College, the awards he had won, and his friendship with the defendant, Rick Kuhn. As he spoke, Sweeney's eyes never once strayed toward Kuhn, who sat at the defense table staring at his former friend and teammate.

McDonald got Sweeney to describe the first time Kuhn approached him about shaving points, during a trip to Harvard Square in the fall of 1978. Then Sweeney told about the Logan Airport Hilton meeting, at which point Sweeney identified Tony Perla, sitting in the courtroom, as the man who had answered the door when he and Rick arrived at the room.

Sweeney recounted how Henry Hill and Perla had told him that he was the "perfect front" for the scheme because no one would ever suspect him, that it would be financially rewarding for him, and that he should not say anything to anybody about it. He then recalled a man named "Paulie" entering the room, who was short with brown curly hair and a receding hairline, and who told him that he would bet their shares for them if they wanted.

"What did you say in response to what was proposed?" McDonald asked.

"At first I said nothing," Sweeney replied, "and then I agreed to cooperate."

"What was your state of mind at that point?" McDonald said.

"I was frightened," Sweeney answered.

As Sweeney described the rest of the meeting, the contrast between his version and Hill's became more pronounced. In the *Sports Illustrated* article and on the witness stand, the mobster had portrayed Sweeney as a hustler, well-versed in the art of point-shaving and eager to make a buck. Sweeney painted a scenario in which a twenty-year-old college kid too scared to say no to a couple of tough guys decided to go along with something he knew was wrong.

McDonald used the rest of his direct examination of Sweeney to elicit the details of the games involved in the scheme, beginning with the Providence debacle and including the Harvard game, during which Sweeney said Kuhn had told him that Ernie Cobb would be cooperating. Throughout, Sweeney defended his decision not to notify school officials or his coach by saying he was frightened of what might happen to him or to Kuhn. He admitted taking the five hundred dollars from Rick before the trip to Hawaii even though he realized it was wrong.

Sweeney testified that he refused Kuhn's entreaties to shave points in the UCLA and Rhode Island games, that he pretended to go along with the plan for the February 3 Fordham game, that he gave no indication of going along for the St. John's game, and that he fouled out of the Holy Cross game intentionally.

"What was the reason for that?" McDonald asked in reference to the latter contention.

"I thought to myself, 'If these bettors are paying each player ten thousand dollars apiece to participate in this game, they must be placing extraordinary amounts of money down on these games,'" Sweeney said. "I didn't want to be any part of it. I didn't want to be a part of that game so someone could say, 'That kid Sweeney was the person that participated in the point-shaving scheme.'"

McDonald ended the session by eliciting from Sweeney that he was not testifying under any agreement from the government.

• • •

The cross-examinations began, as so many had before, with Coiro asking for a connection, any connection, with Burke and finding none since Sweeney had never met Burke or even heard his name. Then, it was Zimmerman's turn, and he began to chip away at Sweeney's story.

He focused on the fact that Sweeney had initially told the FBI agents at his home that he knew nothing about a point-shaving scheme, and that he could not remember Tony Perla's last name during that interview. Zimmerman implied that Sweeney had asked for more than the twenty-five hundred dollars per game that Hill and Perla were offering during the Logan Hilton meeting, which Sweeney denied.

Zimmerman's true focus, however, was Sweeney's agreeing to shave points, even in jest, and his failure to notify the school, or anyone in authority, about the scheme. When Sweeney repeated his contention that he was scared of Hill and his associates, Zimmerman pressed him:

"You spent how much time with Henry Hill, about an hour and a half?"

"Yes."

"Then you saw him one other time after the Harvard game?"

"Yes."

"After that, you never saw him again, did you? . . . Did he ever call you up and make threats to you?"

"No."

"But, you tell us you were still fearful of him, is that correct?"

"Yes, I was."

Zimmerman also focused on Sweeney's lack of an immunity agreement with the government; this did not make sense, he suggested, if Sweeney had agreed to shave points with more than one other person, which constituted a conspiracy.

During a short recess, Sharon got into an argument with one of the court deputies that culminated in an offer to step outside and settle it with fists.

"You are going to have to control yourself," Bramwell told Sharon. "I understand these things happening. I understand you are in the heat of battle, and you have a problem."

"I think the problem is that Your Honor has shown nothing but bias toward me," Sharon answered back.

This raised Bramwell's hackles.

"Oh, I love you like a brother," he said, his words soaked in sarcasm. "I even love you more than I love the rest of these fellows. I love you so much, it is flowing all over the place. I just love you, Mr. Sharon. That is the way it is, you know."

Out of earshot of the court reporter, Bramwell added, "I hope you don't mind if I say something about our mother."

● ● ●

When court resumed, O'Malley homed in on Sweeney's FBI interview and his initial statement to the agents that he didn't know anything about any point-shaving—the reason being, Sweeney said, that he felt he "hadn't done anything wrong." There also was no mention of Rocco Perla in the report of the interview, and Sweeney initially mistook the Logan Airport

Hilton for the Boston Sheraton as the site of the November 16 meeting with Hill and Tony Perla.

O'Malley's questions then began to lead toward alternate theories for why the games turned out the way they did. UCLA, for example, shot a lot of late free throws, which could explain their twenty-two-point margin of victory over B.C., while Harvard used the press to get back into the game against the Eagles. Fordham, meanwhile, simply played at a slow tempo.

Finally, O'Malley charged that Sweeney had double-crossed the gamblers if he indeed took the money but was not shaving points. It was a moral wrong, not a legal wrong, Sweeney countered. O'Malley then finished by implying that Sweeney had been dishonest with the people he'd been dealing with, dishonest with himself for accepting the five hundred dollars, dishonest with his coaches and school for not divulging the scheme, and dishonest with the FBI when they first questioned him. The implication was clear: Why should the jury assume he was being honest now?

Following a brief recess, Zimmerman made a motion that even now, twenty years later, seems perfectly logical. But it was immediately shot down by Bramwell.

"In this particular case we have a witness on the stand who has made a judicial confession to everything that Mr. Kuhn is charged with, and this particular person has not been prosecuted," Zimmerman said. He then moved for a dismissal of the charges against Kuhn.

"I couldn't agree with you less," Bramwell intoned, "and I don't feel that this witness has in any way done something which is consistent with what you say is the position of Mr. Kuhn."

Zimmerman then charged that Kuhn was being made the subject of selective prosecution and denied equal protection under the law. After Bramwell again disagreed, McDonald termed the motion "so ludicrous that it wouldn't warrant a reply."

After lunch, Sharon took over the cross-examination, and he focused on Sweeney's powers of observation as a point guard and how he needed to be able to judge the height of opposing players to create mismatches on the floor. The line of questioning seemed a bit odd, but Sharon eventually got around to the point, which was Sweeney's somewhat shaky identification of Mazzei as the man he had met at the Logan Airport Hilton and saw in the bleachers at the Harvard game.

Sharon pointed out that in Sweeney's grand jury testimony, taken in September 1980, he had only mentioned one person coming into the hotel room while he was talking to Hill and Tony Perla, but now was saying that two people had entered the room, and that second man was about 6-foot-2 or 6-foot-3. He also remembered Mazzei—"Paulie," as Hill had referred to him—as being about 5-foot-10 with a potbelly and a receding hairline. Mazzei stood about 5-foot-7 or 5-foot-8 and was bald. Perhaps more damaging, Sharon elicited that Sweeney had never mentioned the name "Paulie" in his grand jury testimony, and had only mentioned it in his trial testimony the previous day.

The matter of Sweeney's identification of Mazzei at the Boston College–Harvard game, the one where Mazzei and Hill made such a ruckus in the B.C. cheering section, also was called into question. Sharon brought out that Sweeney had told the grand jury he had not been able to identify the people in the stands, but was testifying now in court that he could.

"Between today and the time you testified at the grand jury, did they move the seats closer at Boston College?" Sharon asked, then withdrew the question after McDonald objected.

He closed the cross with one more key piece of information: that Sweeney had failed to identify a picture of Mazzei shown to him at his FBI interview in 1980.

At the defense table, Rick Kuhn watched as Sweeney stepped down from the witness box and walked out of the courtroom. "All I wanted him to do was look at me," Kuhn later told the *Boston Globe*'s Lesley Visser. "He never did, not once."

• • •

If seeing his former buddy Sweeney look right past him from the witness stand was humbling, what followed had to have been doubly traumatic for Kuhn. Like an episode of *This Is Your Life* gone haywire, the next witness was Barbara Reed, the woman Rick had shared his life with for more than two years and who now was going to follow in Sweeney's footsteps and tell the world what an ogre he was. Like Sweeney, she would give her testimony without so much as casting an eye in Rick's direction, as if she were talking about someone who was not even in the room.

Reed had been well-prepared for her day in court by McDonald's office. Not long after her interview with the FBI at her home in Syracuse in late September 1980, she had come to New York and met with the prosecutor at the Strike Force office for about five or six hours. Later, between her grand jury testimony in July and the trial in November, she had met with him three more times for a total of about eighteen hours. Clearly, the government was planning on making Reed's testimony one of the centerpieces of the trial, and they wanted her well-rehearsed.

Before Reed took the stand, however, Zimmerman tried a novel approach to keep her testimony out by attempting to invoke spousal privilege for Kuhn against Reed, noting that the courts had begun to recognize the legal standing of relationships that were not traditional marriages. This would have made any conversation between the two inadmissible. But Bramwell ruled that the privilege belonged to Reed, and he followed by refusing even to advise her that it was her choice.

McDonald took Reed through a basic chronology that began with her meeting Kuhn in the fall of 1977, her senior year at Boston College, and progressed through the end of the 1978–79 basketball season. She described meeting the Perlas on one of her trips to Pittsburgh, and told of how Rick had had the phone installed in their apartment on Peterborough Street in the fall of 1978. She recalled how he had told her about the Logan Airport Hilton meeting with "Henry" and "Paul" and how he had counted out $250 when he got back, money they had used for a shopping spree at the Natick Mall.

She described Rick's relationship with Jim Sweeney, and how Rick had deflected her concerns about "the betting thing" by telling her that Sweeney was not the type of person to be involved in anything illegal. She recalled the scene at Boston Garden during the B.C.–Harvard game, when Henry and Paul made her "very upset" by cheering whenever a Boston College player made a mistake, and recounted her argument with Rick after the game when she accused him of trying to lose and he responded by saying they were "trying to win in smaller ways."

McDonald elicited from Reed the events of late December through early February: picking up the money order at Western Union after the Harvard game; the gifts Rick brought back for her from Hawaii; overhearing him discuss the Rhode Island game on the phone at the apartment; the night before the game against Fordham when Ernie Cobb came to the apartment and spoke to Rick and Rocco Perla; picking up the second money order, when Rick did not want Joe Beaulieu to see how much money he was receiving; and overhearing more phone conversations before the February 10 game against Holy Cross.

McDonald took considerable care in going over the events surrounding the Holy Cross game, as Reed's testimony could establish that Kuhn had been given the point spread for the game. She described Rick's giving her a piece of paper with a number on it, and making two attempts to call the number on the way to Worcester that Saturday morning before seeing Rick during warmups before the game. When Rick told her to make the call again, she was successful, and remembered a voice telling her the number "seven." She testified she recognized the voice as that of Tony Perla, and that she relayed this to Kuhn back inside the gym and that he said, "Beautiful," and gave her a kiss.

Reed's direct testimony ended with her telling the court how Kuhn had threatened to kill her if she told anyone about the betting scheme. As Reed finished describing the scene, she began to cry.

A short recess was taken, and by the time Reed returned to the stand for cross-examination she had regained her composure. It was a short reprieve, however. Zimmerman began his cross by getting Reed to establish that she and Kuhn were in love at one time and had planned to marry. Then, he went for the jugular, and ended up getting more than he bargained for.

"Did you ever become pregnant by Mr. Kuhn?" he asked.

"Twice I did," Reed answered.

"Did you have any of those children?"

"No, I did not."

"And why didn't you?"

"Because Mr. Kuhn gave me gonorrhea."

The last answer threw Zimmerman momentarily, but he immediately pressed Reed on the name of the doctor who had diagnosed her. Before she could answer, McDonald objected and a sidebar was called. Zimmerman claimed that Kuhn had warned him that Reed might lie about contracting gonorrhea from him, and that her statement would be prejudicial to Kuhn in the eyes of the jury. But Bramwell sustained McDonald's objection and ruled that the whole line of questioning was prohibited, and instructed the jury to disregard Reed's statement about the gonorrhea.

Something had happened in the courtroom, however, that seemed to bode ill for the defendants. From the defense table, Rocco Perla noticed that when the attorneys moved to sidebar, Reed began to cry again.

"She was all shook up," he recalled. "The lawyers and the judge didn't see it because they'd called for a sidebar, and she was actually sitting there on the witness stand breathing real heavily and crying. Nobody was really paying attention to her except the lead juror, the jury forewoman. (She) actually got up out of her box and walked over to the witness stand and offered her some water and a Kleenex. And then she turned and glared right at Rick.

"Right then we said, 'Well, this is history. There's no coming back from this.' It was just enough to make (Rick) lose any sympathy that anybody might have felt for him."

Zimmerman continued to try to paint Reed as a woman scorned by bringing up the former girlfriend Rick had visited in Pittsburgh in October 1978.

"What does this have to do with anything?" Reed asked.

"I ask the questions and you answer," Zimmerman chided. "We will get along a lot better. That's the rules of the game."

McDonald got up from his chair. "The judge does the talking and the lawyers ask the questions. That's the rules of the game," he said.

This drew in Coiro, who said, "I object. This is not a game, period."

Sharon interjected, "I think also one of the rules of court is that the attorneys make the objections and not the witness." This only earned him more goading from Bramwell, however, and the issue was dropped.

When Zimmerman changed his line of questioning to the facts of the case, he was able to show that virtually all of Reed's knowledge of the alleged point-shaving scheme derived from what Kuhn told her or what she overheard him say on the phone—and that he had told her initially that his friends in Pittsburgh were paying for inside information. The sole exception was the phone call Reed made before the Holy Cross game to get the point spread from Tony Perla.

As for the other defendants, Sharon was able to bring out that Reed had never heard Rick mention Paul Mazzei's last name, and that she had never overheard him speaking to Mazzei on the phone. And O'Malley elicited that there was no mention of either Rocco or Tony Perla in the FBI report of her interview in September 1980, nor was there mention of anyone named "Henry" or "Paul."

"It doesn't say that here, but that's what I told them," she said.

• • •

Of all the defendants, Paul Mazzei might have been feeling the most confident at this point of the trial. Sweeney's identification from the Logan
Hilton meeting had been disputed and his identification from the Harvard
game discounted. Furthermore, Reed's recollection of meeting him at the
Harvard game was balanced by the absence of Mazzei's name from her FBI
statement and by her admission that Kuhn had never mentioned Mazzei's
name in connection with the scheme.

"There wasn't really a whole lot of evidence against Paul," Leonard
Sharon says. "Henry implicated him, and then Sweeney said that he had
met with a guy named Paul, but gave a description that didn't really match
Mazzei. . . . Sweeney described a person much older than Paul, and he said
he was losing his hair, and Paul was bald, and the height and weight was off
significantly."

Something must have convinced Mazzei not to roll, which is what Hill
says the government was still trying to get him to do.

"He was going to cooperate at one point during that trial," Hill claims.
"He spent hours and hours with me and McDonald and Sharon. They just
couldn't come to the right deal. I tried to convince him, saying, 'Paul,
you're going to lose here.' But he was taking the advice of Sharon, and he
was also afraid of getting whacked."

• • •

Joe Beaulieu's testimony enlivened the afternoon session when the former
Boston College center recounted how Kuhn produced a small vial of
cocaine in the hotel room they were sharing in Los Angeles on the night
before the UCLA game. Zimmerman immediately moved for a mistrial,
claiming that Beaulieu's testimony had nothing to do with the charges in
the indictment and could only raise prejudice against Kuhn. But Bramwell
denied the motion, ruling that a "reasonable person" could form a nexus
between the two.

Beaulieu described on direct examination how Kuhn broached the
point-shaving scheme to him in the days leading up to the Harvard game,
but O'Malley and Zimmerman brought out on cross that Beaulieu hadn't
noticed any difference in the quality of play of any of the players during the
season, and that if any players had been slacking off, Davis would have
taken them out of the game. Zimmerman also focused on Beaulieu's initial
interview with FBI agents in September 1980, when he lied about being
approached by Kuhn.

Beaulieu's testimony closed Wednesday's session, and when court
reconvened on Thursday morning, the proceedings took on a different tone.
Absent was any testimony offering personal recollections of the 1978–79
season. In its place was the introduction of evidence by McDonald that was
designed to establish the connections between the defendants and to corroborate previous testimony about who was where, and on what dates.

Joseph Dragone, a school district official in Rockville Centre, New York, produced a note that the Morris School had received from Karen Hill on January 19, 1979, saying that her daughter, Gail, would be traveling to Florida that week and would be absent from school. He also produced school attendance records to that effect. This was the week that Henry Hill said he had driven to Florida to meet with Burke and had brought Gail along.

McDonald then called Thomas Spitzer, a document examiner from the FBI lab in Washington, who testified that the money orders sent from Pittsburgh to Boston on December 19, 1978, and January 8, 1979, had been signed by Rocco Perla, and that Perla had signed Kuhn's father's name, Frederick, on the second one. But under cross-examination by O'Malley, Spitzer admitted that he could not tell if the January 19 money order had been written by Perla.

Sharon took the opportunity to show that no records from any of the hotels allegedly used by Paul Mazzei in Boston or New York had been examined for Mazzei's signature or that of Tom Musca, the name the government was alleging Mazzei used at the Rockville Centre Holiday Inn. Harking back to Hill's testimony, he questioned why the government had produced no records of money orders that had been sent from Jamaica, New York, to Pittsburgh, as Hill claimed he had done.

The rest of Thursday's session consisted of testimony regarding phone calls: who called whom, which phone was registered to which person, and when the calls were made. Edgar Turner, a representative of Bell of Pennsylvania, confirmed the phone numbers for the Perlas, Paul Mazzei, Mazzei's girlfriend, and his father. Gerald O'Connor, an investigator for the New York Telephone Company, then produced records of phone calls from James Burke's house to various numbers, including the Logan Airport Hilton on November 17, 1978—the morning after the infamous meeting—and numerous calls to Pittsburgh during late December, January, and February.

The afternoon session featured a revisiting of the issue of McDonald's phone booklets. The prosecutor had highlighted calls between the defendants in red or green, which Coiro objected to as prejudicial; he also noted at sidebar that there still was no proof that the calls made from the Rockville Centre Holiday Inn on November 4, 1978, were made by Mazzei allegedly posing as "Musca."

O'Malley objected to the very introduction of the booklets, claiming it was a veiled attempt by McDonald to "summarize his own evidence and highlight it and reintroduce it." McDonald countered that the rules allowed for the preparation of charts and summaries to aid the jury.

Coiro then insisted that the entries should say "Burke home to Savino home," since it could not be proved who had actually answered the phone.

"This was gone over," an exasperated McDonald said. "We had a conference on this. If they had any complaints, they should have renewed their complaints earlier, not two minutes before the agent is going to take the stand."

But Bramwell ultimately ruled that the booklets could come in, judging that their probative value outweighed any potential prejudice. But he also instructed McDonald to change the listing of calls as "home" or "station" instead of to specific persons.

McDonald couldn't hide his anger.

"It's just too late to make this argument," he said. "You ruled that the book was admissible. If they had any complaints about it, they should have told us about it so we could have gone back to Washington."

"If the time is taken and the books are changed, you can write it in," Bramwell said. "It doesn't bother me how you do it."

"It will take an incredible amount of time," McDonald complained.

"He needs thirty FBI agents, one a book, and it will take him ten minutes," Zimmerman cracked.

"From our government, yes, Mr. Zimmerman," Bramwell said, sarcastically using a phrase Sharon had used earlier to make fun of the defense attorney.

McDonald, still fuming, said, "This is a complete surprise to the government. Your ruling was made some time in late September—"

"You see, you have got something that is highly prejudicial," Bramwell said, interrupting the prosecutor. "I might let you go with that, but it could be all for naught."

The matter appeared closed, until Bramwell began to take a look at the booklets. Within a few minutes, he declared, "I am going to permit this to be used just as it is." The reversal was yet another example of the judge's pro-prosecution leanings.

With the jury looking on in the booklets, FBI agent Edmundo Guevara went over calls from James Burke's house to numerous bookmakers named by Hill as being involved in the scheme, and from the Rockville Centre Holiday Inn, Logan Airport Hilton, Boston Sheraton, Colonnade Hotel, and MGM Grand Hotel in Las Vegas—all locations where the defendants were alleged to have been.

On cross, Coiro was able to elicit that the only calls that Guevara could say with certainty had been made between the parties listed—and not someone else at the number—were the call from Hill to Burke on November 16, 1978, from the Logan Airport Hilton, and the call made from Burke's house to the Hilton the next morning. And, he pointed out, this was only according to the testimony of Henry Hill.

McDonald then tried to have Guevara present an exhibit that consisted of a chart showing the chronology of the case. This brought an immediate objection from Sharon, and for what seemed like the first time during the trial, Bramwell agreed with his nemesis.

Above McDonald's objection that he had used similar aids in the Abscam trial, Bramwell ruled that McDonald could use the chart in his final summation, but not during testimony.

"It's just like a juror taking notes," Bramwell reasoned. "If I let you do it, I'll have to let them (motioning to the defense team) put in a chart."

"It's discretionary whether a juror can take notes," McDonald pointed out.

"I don't let them do it," Bramwell said matter-of-factly, then added, "I figure the smart ones will have notes and the dumb ones won't have any."

The afternoon session found McDonald in more hot water. The day before, when some reporters noticed McDonald's phone booklets sitting on the prosecution table, he had not objected to some of them taking a look. Now, Coiro said, they were writing articles based on what was in the booklets.

Bramwell was not amused.

"Well, you shouldn't have given it out," he said. "That is no way of doing things. That is very careless."

"I apologize to Mr. Coiro and the other attorneys—" McDonald began.

"You have a serious situation here, and that type of handling is uncalled for," Bramwell interrupted. "Also, I might say that there appears to be a cozier relationship with the press than should properly be. In fact, I saw one of the defendants the other day with one of the reporters and it looked like they were returning from lunch. . . . This is not my cup of tea. You people choose to proceed in this fashion, it won't be to anyone's benefit around here."

The sequence would not have been complete without someone moving for a mistrial, and Coiro obliged, and added a motion for severance based on Bramwell's seeing Kuhn coming back from lunch with a reporter.

"They were coming from the IRS building," Bramwell said. "They could have been in the snack bar, you know, for a quick, for one of the fast, quick ones."

The reporter was the *Boston Globe*'s Lesley Visser, who did not find Bramwell's double entendre amusing, and lodged an official complaint with the court.

The next prosecution witness was Zach Franzi, the bookmaker who had exaggerated his credentials in order to get on NBC back in August. McDonald presented him as an expert in the field of sports gambling, and had him explain what makes a point spread move up or down and why a game might be taken off the board in a casino.

The problem was, though Franzi claimed he had noticed "radical" changes in the spreads for several Boston College games that season, when Coiro cross-examined him he was unable to name specific games in which the line had shifted. He also admitted that he did not remember any B.C. games being taken off the board that season. Coiro then hit the hanging curveball offered by Franzi's bogus appearance on television, and summed up by asking, "Is it also true that there are many other people who are more qualified than you to discuss oddsmaking and linemaking and gambling?" to which Franzi had no choice but to agree.

Franzi's testimony finished Friday's session and brought to a close a week that had gone exceedingly well for the prosecution. McDonald had presented Jim Sweeney and Barbara Reed, two credible witnesses who had been able to counter the defense's attacks on Hill by offering corroboration on many of his contentions. The phone records had established that the defendants had called each other's homes as well as the hotels where they were alleged to have stayed, which any jury would glean was more than mere coincidence.

All in all, there was reason to be optimistic, particularly since one of the first witnesses on Monday was going to testify that Rick Kuhn already had confessed to his crimes.

• • •

Before anybody took the stand on Monday, November 9, however, a crisis presented itself in the form of an article in that morning's *New York Daily News*. The story linked a series of murders to the Lufthansa robbery—including the killing of "Fat Louie" Cafora, who had scoffed at Ed McDonald's warning at the Strike Force office more than a year earlier—and listed James Burke and Tommy DeSimone as the ones who had plotted the heist. With the jurors not sequestered per Bramwell's order, any of them could have read the article and been prejudiced toward Burke as a result.

Before the jury entered the courtroom, Coiro was all over McDonald, insinuating that a leak from the prosecutor's office was behind the story.

"They're dredging up old news. How this came about, I have no idea, Your Honor," McDonald said in defense.

"Old news at a particular time when Mr. Burke is on trial and we are hearing the close of the government's case?" Coiro asked.

McDonald tried to rationalize, though somewhat lamely.

"I have relatives named Burke," he said. "Somebody reading this thing would not necessarily connect the James Burke here with the James Burke on trial here."

Bramwell sensed the gravity of the moment and ruled that he would question the jurors individually in his chambers to see if any of them had read the article. This process, known by the French term *voir dire*, is used by lawyers in selecting a jury, to weed out any jurors who might be biased toward either side in a trial.

As the jurors trooped into Bramwell's chambers one by one, like students being summoned to the principal's office, they found themselves face-to-face with the attorneys, Bramwell, . . . and James Burke.

Three jurors said they had read all or part of the article, but each insisted that it would have no bearing on his objectivity—a wise choice given that the man who was alleged to have ordered all these killings was staring right at them.

When Bramwell was through, Coiro contended that since jurors usually are reluctant to disobey an order—in this case, Bramwell's order not to read the papers or watch television—it was significant that two had proceeded to read the whole article anyway. On this basis, he applied for a mistrial, claiming that Burke's right to choose the jury had been taken away from him, and that the article was prejudicial. Sharon and O'Malley joined in, pointing out that while they had been prohibited from mentioning Lufthansa during the trial, some of the jurors had admitted reading an article linking Burke—and, by extension, their clients—to the robbery. But Bramwell denied their joint motions.

Christine Siano then took the witness stand, and the former childhood neighbor of Rocco and Anthony Perla recounted the day in February 1981 that Tony Perla came over to her house and admitted his involvement in the point-shaving scheme. Her testimony would have passed without incident, except that in response to one of O'Malley's questions she mentioned that Tony Perla had been a school librarian. McDonald jumped on this during his redirect questioning, claiming that any discussion of what Perla did for a living would open the door for him to cross-examine Siano on whether Perla was a bookmaker.

Bramwell allowed the questioning, and it came out that Siano's brother, David Ludwig, used to bet with Perla, and that she had given a football pool card to him to pass along to Perla.

• • •

Their first meeting had been more than a year ago, under quite different circumstances. It was 6:30 on a cool September morning, and Rick Kuhn was clad only in a pair of shorts as he stepped out of his parents' house in Swissvale and walked across the street to a Ford with two FBI agents. Now, one of them, James Byron, was sitting in a suit across the courtroom from him, preparing to tell the jury what Kuhn had said during their fateful thirty-minute conversation.

Byron, who had been an agent for the Internal Revenue Service in Boston before becoming an FBI agent in 1977, began to describe the interview he and partner Thomas Sweeney (no relation to Jim) had conducted with Kuhn, beginning with the moment they knocked on the door and asked Kuhn's father to rouse his son out of bed.

Once the three men got to the car, Byron told the court, "He said that during the summer of '78 he was approached and asked if he'd be interested in making some money. He asked how. He was told by point-shaving . . . keeping Boston College games manipulated."

Byron recounted Kuhn's description of the meeting at the Logan Airport Hilton, in which Rick said he and Sweeney were given five hundred dollars by Henry Hill, and in which Sweeney was reluctant to go along with the scheme but eventually gave in. He described Kuhn telling him how Ernie Cobb had agreed to go along with the scheme for the Harvard game, and how he split three thousand dollars with Sweeney and Cobb.

The jury had heard other witnesses speak of Kuhn's words and deeds during the time period of the alleged scheme; now, they were hearing Kuhn's own words, in effect admitting his complicity in the crimes with which he was now being charged. It was persuasive stuff . . . yet some things didn't quite fit.

Two weeks earlier, Zimmerman had used all his considerable skills as a defense attorney to try and keep Kuhn's FBI statement out of the trial. He had failed in that endeavor, but now he was primed to take aim at Byron on cross-examination.

First, he elicited that Byron was an inexperienced interviewer who had questioned only five or six criminal suspects during his four years with the Bureau. Then, he brought out that Byron and Tom Sweeney differed on what Kuhn was wearing when he left the house that morning. He also got Byron to admit that he had told Kuhn he was under no obligation to talk to them before he told Kuhn of the allegations against him, and only when Kuhn asked. After the allegations were brought up, there was no mention of Kuhn's right to end the interview. Byron and Sweeney also did not tell Kuhn that his statement could be used against him at a later date, or that he should talk to a lawyer before he talked to the agents.

Zimmerman was playing his hand expertly at this point. Bramwell had ruled earlier that the interview of Kuhn had not been custodial, which meant the agents were under no obligation to read him his Miranda rights. But that did not prevent Zimmerman from playing on the image of the half-dressed Kuhn being duped by the government agents while he sat shivering in a car at 6:30 in the morning.

Byron explained that the interview was intended as a question-and-answer session designed to try and get Kuhn's cooperation, not to arrest him. He also said the interview was not tape-recorded, per FBI policy.

The specific games Kuhn mentioned did not jibe with the government's theory, either. According to Kuhn's statement, the only game Kuhn admitted to fixing was the Harvard game, for which he was paid three thousand dollars and in which he admitted shaving "five points." The two UConn games mentioned—January 17 and the ECAC playoff game on March 1— were games Boston College was supposed to win. Kuhn said that he told Tony Perla before the Holy Cross game on February 10 that there was "no way" B.C. would lose by more than the point spread. The agents did not ask Kuhn about the Providence, UCLA, Fordham, or St. John's games that later appeared in the indictment.

On redirect, McDonald tried to get Byron to explain why Kuhn was not read his Miranda rights, but Zimmerman objected and a sidebar was held. Bramwell would not let McDonald mention Miranda, even though, as McDonald correctly argued, Zimmerman had just alluded to Miranda in his cross of Byron. McDonald then got Bramwell to warn Zimmerman not to make any mention of the subject in his summation, which the judge did.

McDonald then rehabilitated Byron by asking the agent whether Kuhn had been handcuffed during the interview (he was not), whether Byron had ever put his hands on Kuhn (he had not), or whether Sweeney had restricted Kuhn's movement in any way (he had not).

When Byron stepped down, McDonald entered a stipulation to phone records for "Robert Smith" at a phone number known to have been used by Richard Perry. After the clerk marked the phone slips Government Exhibit

39 for identification, McDonald said, simply, "That is the government's case."

It had taken two weeks to present the prosecution's witnesses, but it was clear that the stars had been Hill and Sweeney, two men of opposite temperaments, backgrounds, and aspirations whose stories meshed well enough to provide the jury with an accurate picture of a conspiracy.

Following standard legal procedure, Bramwell ruled that the prosecution had "presented in its case sufficient evidence . . . to permit the question of whether or not a conspiracy existed and whether or not [the defendants] were participants in that conspiracy." The defense lawyers then went through the motion of moving to dismiss the charges against their clients, all of which were denied by the judge.

It was time for the defense to present its case, but Coiro, Zimmerman et al would have to wait a bit. Bramwell had a hearing scheduled for the next day, Tuesday, November 10. The next day was Veterans Day, and on Thursday and Friday he would be at a judge's conference in New Paltz, New York. The trial would thus resume the following Monday.

"How long do you fellows think you'll take?" Bramwell asked the defense attorneys.

"One day for me, Judge," Coiro replied.

"Very short," O'Malley answered.

"One day at the very most. Probably a half day," Zimmerman said.

"Likewise," Sharon chimed in.

This must have come as a pleasant surprise for Bramwell after Hill's marathon on the stand, and he cracked, "I would like to twist your arm, and it doesn't show on the record, but I'll have to go along."

• • •

For all the hand-wringing over the fate of the now-infamous *Sports Illustrated* article, when Doug Looney, its author, took the stand on Monday, November 16 to open the defense's case, there was still a good deal of confusion over how the questioning would be conducted.

Coiro began by asking the writer if Henry Hill actually told him, "I am the Boston College fixer," as the article's first sentence stated.

"Henry Hill did not in that case use those exact words," Looney admitted. When Coiro asked what words Hill had used, Bramwell interjected, McDonald objected, and the wrangling began.

What followed was a protracted do-si-do as the attorneys haggled over how the questions to Looney would be framed. McDonald steadfastly objected to anything from the article being read in open court, since the article had not been admitted into evidence.

After another false start and another objection by McDonald, Bramwell ruled that Coiro would have to ask Looney questions based on what was in the article—without specifically quoting the article—but related directly to Hill's testimony.

When the jury finally returned, they were met with a scenario that bordered on the surreal. Coiro was prevented from asking Looney what Hill had told him; nor could he quote directly from the *Sports Illustrated* article. What he was allowed to do was to read Hill's testimony, then ask Looney whether Hill's testimony—about what he had told Looney—was true or untrue. As McDonald noted in an objection, Looney could not testify as to the truth of Hill's contentions, because only Hill could know that.

For his part, Looney never strayed from simple, unadorned responses that left open no room for misinterpretation or further inquiry. "Yes. . . . Correct . . . I might have. . . . That is the truth. . . . I did. . . . That's correct."

What the convoluted format merely established was that Looney had printed what Hill had told him, with some embellishments, and that the writer had been told by Hill that what Hill was telling him was true. Looney did, however, clarify a point that Hill had waffled on, that Looney had indeed read the article to Hill before publication and that Hill had confirmed its accuracy.

Much confusion could have been avoided if the defense had only been a little savvier.

"One of the things they never asked for, but probably should have, was whether or not there were tapes that existed" of Hill's interviews, Robert Simels says. They could also have subpoenaed Simels, since he had been present at all interviews between Hill and Looney and any conversations between the two that were overheard by Simels would not fall under attorney-client privilege. But the defense attorneys failed to do either, and as a result, Looney's testimony helped little, if at all.

• • •

The jury got a firsthand look at a real, live, New York gambler when the next witness, John Yarmosh, took the stand. Yarmosh had been booking bets for decades in New York and had known Henry Hill and Jimmy Burke for years. The defense's purpose for calling him was to refute Hill's claim that Yarmosh and Milton Wekar, another bookie, had met with Hill and Burke at a Manhattan restaurant to discuss the point-shaving scheme.

Yarmosh's performance should have earned him awards for evasiveness. He tried mightily to avoid saying that Wekar was a bookmaker, even though he said he had been a "runner" for Wekar for forty years. As for Hill's contentions, all Yarmosh would admit to was being in Bobby's, the restaurant at Twenty-seventh Street and Seventh Avenue in New York where wiseguys hung out, at the same time as Burke and Wekar on several occasions. When McDonald asked him on cross if he had ever sat down at a table at Bobby's with Burke and Wekar, Yarmosh replied coyly, "Well, a lot of times there are two or three tables together at the restaurant."

On redirect, Yarmosh told Coiro that he never discussed Boston College games with Burke or Wekar when he was in the restaurant—and also said that he had seen Hill use the phone in Burke's house, which was a key defense point that the next witness, William Bored, would elaborate on. Their testimony would plant a seed of doubt in the jury's mind about whether it was Hill, not Burke, who had made the calls to the other con-spirators.

Bored was a thirty-six-year-old general contractor who had known Henry Hill since grammar school and had spent about eight weeks in early 1979 doing interior work at James Burke's house in Howard Beach. Bored testified that he saw Hill using Burke's phone frequently, sometimes when Burke was not there. Bored also said that he stopped bringing his son to Hill's house when he was doing work there because he "didn't want my son influenced" by Hill's habit of smoking marijuana in the morning.

When Bored finished testifying, Coiro rested Burke's defense. O'Malley and Sharon had some final business to take care of, and O'Malley called Edward Medo, a former bookie who ran a sports information service in Las Vegas aimed at gamblers that Tony Perla had subscribed to during the 1978–79 basketball season.

Medo explained how a point spread works, how a bookmaker would react if heavy money was being bet on a game, and how inside information can be used to a bettor's or bookie's advantage. He then testified that he could not recall any fluctuations in the point spreads of Boston College games during the 1978–79 season. "If it did happen again and again, we'd be aware of it," he said.

• • •

Tom Davis had coached in hundreds of basketball games, given countless lectures at camps, and been in the spotlight for a good portion of his pro-fessional life. During that time, he had become known as a coach who stressed preparation as the key to success, and who never left anything to chance. But appearing in court to testify about his team, his coaching style, and his players—particularly the one whose future he was holding in his hands on Tuesday, November 17, 1981—gave him a serious case of butter-flies.

"When you go in there to testify, you're pretty well informed as to what you're going to see and what you're going to do," Davis recalled. "It isn't like you're going in there blind. You pretty much know the types of ques-tions you're going to have to respond to. But it's still . . . it's a really nerve-wracking experience. It's not a pleasant kind of a day, that's for sure. The whole process is a little uncomfortable to be a part of. It's not a walk in the park. It's really serious, because you're talking about people's lives, people that you've been involved with.

"One thing that really helped me was that the lawyers that B.C. had provided told me how to handle it, and I met with McDonald's guys before-hand and they said, 'This is what they're going to ask.'"

What the defense elicited from Davis was that he could not remember one instance during the 1978–79 season when he felt any players were shaving points, and that no player ever contacted him about being approached by gamblers.

McDonald was ready on cross, however. The prosecutor, using his knowledge of the history and intricacies of basketball, got Davis to agree that even legendary coaches like Clair Bee, Nat Holman, and Adolph Rupp had been unable to detect point-shaving by their players. He also had Davis explain how anyone connected to the program—a coach, assistant coach, even a student manager—could provide inside information to gamblers, and that the school policy was to make information about injuries or suspensions available to the media. It would not be necessary, then, to approach a player solely for inside information—but it would be necessary if the objective was to shave points.

Even after Sharon pointed out that other intangibles that could affect a player's performance, such as a fight with a girlfriend, would not be made public by the school, McDonald appeared to have won this round.

• • •

Zimmerman opened the afternoon session by announcing he was going to call Kuhn's father, Fred, to testify about what Kuhn was wearing when he was interviewed by the FBI agents in 1980. Realizing that McDonald would be chomping at the bit to question Mr. Kuhn on a whole host of topics, he tried to get Bramwell to limit the scope of questioning, but the judge would not bite. So Zimmerman opted against putting him on the stand, and charged that the court was "preventing Mr. Kuhn from setting forth some essential elements in his defense."

Instead, Sharon called Paul Mazzei's mother, Florence, to the stand. In an attempt to discredit Sweeney's identification of Mazzei at the Logan Airport Hilton meeting, he had her explain that her son was 5-foot-6 ("Has he grown at all since 1978–79?" he asked her.) and 165 pounds, and had been bald on the top of his head for about eight or nine years. She also said that he did not have a potbelly, as Sweeney had claimed in his testimony.

She also testified that Hill would call her house occasionally and ask her about recipes, though she said Hill "seemed like he was interested in cooking, [but] maybe he was more interested in eating." She also said Hill never called her son "Paulie," but instead called him by his nicknames, "Maze," or "Kojak." This appeared to contradict Sweeney's testimony about Hill referring to Mazzei as "Paulie" at the Logan Airport Hilton meeting.

"Do you love your son?" McDonald asked her.

"Yes," Florence Mazzei replied.

"Would you perjure yourself for the love of your son?" Sharon said in answer to McDonald's question.

"No, I wouldn't," she said.

That closed Mazzei's defense . . . or so it seemed. McDonald, demonstrating the tenacity for which he was known, tracked down the U.S. deputy marshal at the courthouse who had processed Mazzei at the time of his drug arrest earlier in 1981. The marshal, Michael Hollander, produced a photograph of Mazzei taken against a height board. He also testified that

Mazzei had told him he was 5-foot-8. Sharon was unable to shake Hollander's testimony, though he tried to point out that in the photograph it might have been Mazzei's "wisps of hair" that were between five-seven and five-eight.

McDonald offered the photo into evidence, and then announced that the government rested its case. The defense lawyers followed suit in alphabetical order—Coiro, O'Malley, Sharon, and Zimmerman—and Bramwell declared, "The case is over."

The defense attorneys moved for acquittal based on the grounds that the government had failed to prove its case beyond a reasonable doubt, which Bramwell denied. Then, with the jury excused, the lawyers met with Bramwell to go over the charges he would read to the jury after final summations. When the subject of charts came up, Coiro again became animated. When McDonald asked if the defense planned to use any charts, Coiro replied, "I intend to use thirteen of them, as big as yours . . . the same colors and background as yours, with pink for Henry Hill."

"Don't be surprised if he doesn't show up with them," Bramwell added.

McDonald requested that the jury be sequestered during deliberations, but Bramwell demurred. "I go for seven, eight days, and everybody shows up the next day, and I sleep every night," the judge said. "Some judges can't send a jury home after five, six days and wondering if you are going to have twelve the next day."

"I think it shows a lot of confidence in the jury, Judge, when you do something like that," Coiro said. "I think it does, and I think the jurors are a lot more comfortable being at home."

"I know they are," Bramwell agreed. "No question. Anybody is."

"Especially those of us from Pittsburgh," Zimmerman added, ending the proceedings.

It was Tuesday, November 17—three weeks since Ed McDonald stood in front of the courtroom and, in his opening statement, characterized the defendants as bumblers who had fallen victim to "greed, corruption, disloyalty, and carelessness." Now it was up to the twelve men and women in the jury box who had sat silently through all the sidebars, snide remarks, and shouting matches for those three weeks, to cut through the rhetoric and render a verdict. It would not come easily.

CHAPTER FIFTEEN

End of the Line

The prosecution has a built-in advantage at the end of any criminal trial simply because it has the last word. The lead prosecutor makes his closing argument first, followed by the defense. But the prosecution then is allowed a rebuttal summation to counter the charges made by the defense in its summation. This seeming disparity arises out of the fact that it is the prosecution's burden to prove the facts, while the defense is given latitude throughout to poke holes in the case and engage in general obfuscation.

For the jurors in *U.S. v. Burke*, this meant that after nearly four weeks of testimony they would have to sit still for a total of six more summations. It also meant that the last words they would hear from any of the attorneys would be McDonald's. And he would be summarizing a case that appeared to contain an overwhelming amount of evidence against the five defendants.

When McDonald stepped to the podium on Wednesday morning, November 18, 1981, he took the customary tack of thanking the jurors for their attention during the trial and giving a brief description of the charges on which they would be deliberating. He then went through the government's version of the chronology of the scheme, pausing along the way to remind the jury that the case did not hinge solely on the say-so of Henry Hill.

"You have much more than Henry Hill to prove it. And much more to prove that Henry Hill was telling the truth," he reassured the jury, citing Rick Kuhn's confession, as well as the testimonies of Jim Sweeney and Barbara Reed. Common sense, too, confirmed Hill, McDonald said; it followed that the Perlas would need the help of big-time bookmakers in New York, and that they would have to go past Hill and get to Burke to help them realize the scheme.

To establish the connection between Hill, Burke, and the rest of the defendants, McDonald went over the telephone calls from the Burke home to various bookies, Paul Mazzei's two trips to New York, the meeting at

Robert's Lounge, the trip to Boston, and the meeting at the Logan Airport Hilton.

Burke was the man from New York, McDonald said. "Nothing was ever said about inside information. It was point-shaving for money. That was the only thing discussed."

The calls between Hill and Burke from the Logan Airport Hilton in Boston on the night of the meeting with Kuhn and Sweeney, as well as the morning after, proved Burke's involvement, McDonald contended. "Why else would (Hill) be calling Burke's number at 12:24 in the morning?" he asked rhetorically. "Do you make phone calls at 12:24 in the morning? Do you think he wanted to tell Burke about how nice the weather was in Boston at 12:24 in the morning? . . . Do you think Hill is the kind of person who gets up at 8:14 in the morning when he is in another city and staying up all night?"

He contemptuously characterized Kuhn coming up with the infamous line to Barbara Reed, "as if some sort of poet," telling her that "we are not trying to lose the games, we are only winning in smaller ways." He repeated the phrase for emphasis. "Winning in smaller ways. That is exactly what point-shaving is, ladies and gentlemen: winning in smaller ways."

McDonald reeled off the games that allegedly had been fixed—Rhode Island, Fordham, St. John's, Holy Cross—and reminded the jury about the wire transfers from Pittsburgh to Boston made by Rocco Perla during that time frame. He summoned up Kuhn's comment before the Holy Cross game to Reed: "If we win, we win, and if we lose, we win," and recounted Reed's testimony about calling Tony Perla in Las Vegas, and phone records of calls made by James Burke to the MGM Grand, where Perla was staying.

"I suppose Mr. Burke just happened to have another friend out in Las Vegas that day, or maybe somebody else in his household did," McDonald said sarcastically.

After the jury was given a short recess, McDonald attempted to place Hill as just one witness of many who could corroborate the government's theory. There was Sweeney, who had no motive for lying, the prosecutor said, since Rick Kuhn was his friend. "He had no axe to grind with Rick Kuhn. . . . Why would he want to get involved as a witness in this case?" conveniently forgetting to mention that Sweeney had admitted taking money and agreeing to shave points.

Similarly, why would Barbara Reed come into court and "expose her past, expose herself, subject herself to cross-examination just to get back at Mr. Kuhn and some of the other people a year and a half later?" Joe Beaulieu, too, had no reason to lie about being approached by Kuhn during their night of partying before the Harvard game.

But what really damaged Kuhn, McDonald implied, was Zimmerman's promise of a surprise that never materialized.

"You know, in his opening statement, Mr. Zimmerman told you that he did have an explanation for Mr. Kuhn's confession," McDonald said.

"He told you you're entitled to a little suspense, a little surprise. You are going to get it at the end of the case. Well, I'm waiting. I'm asking Mr. Zimmerman to end the suspense and explain away Rick Kuhn's confession. I submit to you that he can't do it. There is no explanation for what Rick Kuhn said other than guilt."

As for the other defendants, McDonald went on, Mazzei's guilt was established by Hill's and Sweeney's testimony, and by hotel records that placed him in New York for the November 4 meeting with Hill, and phone records that showed Burke calling Mazzei's parents' house in Pittsburgh. On the question of Mazzei's height that had caused so much debate near the end of the trial, McDonald quipped, "I submit to you that you have also seen the Pittsburgh style in the courtroom, big guys and little guys wearing cowboy boots," a not-so-veiled reference to the tallish Sharon and the shorter Zimmerman.

Sharon immediately objected.

"You can't make it personal," Bramwell chided McDonald.

"He can, it's for me," Zimmerman chimed in.

McDonald resumed the assault when the jurors returned from lunch. Tony Perla had confessed to Christine Siano in February after the *Sports Illustrated* came out, he said, and was tied to the scheme by testimony from Hill, Reed, and Sweeney. Rocco Perla's guilt was established by Reed, who "incriminates Rocco right down the line. She puts him right in the middle of the conspiracy," and by the handwriting analysis of the Western Union money-order receipts.

The prosecutor returned to Burke, who had the most tenuous connection to the scheme of any of the defendants. After positing that since Hill had been corroborated so thoroughly with respect to all the other defendants that it was hard to imagine he could have been wrong about Burke, McDonald described Burke as "like Henry Ford . . . he doesn't do the dirty work, he doesn't go into the factories to make the cars. . . . Henry Ford would speak with the chairman of the board and directors of other companies and discuss important deals with them; likewise, Jimmy Burke would meet with the chairman of the board and director of the Pittsburgh connection, Tony Perla and Paul Mazzei. He wouldn't meet with the people who could get him into trouble."

Meanwhile, as McDonald read off a list of phone calls from Burke's house to other members of the conspiracy, Coiro was lying in wait. When he sensed an opportunity, he stood up and objected and moved for the withdrawal of a juror and a mistrial, on the grounds that McDonald was disobeying Bramwell's earlier ruling about assuming which person had answered the phone at the various numbers Burke had called.

"Mr. McDonald's conduct is clearly prosecutorial misconduct," Coiro charged, "when he stood here and, knowing full well when he said a phone call from James Burke to John Savino. . . . I let him do it three or four times and I made sure that he did it enough times to louse himself up. . . ."

"I don't agree with you," Bramwell said and denied the motion.

Sharon then entered the fray and asked for a mistrial based on McDonald's "cowboy boots" comment, which he claimed was prejudicial because an attorney is not allowed to "personalize the defendant through his attorney." Zimmerman and O'Malley joined both Coiro's and Sharon's motions, which were, predictably, denied.

By the time McDonald finished, he had been talking for nearly three hours. If the case had ended right then, it would have been a slam-dunk for the prosecution; such is the power of a skillful summation.

Now, though, it was the defense's turn at bat, and the four lawyers were itching to take their cuts at McDonald's version of the case.

• • •

The defense attorneys had changed the order they had used throughout the trial, so it was O'Malley who took the podium after McDonald. Coiro's histrionics would be saved for last.

"I am a firm believer of the old adage that a human being can only absorb so much," O'Malley told the jury. "I will restrain myself to those items which pertain particularly to the Perlas. But of course, that might be somewhat difficult."

After spending what seemed like a long time going over the law, particularly on the difference between reasonable doubt and a preponderance of evidence, O'Malley raised several questions about the government's witnesses. If Hill was saying on one hand that Ernie Cobb was not involved until the final five games of the scheme—using the list of nine games from the *Sports Illustrated* article—what about the first four games, which included Providence, Harvard, and UCLA, which the government now was alleging were fixed? And, if Hill was confused over whether the gamblers won or lost money on the St. John's game, how could he be sure that the Holy Cross game was fixed because the gamblers wanted to make up their alleged losses?

O'Malley saved some of his barbs for Sweeney, and asked what seemed a logical question: If Sweeney supposedly was so afraid of the gamblers, how did he suddenly get the courage to double-cross them during the season?

"'Just his demeanor tells you Jim Sweeney is telling the truth,'" he said, repeating McDonald's words. "Well, Jim Sweeney admitted, the All-American Jim Sweeney admitted, 'Yes, I deceived my coach about being approached by gamblers.' He also deceived his cohorts and later lied to the FBI. If he's not even going to be honest with himself, and deceive his coach and the people he's dealing with, then the All-American façade starts to crumble a little, [and] a little of the glitter comes off the man . . . it seems to me that is a lot of deception for being an All-American."

The defense attorney then described Hill as if he were describing a wild animal in captivity for the first time.

"Henry Hill is the kind of person that I suspect not one of you ladies and gentlemen have ever met before. I know I have not. I know I've read about and studied about the kind of person Henry Hill is, but I've never seen one in the flesh before.

"Henry Hill is an amoral person. . . . An amoral person doesn't recognize guidelines. He doesn't recognize standards. He doesn't recognize sin. . . . He doesn't care about anyone else in the entire world except himself. He cares only for self-gratification. . . . [This] is important because the government's case is built around Henry Hill."

Barbara Reed's and Jim Sweeney's testimony should be scrutinized as well, O'Malley cautioned the jury. Reed testified that Rick Kuhn and Rocco Perla were close friends, and it would have been normal for Rocco to travel to Boston to visit Rick; she also said he told her that he was giving inside information to the gamblers.

Sweeney, meanwhile, claimed that he had met with Rocco and Rick early in the evening on the night before the Fordham game, O'Malley pointed out, when hotel records showed that Rocco and his girlfriend had not checked in at the hotel until close to midnight, and allegedly had gone straight to the hotel from the airport.

O'Malley finished by recalling the testimonies of witnesses who had spoken of the value of inside information, and questioned why Tony Perla would need to fix games when he belonged to the handicapping service run by Eddie Medo. He also noted that no one had testified about any Boston College games being taken off the board during the 1978–79 season because of point-spread fluctuations.

• • •

Despite his run-ins with Bramwell throughout the case, Sharon had proved himself to be the most erudite of the attorneys in Courtroom 9 over the past four weeks, and his summation held true to form.

"My name is Lenny Sharon, and as you know, I represent Paul Mazzei," he began. "As Mr. McDonald told you, my practice is in Pittsburgh, Pennsylvania. That's where I'm from, and I want to thank you for your hospitality, and the hospitality of the court. Other than getting my wallet pickpocketed at Madison Square Garden during a Knickerbocker game, it really hasn't been a bad stay here," he said, and added some humor by mentioning, "but, all I had in there were three dozen Boston College schedules, like Jim Sweeney."

Sharon proceeded to give a brief history lesson, evoking the English "star chamber" to demonstrate how an indictment in itself does not mean anything, and he explained the difference between a preponderance of evidence and reasonable doubt by having the jury visualize the scales of justice.

"Henry Hill's testimony alone would be like putting a grain of sand on these heavy scales," he said, then impugned Hill's testimony by using an analogy of a house buyer who finds out that the seller has lied about the age of the house, the wiring, the plumbing, and other features. "Would you move your family into a house that Henry Hill built?" he asked the jury.

Sharon described the many inconsistencies in Hill's various statements and testimony, and implied that between Hill's first statement to the FBI in the summer of 1980 and his next interview on the subject eleven months later, the government had started from the assumption that Mazzei and the others were guilty and had tailored bits and pieces of testimony to that end.

"You have heard it referred to as a 'search for the truth,'" he said. "Hill couldn't search for the truth if it jumped off the ground and bit him on the nose."

Sharon turned around McDonald's "common sense" argument and questioned why, after the Harvard game, Mazzei would need to fly to New York to pick up money from Richard Perry and take it personally back to Pittsburgh, then give it to Rocco Perla and have Perla wire it to Kuhn. "We have to get him in," Sharon said. "We've got to get the organized syndicate together. We always have to have everybody doing everything."

McDonald's comments about "Pittsburgh style" also came in for ridicule, focusing on the Logan Airport Hilton meeting where there was no solid evidence that Mazzei was there, beyond a shaky identification by Sweeney that the government was trying to make fit by saying Mazzei might have seemed taller because he was wearing cowboy boots.

"You can infer, because it is a Pittsburgh style and because I wear cowboy boots, that Mr. Mazzei must wear cowboy boots?" Sharon said. "Come on.

"Check the registration," he continued. "There are four people registered for those two rooms. Where do the documents show that there is a fifth person? Maybe Mr. Perla slept on the floor—as is the Pittsburgh style. . . . When we cut the pieces so four people checking into a hotel become five, are we corroborating or searching for the truth, or are we straining or groping at straws?"

There was no evidence, he continued, that placed Mazzei at the Rockville Centre Holiday Inn on November 4, 1978, or at the Sunrise Motor Lodge or Logan Airport Hilton on November 15 and 16; and, by the way, the names Mazzei was alleged to have used as aliases—"Musca" and "Thompson"—were the names of real people "who do exist, and have the ability to travel."

In addition, Hill had said nothing to the FBI or grand jury about Mazzei being at the November 4 meeting with Hill and Burke at Robert's Lounge, but now was claiming Mazzei was there. Sweeney could not identify Mazzei from pictures the FBI showed him and made no mention of Mazzei in his FBI statement. "And this is a Rhodes Scholar candidate here, a sports leader, a creative writer," Sharon characterized Sweeney. "An executive in a high-level job. This is not a run-of-the-mill idiot who can't describe people."

Sharon focused on the fact that Sweeney, whom he said "even looks like Beaver Cleaver from the TV show," had told the grand jury that he came out of the locker room at Boston Garden after the Harvard game and saw "Hill and a guy I didn't know," but was now saying that the man he saw with Hill was Mazzei.

After a short recess, Sharon lit into McDonald's phone evidence. Instead of Mazzei posing as his friend Tom Musca and making an eleven-minute call to his parents from the Rockville Centre Holiday Inn on November 4, could it not have been the actual Musca, whom Hill admitted to knowing, calling Mazzei in Pittsburgh at his parents'? And where, Sharon wondered, were the records of calls between Hill and Mazzei in the weeks leading up to the Providence and Harvard games, the first two games in the scheme? And how convenient for the government that Hill had called in his bets on the Harvard game from a pay phone in the lobby of the Boston Sheraton instead of his room, so they could not be checked against the hotel's phone records.

Turning the tables on the government's theory, Sharon wondered aloud, "Do these documents corroborate Henry Hill, or does Henry Hill corroborate these documents?"

Much evidence was absent, too. For instance, there were no betting slips or receipts from Tony Perla's alleged trip to Las Vegas to make a big score on the Holy Cross game. And there was not one phone call on McDonald's lists from the Burke residence to any of the syndicate of bookies on the day of any of the games in question.

"How were these games bet? By carrier pigeon?" Sharon asked.

In closing, Sharon urged the jury not to be swayed by the fact that Mazzei didn't testify, or that the government presented more witnesses than the defense.

"It is not like Boston College games where we are trying to shave witnesses," he said. "The government . . . must produce enough evidence to tip that scale of justice far enough to convince you beyond a reasonable doubt that Mr. Mazzei is guilty. This they have failed to do.

"Henry Hill has gained enough from ill-gotten benefits from the government without his getting more than enough, without allowing his testimony and this evidence to remove Mr. Mazzei's cloak of innocence and remove him from his living."

• • •

It was Zimmerman's turn next, and his challenge was a tall one. Despite the charge that Bramwell would give them about not looking askance at a defendant's decision not to testify, the jury would remember that his client, Kuhn, had not taken the stand in his own defense. They also would remember that in his opening statement Zimmerman had promised the jury a surprise regarding Kuhn's statement to FBI agents but had not produced one, as McDonald had already been nice enough to point out during his summation.

But the crafty defense attorney had a few tricks up his sleeve. Unlike his colleagues, he spent very little of his summation attacking Hill's credibility, and instead Zimmerman focused on Jim Sweeney and Barbara Reed—witnesses who, Zimmerman contended, contradicted each other and thereby cast doubt on the charges against Kuhn.

"I submit, ladies and gentlemen, that if you believe fully what every witness has said, that it would be absolutely, entirely impossible for you to reach a verdict of guilty for Mr. Kuhn," he boldly stated.

Sweeney's primary contention was that he had taken money but not shaved points, Zimmerman said. But Reed testified that she overheard Kuhn and Sweeney the night before the Fordham game in February 1979 talking about mistakes they had made during games. "How can you reconcile [these] two opposite statements that the government is asking you to believe?" he asked. "Which one are you going to disregard?"

Then there was Reed's testimony that Kuhn told her he was giving inside information to the gamblers in exchange for money. Later, she claimed he said he was "trying to win in smaller ways." Which one was the truth?

If Rick Kuhn gave inside information, he may not be a nice guy, Zimmerman said, but he was not guilty of a crime, and Reed's testimony that Kuhn made a bet on the Holy Cross game and that he threatened her near the end of the season were designed only to prejudice the jury.

There also were problems with the testimony that was supposed to support Hill's contentions. Jim Sweeney "admitted he was a liar" when he was first interviewed by the FBI, and his account was contradicted by Reed anyway.

"What is the truth about Jim Sweeney?" Zimmerman asked. "He gives you the impression of being the All-American boy, the kid next door, apple pie and all that. . . . Sweeney is here to help you believe Hill, but Hill said Sweeney did it but Sweeney said, 'No, I didn't do that.' . . . We hear Mr. Hill saying Mr. Sweeney is not telling you the truth. And Mr. Sweeney saying Mr. Hill is not telling you the truth. And Barbara Reed is saying Sweeney is not telling the truth. What do we have? How can you put it together?"

Joe Beaulieu's testimony, too, had to be viewed with skepticism, according to Zimmerman; after all, like Sweeney, Beaulieu had lied to the FBI when first interviewed, and admitted using drugs and alcohol for several hours on the night he said Kuhn approached him about shaving points.

"Ladies and gentlemen," Zimmerman summed up, "we have in essence, three liars trying to corroborate a fourth."

As for Kuhn's alleged confession, Zimmerman revisited the issues that he had focused on during his cross-examination of FBI agent James Byron: specifically, that even though Kuhn had not been "locked in a room for hours," the circumstances of the interview were designed to intimidate him.

In addition, why were only three games written up in Byron's report if the FBI agents had information on eight games that allegedly were fixed?

Where was the big admission Kuhn was supposed to have made? And, if no tape recorder was used and no notes of the interview were produced during the trial, how reliable could Byron's account be? After all, Reed had testified that the FBI's report of her own interview omitted some information.

"When you put a twenty-two-year-old kid in shorts in an FBI car at 6:30 in the morning, you have not only coercion, but evidence coming from the stand from the agent who was going to tell you about this big admission that, 'I don't know if it's right or not, it's what's said on the report,'" Zimmerman said.

One of three things could have happened during Kuhn's interview, Zimmerman suggested: one, the statement Kuhn made was not what was on the FBI report; two, the entire report was made up; or, three, Kuhn may have said it, but done so involuntarily.

The summation concluded with Zimmerman equating the government's case against Rick Kuhn with a story about a boy throwing horse manure around a room because "there's got to be a horse in here somewhere."

● ● ●

With that analogy still fresh in their minds, the jurors were excused for lunch. When they came back at about 2 P.M., Coiro was waiting with what promised to be the defense team's coup de grâce.

Alternately blustery and self-deprecating, Coiro did not disappoint. From the beginning of his summation, when he told the jurors that in the American justice system they were "as close to God as you can get," until his conclusion, he summoned up various colorful images to convey his points.

He began by painting Henry Hill as a shiftless, immoral, bald-faced opportunist who was offering up James Burke to the government in return for his freedom, and implied that Hill, not Burke, was the infamous "man from New York" referred to in Barbara Reed's testimony.

"I welcome you to the production of 'The Man from New York,' alias 'The Boss,'" Coiro said. "Authored, directed, produced, and starred in by Henry Hill. With the choreography by McDonald. That's just what it is, making a movie of the system. When Frank Sinatra stars in a production, as I told you in my opening, he wants a salary. He wants good accommodations, good acoustics, good equipment. When Henry Hill produces a production, he wants money, he wants liberty, and he wants a right to keep making more money. That's Henry Hill."

Coiro then questioned Burke's connection to the alleged scheme, since hardly anyone who testified had mentioned him. Jim Sweeney never mentioned him. Barbara Reed never mentioned him. Kuhn never mentioned James Burke's name to Reed. Hill, it seemed, was the only one who tied Burke to the scheme, and even he never mentioned Burke in connection with the case in his 1980 FBI statement or during his grand jury testimony in June 1981.

"An inference on an inference, that's what the government's case is against James Burke," Coiro said.

The phone calls from the Burke residence also were suspect, Coiro contended. Joseph Razzano had testified that he, not Burke, made the call to Henry Hill at the Logan Airport Hilton on the morning after the meeting with the players, and Coiro pointed out that during his cross-examination McDonald never asked Razzano why he had made the call. Similarly, a call from bookmaker Martin Krugman to Burke's house on December 16, 1978—the day of the Harvard game—had been offered by the prosecution as evidence of Burke's involvement, yet Hill had testified that Burke was in Florida on that day.

"Ladies and gentlemen, the way that the government wants you to infer that every call from the Burke house is of a sinister nature, I am going to ask you to give it an innocent connotation," Coiro said. "James Burke was a gambler. Is that so terrible?"

Using McDonald's "common sense" argument, Coiro asked: Why would Burke just hand over five thousand dollars to give to the players for fixing the Harvard game when they had blown their first assignment by covering the point spread against Providence?

This set the stage for the grand finale. Referring to the charts he had introduced that detailed Hill's lengthy list of crimes, Coiro delivered his final attack on the government's star witness. It was a bravura performance even by his lofty standards:

"I would like you to picture . . . all of those crimes painted on a boulder that would cover this entire area, a rock, with all those crimes and everything listed on it, and out from underneath that rock comes the most vicious, slimy viper you ever saw in your entire life. A viper that deals in narcotics, that robs, steals, cheats, swindles, and crawls out to be let loose in a community to destroy our community and children."

Then, in a move that would have seemed bizarre at most other trials but somehow didn't seem much out of place here, Coiro ended by reciting the Ten Commandments one by one, and enumerating how Hill had violated each one of them:

"Thou shalt not commit adultery—with him, it's a question of how many and how much," Coiro sneered.

"Thou shalt not covet thy neighbor's wife. If I ever lived next door to Henry Hill, I'd build a fence one hundred feet high, made of steel."

"Thou shalt not covet thy neighbor's goods. I think if you had a dog, he'd steal the dog."

It went on until Coiro got to number eight, "bearing false witness against thy neighbor." He paused.

"He is going to use you and you and you," he said, pointing to the jurors individually. "He's going to use the twelve of you, because if you walk into this courtroom and put the stamp of approval on his testimony, then he will have violated that commandment, and not only that, you will have stamped with approval that act."

When Coiro finished, the jury was given a ten-minute recess before the prosecution's rebuttal summation.

• • •

Ed McDonald had sat at the prosecution table over the last two days and listened as the four defense attorneys tried to make the jury believe that understanding the nuances of a conspiracy case was like doing advanced calculus. He had also heard them attack his case and his evidence, and particularly his reliance on Henry Hill, who by now had been flown safely back to an undisclosed location in the Midwest but whose name was still being dragged through the mud every day in U.S. District Court.

There were plenty of charges to answer, and McDonald was ready to address them, one by one. It was 4:19 P.M. when the jury reentered the courtroom.

McDonald began by talking about the law. Listening to the defense summations was like being in law school again, he said, with all the talk about the responsibility of the jury and the difficulty of trying a conspiracy case. The problem was, he reminded the jury, the law was the province of Judge Bramwell and not the defense attorneys.

The conspiracy charges, he continued, really were very simple. All the prosecution had to do was show that the defendants agreed to do something illegal. That was it. They did not even have to be successful in doing what they set out to do.

Turning to Hill, McDonald charged the defense with trying to deflect attention from their clients by attacking him—and, by extension, McDonald. "Listening to Mr. Coiro, I thought I had become a codefendant in this case," he said. "I am not on trial, either. Those five people sitting over there are the ones who are on trial," he added, motioning to the defense table. Besides, he added, Hill had more motivation to tell the truth because of his deal with the government.

"You don't go out and audition witnesses," he went on. "You take them as you find them, and in this case you find the Henry Hills of the world, and you have to make deals with them or otherwise these cases can't be made."

Then, in a shrewd move, McDonald turned the defense's strategy back on itself.

"Their argument, in effect, is a double-edged sword," he said. "By attacking Henry Hill and showing him to be a criminal, they add to our proof that Henry Hill is just the type of person who would be involved in fixing college basketball games. . . . They painted him with too broad a brush. By painting Henry Hill, they painted themselves. . . . By attacking Henry Hill, they add the ring of truth to his testimony."

In other words, if Hill was such a lowlife and criminal, what was Burke doing welcoming him into his house? What were Tony Perla, Paul Mazzei, and Rocco Perla doing with Hill in Boston? Why was Rick Kuhn giving Hill his phone number and meeting with him at Boston Garden after the Harvard game?

The inconsistencies between Hill's statements in the *Sports Illustrated* article and his testimony could be explained, McDonald claimed, by the fact that Hill had not been debriefed on the details of the case when he talked to Looney. So, in fact, his memory actually was better in late 1981 than it had been in February. Besides, did it matter who actually circled the games on the schedule at the Logan Airport Hilton meeting? Did it matter how Rick Kuhn got the money after the Harvard game, or merely that he got it?

McDonald used a similar thread of logic with Sweeney's testimony. If Sweeney was, indeed, a liar as the defense charged, then that only proved that there actually had been a point-shaving scheme and that he had taken part in it. "By arguing that he lied to you, I submit that [the defense] disproved their inside-information defense," he said.

Kuhn's inside-information defense "is a defense that has been fashioned out of desperation. I submit to you it is an explanation that insults your intelligence," he said. It was clear since the day that Kuhn approached the team's most important players—Sweeney, Cobb, and Beaulieu—that the scheme was about point-shaving. And, lest anyone on the jury feel too much sympathy for Kuhn, McDonald reminded them of the testimony about how Kuhn was "double-dealing," taking Sweeney's money and sticking it in his own pocket.

McDonald then took a page out of Coiro's book of imagery.

"I submit to you, ladies and gentlemen, Rick Kuhn is the Judas of Boston College basketball," he said. "He sold himself and his school right down the drain for some cocaine, some quaaludes, and a few thousand dollars. There is no doubt about his guilt.

"I ask you on behalf of the federal government to find the defendants, James Burke, Tony Perla, Rocco Perla, Paul Mazzei, and Richard Kuhn, guilty. Thank you."

McDonald sat down, and Bramwell made a short statement to the jury and asked them to report for their charge the next morning at 9:30, then dismissed them. It was 5:51 P.M. on Thursday, November 19, 1981—almost three years to the day since Jim Sweeney took a fateful ride with his friend Rick Kuhn to the Logan Airport Hilton in Boston one night after basketball practice.

• • •

When court convened on Friday morning, Bramwell spent the first two hours giving the charge in the case, in which he reviewed the counts in the indictment and the points of law that the jury would need to consider during its deliberations. Much of the charge covered basics tenets of criminal law: the difference between direct and circumstantial evidence; the role of accomplice or informant testimony; and definitions of "presumption of innocence," "burden of proof," and "reasonable doubt." Some of it dealt with specific issues raised by the defense after McDonald's rebuttal; for example, Bramwell instructed the jury that the defendants were not obligated to come forth with exculpatory evidence, something he claimed McDonald had implied in his summation.

Bramwell also went over the three counts mentioned in the indictment, paying particularly close attention to the definition of conspiracy: "a combination of two or more persons, by concerted action, to accomplish some unlawful purpose, or to accomplish some lawful purpose by unlawful means." He told the jury how a person can be a member of a conspiracy without having full knowledge of its details, and how a person's mere presence at the scene of a crime or knowledge that a crime is being committed are not sufficient to establish that the person aided and abetted the crime.

The rest of the morning was spent putting into evidence such exhibits as telephone slips from the Colonnade Hotel in Boston, where Rocco Perla was alleged to have stayed with his girlfriend on the weekend of the Fordham game; a registration card from the Rockville Centre Holiday Inn, where Paul Mazzei, allegedly posing as "Musca," had stayed when he first met with Jimmy Burke about the scheme in November 1978; and various sales receipts from stores where Rick Kuhn had bought items in the winter of 1979.

Bramwell excused the jury to begin its deliberations at 1:15, but the jurors were back in the courtroom at a little before 4:00 to have the last portion of Bramwell's charge reread to them—a section that covered, among other points, the nature of immunity agreements for government witnesses. The jury left again, but within ten minutes had returned to the courtroom and asked to have the entire testimony of Jim Sweeney and Barbara Reed read back, as well as the testimony of Gerald O'Connor and Edgar Turner, the two phone company representatives. With Friday's session nearly over and Sweeney's and Reed's testimony alone consisting of more than 350 pages of the trial transcript, the bulk of the session spilled over and took up most of Saturday.

With each successive request by the jury, the Perlas, Mazzei, and Kuhn clung to what little hope presented itself.

"When the jury went out, we actually felt there was no chance," Rocco Perla remembers thinking. "We thought they were leaning toward a conviction, because of the way the closing arguments went, and because the prosecuting attorney gets to go last and he gets to recap and keep everything fresh in their minds.

"For some reason, it took a couple of days. . . . [The jury] sent back notes that picked up strange, small things. And that kind of gave us a false sense of hope. Like, they asked for rereads of testimony about things that seemed to us unrelated to the case, like the car somebody had driven, or guns that somebody had sold, and so on. And so for some reason we thought, 'Maybe somebody's picking up on something.'"

During the deliberations, the defense team was rocked by news unrelated to the trial. Gary Zimmerman's father, who had been in the hospital with a heart condition but had seemed to be in stable condition, passed away, forcing Zimmerman to go back to Pittsburgh and miss the reading of the verdict.

By late afternoon on Monday, November 23, the jury had been deliberating more than twenty hours. As 5 P.M. approached, it looked as though court would be adjourned until Tuesday—especially since the jury had just asked Bramwell for yet another rereading of his charge, this time the part that defined conspiracy to commit sports bribery and what was required to return a guilty verdict.

But within twenty minutes, they filed back into the courtroom.

At 5:25 P.M., jury forewoman Jane Klimpel announced: "We have reached a verdict."

Before she had a chance to read it, Paul Mazzei knew his worst fears were about to be realized. Unlike the Perlas and Kuhn, he had been through several trials, and he had spotted something when Klimpel and the rest of the jury came back in.

"It's over. It's no good," he murmured to the Perlas. "She has no paper."

"What are you talking about?" they asked.

"She's not reading any paper, she couldn't possibly read some people innocent and some people guilty on all those counts without a paper," Mazzei said. It was either all guilty or all innocent, and no one was giving the latter much chance.

Mazzei did not need anyone shaving points to pick this one right. Klimpel read the verdict: all defendants guilty on all counts.

Kuhn, who had sat staring at the jury box with his hands folded together when the jury came into the room, looked dazed and pale. His father, Fred, who had been attending the trial since the beginning of summations the week before, held back tears in the spectators' gallery. The Perlas and Mazzei, the buddies whose small-time scheme had blown up into a national scandal, stared straight ahead as their relatives wept or held their hands over their faces.

Leonard Sharon sat slumped at the defense table, his head in his hands. Michael Coiro told reporters he would appeal, no question. Judge Bramwell announced that sentencing would be deferred until January.

Later that day, Boston College released a statement that said, in part, "The entire Boston College community is saddened by the fact that one of our former student basketball players has been found guilty of the serious charges of which he has been accused. The verdict returned against Richard Kuhn, for his actions during the 1978–79 season, is indeed grave. . . .

"Boston College's tradition in athletics rests upon the accomplishments of many thousands of men and women. We trust that this incident will not be allowed to detract from that tradition. For this university, this episode provides incentive to redouble vigilance in pursuing the ideals of that tradition."

• • •

If the defendants in *U.S. v. Burke* felt the cards were stacked against them during the trial, they were in for a rude awakening when it came time for Bramwell to hand down their sentences. Before sentencing guidelines were adopted in 1987 that effectively removed much of the judge's discretion from the process, every unsavory detail of a defendant's background that was kept out of a trial was allowed into play at the sentencing hearing. For James Burke, Paul Mazzei, and Tony Perla, this was not good news, particularly for Burke, whose proven and reputed criminal acts and associations went back three decades.

Freed from the constraints of a criminal trial, government prosecutor Ed McDonald could thus stand in front of Judge Bramwell and say that Burke was "an upper-echelon figure in organized crime circles in New York and has been involved in serious criminal activity for the last thirty years" without introducing any direct evidence.

What McDonald did introduce was the testimony of New York City Detective Kenneth McCabe and Organized Crime Strike Force Detective Douglas Le Vien, both of whom cited numerous informants who had detailed Burke's assorted extralegal activities. Yet as Coiro rightly noted, there was no explanation of how the informants' information had been verified, and there was the small detail that none of the information cited had led to any arrests of Burke.

Tony Perla's unsavory reputation preceded him as well. At a hearing five days before Burke's on January 14, Henry Hill testified that the former school librarian was a "heavy narcotics dealer" who made drug deals in the basement of his house while his wife and kids were upstairs. FBI agent Edmundo Guevara testified about Perla's alleged connections with several well-known Pittsburgh bookmakers. Former Boston College center Joe Beaulieu testified that Rick Kuhn had approached him to see if he wanted to get involved in selling drugs in the Boston area on behalf of Tony Perla.

"I told him I was too public a figure, you know, being 6-foot-9 doesn't help a lot," Beaulieu told the court. "I was well known in the city of Boston. I was controversial because I transferred out of Harvard, and a lot of people thought I was crazy."

On January 22, three days after Burke's hearing, Bramwell pronounced sentence on Burke and the two Perlas. He prefaced his announcement by reading a list of questions he had drawn up. Among them was, "Does the court have a responsibility to protect the integrity of sports?" His expression and tone gave the answer: yes, it does, and in this case it would.

Bramwell then gave Burke twenty years, the maximum penalty allowable, plus a thirty-thousand-dollar fine, and gave Tony Perla ten years and Rocco Perla four. For Rick Kuhn, already facing almost certain jail time, it was one more reason to worry as his own sentencing date drew near.

• • •

Kuhn's sentencing had been delayed twice since the beginning of the year, and now it was scheduled for February 5. The delay had been caused by Gary Zimmerman's strong reaction to a presentencing report presented by the U.S. Department of Justice's Probation Department that spoke of a "great cloud hanging over college basketball." Where Burke's criminal past had played a major role at his sentencing, it now sounded as though Kuhn, with no criminal record to speak of, was being blamed for the present and future ills of an entire sport.

"It is quite possible that the public will begin to wonder if a particular team lost a game because it played worse than its opponent or because a player, coach, or referee was reached by gamblers who stood to win large amounts of cash based on the outcome," the Justice Department statement read. "It may also generate public criticism and abuse toward a team based on the suspicion.

"It is unfortunate that the college athlete must now come under suspicion for an offense which was carried out by a small group of players, career criminals, and bookmakers."

Zimmerman correctly noted that the report was speculative, with no basis in fact. But he raised Bramwell's ire when he told the judge, "The public does not matter."

"That's ludicrous, Mr. Zimmerman," an angry Bramwell practically shouted. "That is the position a lot of people take—that the public, the victims, don't matter. You are wrong."

Having thus anointed himself the protector of college basketball, who would use his power to shield the sport from the menace posed by the Rick Kuhns of the world, Bramwell set the stage for the day Kuhn would finally be sentenced. Zimmerman already had been through enough trials to know a bad situation when he saw it, and he prepared his client for the possibility of a three- or five-year sentence.

That turned out to be optimistic.

Saying that, "[An] argument can be offered that a substantial term of incarceration imposed on this defendant will be recalled in the future by another college athlete who may be tempted to compromise his performance," on February 5, 1982, Bramwell sentenced Kuhn to ten years in prison, the stiffest punishment ever given a player in a point-shaving case. Even McDonald, who had compared Kuhn to Judas during his summation, seemed surprised.

Zimmerman tried in vain to get Bramwell to give Kuhn an alternative penalty such as public service.

"Unfortunately, I don't give alternative sentences," Bramwell glowered. "I don't believe in them."

The next day's newspapers ran a wire-service picture of an ashen-faced Kuhn, dressed in a corduroy three-piece suit and staring blankly ahead as he left the courthouse. Placing the Boston College case alongside several other recent examples of wrongdoing in college athletics, *Boston Globe* columnist Ray Fitzgerald wrote, "The grass has never been greener in college basketball, but under the slickness and the glitter flows a river of garbage, a sewer streaming through a sport that cannot seem to govern itself."

• • •

Already on a roll, Bramwell swung his axe at Mazzei in early May 1982, sentencing the three-time drug offender to ten years—five years each on the sports bribery and interstate travel charges—and ten years on the racketeering charge, all to be served concurrently and tacked on to his previous drug convictions. In doing so, Bramwell ignored an impassioned plea from Mazzei that detailed how drugs had destroyed his life.

"All my life, growing up, I wanted to be somebody and for the first twenty-eight years of my life I never had a record," Mazzei said at his sentencing hearing. "For the last eleven years I have been involved on and off with drugs, and drugs have caused me to become a criminal and drug dealer. I never dreamed that would happen."

As he would for most of the next fourteen years, James Burke kept a coterie of lawyers busy with various appeals and motions. Two days after Mazzei's sentencing, Gerald Shargel presented a motion for a new trial based on evidence that allegedly showed that Henry Hill had committed perjury in certain aspects of his testimony that pertained to Burke; specifically, that Burke was not at the meeting at Robert's Lounge on November 16, 1978, when the scheme came together. The source of this information was Tony Perla, whom Burke could not have called to testify at the trial because he was a codefendant. Kuhn, too, had filed an affidavit saying he had never received three thousand dollars from Henry Hill after the Harvard game—money that had allegedly come from Burke.

Bramwell denied the motion, saying that all the affidavits did was cast more doubt over "the testimony of a witness who was already shown to have a character of a highly questionable nature," another reference to Henry Hill. His decision was affirmed by the Second Circuit Court of Appeals in February 1983, three weeks after the same court upheld the original conviction of the five men.

As far as the public knew, the Boston College point-shaving scandal was dead and buried once Kuhn was sentenced in 1982, knocked off the sports pages by North Carolina's thrilling win over Georgetown to win the NCAA championship game. But as far as the government was concerned, this game was still in the third quarter.

CHAPTER SIXTEEN

Full-Court Press

From the disclosure of the point-shaving investigation at Boston College in early 1981 through the trial and sentencing of his teammate Rick Kuhn, Ernie Cobb was never far from the center of any discussions about the case, even if he had managed to keep his distance from the circus surrounding *U.S. v. Burke* and its aftermath. His only public utterance on the case was the prepared statement he read on NBC in January 1981, during halftime of the Notre Dame–Maryland game a week after the story broke.

Cobb had taken a trip to Israel with the Harlem Wizards in 1981, and he liked the country and its people enough to take a gamble the next summer and sign on with an Israeli team in Tel Aviv. He prospered there, leading the league in scoring in his first season at a pace of more than thirty points per game. By June 1983, he was back in the U.S. playing for the Wizards and had signed a more lucrative deal to play in Israel again.

Before he could cash in, though, he found himself back in the spotlight, and for all the wrong reasons.

"I had just gone to Israel, I had led the league in scoring and had signed a big-time contract, making big money, and all of a sudden I get to the States and I'm not allowed to leave the country because I'm facing these charges," Cobb remembers. "And after four years, I'm sitting in limbo."

Cobb had avoided indictment along with Kuhn and the others in 1981 because the government felt it did not have enough corroboration for Sweeney saying Cobb was involved in the scheme. The only other person who was not under indictment who could even faintly corroborate Sweeney was Henry Hill, and his knowledge of Cobb's role was based totally on what he had been told by his coconspirators.

Once the guilty verdicts were handed down in *U.S. v. Burke*, though, everyone began to line up against the high-scoring guard. Kuhn was handed a subpoena to appear before a grand jury on his way out of court in Brooklyn after his sentencing in February. In April, he and the two Perlas met

with Ed McDonald to discuss having their sentences reduced if they cooperated with the government's ongoing investigation. Paul Mazzei, who
already was providing information to Western Pennsylvania authorities
about gambling and extortion activities in Pittsburgh, also stepped up to
offer his services.

The result was that on June 23, 1983, more than four years after his last
game in a Boston College uniform, Ernie Cobb was indicted on charges of
taking bribes to fix the Harvard, Rhode Island, and Fordham games. He
faced a maximum five-year prison sentence and a ten-thousand-dollar fine.
Six days later he was arraigned in District Court in Brooklyn, the same
building where his former teammate Rick Kuhn had been sentenced to ten
years in prison a year and a half earlier. With his girlfriend, Laverne
Mosley, in attendance along with Stamford attorneys Franklin Melzer and
David Golub, a visibly shaken Cobb pleaded not guilty.

But it would be almost nine months until the case came to trial. There
were several reasons for this delay, the most obvious one being that Cobb
was steadfastly refusing to accept a plea bargain in exchange for admitting
to shaving points. He had taken (and passed) an independent polygraph
test, and had offered to take one administered by the FBI that McDonald
refused. Cobb eventually was offered a chance to plead guilty to making a
false statement to the FBI, for which he would receive probation, but he
turned it down.

Faced with Cobb's stubbornness, the government asked for a continu-
ance so it could add more defendants to the indictment. But the feds were
running out of time. The statute of limitations was set to expire after
November 16, which would be five years since the infamous meeting at
Boston's Logan Airport Hilton.

Something had to break, and it ended up being Tony Perla, who finally
succumbed to the government's pressure and, in late October 1983, gave
positive identifications of Peter Vario and Richard Perry as the men he had
met at Aqueduct Racetrack in New York on the afternoon of November 16,
1978.

Perla's statement—he had refused to identify pictures of Perry and
Vario until this point out of fear of reprisal, he later claimed—enabled the
government to add both men to Cobb's indictment. On November 15,
1983, with the statute of limitations about to run out on the case, FBI
agents and New York City police officers arrested Peter Vario. At Richard
Perry's Staten Island home, his wife refused to let the agents into the house
for an hour. When they finally got inside, they discovered Perry was gone.
He would not surface again until the following April, when he was appre-
hended crossing the border from Canada into Washington.

"Because they thought (Ernie) was going to plead out, they didn't think
there was even going to be a trial," David Golub, Cobb's lawyer, recalls.
"When he refused a plea bargain, they decided to indict more people on his
indictment, so that if they were going to have to do a trial they'd have
somebody that they were really interested in there. They went back to the

grand jury and added these two organized crime figures so that if they went to a trial, they'd have something more substantial than just a former college basketball player."

By the time the case came to trial in March 1984, Ernie Cobb was working as a substitute teacher in the Mount Vernon school district, making about forty dollars a day.

• • •

Jerry Bernstein felt "pretty cocky" when he was handed the task of prosecuting *U.S. v. Cobb* in early 1984. His confidence was well-founded: He had just won his third case in a row with Henry Hill as his star witness, and he was looking to improve his mark to 4–0.

Bernstein, a special prosecutor with the Organized Crime Strike Force since 1980, had won a conviction in Paul Mazzei's heroin trial in March 1981 in Hill's dry run as professional witness extraordinaire. In late 1983, he used Hill again to convict Philip Basile, a Long Island nightclub owner and music promoter, of providing Hill with a no-show job when Hill was paroled from Allenwood in the summer of 1978. Reputed Lucchese family capo Paul Vario was to have been a defendant in that trial, but a bizarre series of events wound up severing the case into two trials.

At one point, Bernstein convinced the judge to try Vario and Basile together, which required impaneling two juries for the same case that would sit in the same courtroom and hear testimony separately and together. But Vario's attorney, Joel Winograd, took ill after the first day of the trial, negating that unprecedented arrangement. After Basile's conviction in December, Bernstein got Vario convicted in early 1984 in a case in which Hill was his only witness.

By March 1984, a plea bargain again was offered to Cobb, and again he refused. Considering that the government had Rocco Perla, Tony Perla, Rick Kuhn, Henry Hill, and Paul Mazzei all set to testify that Cobb had agreed to shave points, it may have seemed a foolish choice. But there were serious problems with the government's case, as Bernstein would soon find out.

To begin with, Rocco Perla and Kuhn were the only ones who had had direct contact with Cobb. Tony Perla and Hill had never met him, and Mazzei's only conversation with him consisted of saying "Nice game," outside the locker room in Boston Garden after the Harvard Game. And Bernstein would have to convince the jury that these five convicted conspirators, who were coming forward in an effort to get their sentences reduced, really were telling the truth.

Plus, Cobb's "confession" to FBI agents John Bowe and Gary Kirby at the New Jersey Nets training camp in 1980 was not really a confession to shaving points, but a statement to the effect that he had taken money from Rocco Perla. More damaging to the prosecution, though, was the fact that the games Cobb mentioned in his FBI statement did not match the games on the indictment. He was being charged with sports bribery in the Harvard, Rhode Island, and Fordham games, but he had told Bowe and Kirby that he had been paid for the Bentley and Stonehill games, and that he had refused Rocco Perla's offer to shave points in a third game.

For once, it seemed, the government was starting out with a handicap.

"I remember on the eve of the trial, still trying to figure out which games we were going to say were fixed," Bernstein remembers. "We'd sit there and say, 'Well, we'll say this game was fixed . . . but wait a minute, that's not what Henry Hill testified to, so maybe we'll say this other one was fixed.' You can't try a case like that. It was ridiculous."

• • •

David Golub was an experienced defense lawyer who had done more than his share of pro bono criminal work in Stamford and at the University of Connecticut Legal Center, where he taught. But this was not a simple legal matter, a drunk-and-disorderly or a domestic squabble. This was about as high-profile as you could get: the United States government, with its endless resources and manpower, against a college basketball player accused of violating sport's most sacred taboo.

Golub thought it over, then took on the case despite the fact that Cobb had hardly any money with which to pay him.

"Ernie obviously didn't have enough money to pay for a substantial federal trial," Golub remembers. "It was very complicated. It was a lot of work."

One of Golub's first moves was to get the venue shifted from Uniondale, in Western Nassau County on Long Island, to Brooklyn, where Cobb was more likely to get a sympathetic jury, or, at least, one that was more diverse. This choice did not go over well with Judge Leonard Wexler, who had been assigned to the case, his first as a federal judge. Wexler lived on Long Island and was none too happy with having to travel to Brooklyn each morning, Golub recalled.

"This was one of the first days he had ever been on the bench," Golub said. "And he walked into the court, and the court was packed with people. And it was clear he just froze. We had the right to have the trial in Brooklyn, and we wanted to have the trial in Brooklyn. Ernie wanted to have the trial in Brooklyn because there would be a better mix on the jury.

"After we didn't agree to the plea bargain, the judge asked if we would agree to having the trial in Uniondale, and we said no. Which meant that the judge had to get up very, very early in the morning. As a matter of fact, he told us later that he was sleeping on the floor in his chambers because he couldn't make it in so early. [He] was furious about that. Furious. He was very, very angry at me. He made comments to me. And that happens when you defend people; you just try and make sure it doesn't interfere with the trial."

Before the opening statements, Golub moved for a severance for Cobb, which was denied by Wexler. The judge also denied a motion by Joel Winograd, representing Peter Vario, to suppress the identifications made by

Tony Perla of photos of Vario and Richard Perry on the grounds that the pictures were old and not representative.

Wexler also let both attorneys know up front that he was not going to stand for any shenanigans in his court.

In an effort to short-circuit Golub's theme of selective prosecution, Bernstein said he would say in his opening that the reason Jim Sweeney was not prosecuted was because he had cooperated with the government. Golub moved to prevent Bernstein from making the statement, and an argument ensued.

"You may move as much as you want," an impatient Wexler said. "Until you listen to my rules, I won't listen to yours. Mine is, you discuss these things not at 9:30, but before the opening of the court. In chambers. And they are resolved. I said that yesterday. I said it before, and I'm saying it again."

When Golub insisted on arguing the point, Wexler told him, "You abide by my rulings yesterday, or else I'll jump on you in front of the jury."

With the jury finally present, Bernstein began his opening statement. It was Tuesday, March 13, 1984.

The government prosecutor introduced the prosecution's theory that Rocco Perla had been sent to Boston by his brother in December 1978 to meet with Cobb and secure his cooperation in the point-shaving scheme, and that Cobb had shaved points in the Harvard, Rhode Island, and Fordham games. Bernstein also did some advance damage control, telling the jury that Rick Kuhn had lied to the grand jury about dumping the Rhode Island game because he "couldn't face the fact that he had intentionally dumped a Boston College game."

He also offered a different theory on the Holy Cross game of February 10, 1979, the one in which the gamblers took a bath and Jimmy Burke put his foot through his television set. The players actually did not agree to dump the game, Bernstein said, but miscommunication between Kuhn and the gamblers resulted in heavy losses.

"I imagine, ladies and gentlemen, the credibility of all of the witnesses presented by the government will be attacked, but we will show that the testimony is corroborated by the testimony of others and by the documentary evidence," he said in closing.

Golub then used his opening statement to offer the theory that Cobb had been paid for information, which did not equate to sports bribery or shaving points. In fact, he said, Cobb had refused to "lay down" when the gamblers had asked him to. He also pointed out that Cobb was not a defendant at the 1981 trial of Kuhn and the rest, even though the government already had what it now was claiming was a confession from him a year earlier.

The evidence pointed to the fact that the gamblers were trying to get Cobb involved in the scheme as late as the St. John's game, Golub went on, which would cast doubt on whether or not he was involved in the earlier games listed in the indictment. Plus, now the government was saying the Holy Cross game was not fixed per Kuhn's testimony, even though Hill had claimed it was fixed.

At this point Wexler stopped Golub, saying, "I happen to agree with the defendant in this instance, but I disagree with the presentation. You are still coming to conclusions, and if you don't stop, I will stop you in the middle."

"Thank you," Golub said.

"Don't say 'thank you,'" Wexler responded. "Listen to what I say."

About Cobb, Golub said to the jury, "You will judge whether this was someone who was trying to make the pros as a high-scoring guard, but who shaved points for peanuts."

In closing, Golub told the jury, "There was a point-shaving conspiracy at Boston College, make no mistake about it. There were people who violated the law, but Ernie Cobb wasn't one of them."

• • •

If the Cobb jurors had been in District Court two and a half years earlier for *U.S. v. Burke*, they might have had a chuckle or two over the next five days as one after another, the convicted conspirators from the first trial took the witness stand and told their version of what really happened. The same men who had sat silently as their attorneys claimed that no testimony or evidence tied them to the crimes which they were supposed to have committed now were being presented as penitents questing to cleanse their souls of past misdeeds.

It was an exceedingly tough sell. Each successive testimony only seemed to confuse the issue, until before long it became a contest to see whose story had the most holes in it.

Tony Perla, testifying after the opening statements on Tuesday, scored a point during direct testimony when he pointed out that there would have been no point spreads posted on the B.C.–Bentley and B.C.–Stonehill games, thus casting doubt on Golub's claim that Cobb had been paid solely for information about those two games. But on cross, Golub began to lay the basis for his central premise, which was that the government was changing its theory of what happened during the 1978–79 season. He zeroed in on Perla's claim that neither the UCLA game nor the February 10 Holy Cross game was fixed—games that were listed as being fixed on the government's indictment against Perla two and a half years earlier.

This brought an objection from Bernstein.

"It is totally improper," the prosecutor said. "I've never heard of a prior jury verdict being used to impeach the testimony of a witness."

"Overruled. I will allow it," Wexler intoned.

Golub finished by pointing out the discrepancies in payoffs to the players after the Harvard game: the three thousand dollars allegedly given to

Kuhn plus two thousand dollars more wired from Pittsburgh made five thousand dollars, or twenty-five hundred each for two players—Sweeney and Kuhn—was the implication.

The testimonies of Henry Hill and Paul Mazzei only added more reasonable doubt to the government's case. Golub hammered Mazzei on the money discrepancies, getting him to admit at one point, "You know, there was a lot of inconsistencies with a lot of things that happened between these players and these games."

Without Michael Coiro to trade insults with as he did in the first trial, Henry Hill came across as a snitch who could not get his story straight under questioning from Golub.

"He was at that point viewed as this wonderful witness," Cobb's lawyer recalls. "He had never lost a trial. One of the reasons he'd never lost was because when they went after him with his background, he just admitted, 'Yes, I did this, yes I did that, but I'm your guy's buddy.' So that it was a two-edged sword. You were burying yourself if you were a colleague of Henry Hill's. You were burying yourself by showing how bad he was. And he had been very effective as a witness. And basically, he was very comfortable answering anything about his background. He had made his deal, he was going to tell everything—and part of his deal was, he had to admit everything—and it wasn't that he boasted about what he'd done, but he certainly enjoyed telling what he did.

"It was my view that no one had been able to attack him from the facts. It was all general impeachment—what an unbelievable person he was."

After Winograd went first and followed that line of questioning, Golub got up and focused on the inconsistencies between Hill's statements to various law enforcement authorities. For instance, Hill claimed that Cobb was involved as early as the Harvard game because he had messed up the Providence game by scoring too many points, and that he and "his associates" delivered three thousand dollars after the game to Kuhn, who gave a portion to "Cobb's man." But Golub pointed out that this contradicted a statement Hill had made to the FBI in June 1981, in which he said that the St. John's debacle in February happened because Cobb was not involved in the scheme.

Suddenly, Hill was not the glib, wisecracking jokester he had been at the Burke trial when he had had the defense attorneys on the defensive. Now he came across as a witness who, as special prosecutor Douglas Behm had noticed three years earlier, "had a flexible concept of the truth."

"What happened was, it went beyond the mere, 'He's a criminal,' to 'He's inconsistent on the facts,'" Golub remembers. "So from my point of view it was a cross-examination that was easy to succeed at, if it was done right. Because any cross-examination where you're taking a witness and showing he's made inconsistent statements, and that he's changed his testimony—that's a good cross in a criminal trial."

• • •

When Rick Kuhn took the witness stand on Friday, March 16, there was the possibility that, after five years, the whole Boston College mess might finally be laid bare. After all, this was the player at the center of it all, and he would be making his first public statements about what happened during the 1978–79 season.

But any revelations—and there were several—were obscured by the numerous contradictions and denials that came from the witness box.

Kuhn, who by now had been in prison for seven months, told an entirely different story than the one heard in *U.S. v. Burke.* For starters, Kuhn painted Jim Sweeney, his former teammate and friend, as a willing participant who even recruited starting center Joe Beaulieu into the scheme. Sweeney also joined Kuhn in betting his share on the Fordham game, Rick said.

Topping that, Kuhn testified that his grand jury testimony—that the Rhode Island game had not been fixed—had been a lie; actually, the game had been fixed, and Cobb had agreed to shave points that night. As for the February 10 Holy Cross game, Kuhn claimed he told Barbara Reed to call Tony Perla in Las Vegas and tell him to bet *on* Boston College since the players would not be dumping the game.

"She came to me before the game and told me that she called and she didn't get a chance to talk with Tony, that whoever answered the phone told her the number was seven, and they hung up on her," he said. When Kuhn replied, "Beautiful," he said, he was saying it sarcastically, since he knew the gamblers were about to make the wrong bet.

Kuhn's direct testimony gave Golub an opening wide enough for the *Titanic* to sail through, and he took the wheel with enthusiasm. As each point was raised, a new denial came from the witness box.

Kuhn denied telling Barbara Reed to call Tony Perla to get the line for the Holy Cross game. He denied being paid three thousand dollars by Henry Hill after the Harvard game. He denied asking Sweeney to dump the Holy Cross game and denied seeing Cobb and Sweeney argue during the UCLA game. He denied receiving cocaine in a camera from Rocco Perla and denied receiving quaaludes from "John" from Pittsburgh. He denied approaching Cobb before the St. John's game about shaving points and denied telling Hill on the phone after the game that, "We can't control Cobb."

Why, then, Golub asked, would Hill call and threaten Kuhn after the St. John's game if the game had not been fixed?

"I wondered that myself," Kuhn responded.

What followed Kuhn's testimony was reminiscent of the first trial. Golub, incensed at what he felt were repeated lies by Kuhn that were being sanctioned by the government, waited until the jury had left the courtroom at the end of the day Friday and then confronted Bernstein. A reporter from the *Stamford Daily Advocate*, Cobb's hometown paper, overheard the exchange.

"You convicted (Kuhn) of fixing the Holy Cross game and now you have him denying it was fixed," he angrily said to Bernstein. "What kind of responsibility is that? You made him lie on the witness stand."

Bernstein tried to get Golub to lower his voice, then said, "David, do you want to get up on the table and make a speech?"

• • •

There was one way for Golub to confirm his belief that Kuhn was lying about the hours leading up to the Holy Cross game, and that was to put Barbara Reed, his ex-girlfriend, on the stand. So, he arranged for Reed to fly down from Syracuse to appear in court on Tuesday, March 20.

"I thought it was perjured testimony, and I thought the government knew it was perjured testimony," he said. "I put the girlfriend on—I brought her down from Syracuse—to testify about what happened, and the jury had to decide: Was Kuhn's saying, 'Beautiful,' believable enough?"

Before Reed appeared, however, Rocco Perla would take the stand on Monday, followed by FBI agent John Bowe. Both would offer potentially damaging testimony, Perla regarding Cobb's alleged involvement in the scheme and Bowe regarding his alleged confession.

Perla was perhaps the prosecution's most effective witness. He described how he broached the subject of point-shaving to Cobb at Cobb's apartment during the week before the Harvard game, and how Cobb agreed to go along.

"At first he was very skeptical," Perla said. "He didn't want to go along with it at first for fear that somebody would find out. . . . He was concerned that if anyone found out," it would ruin his chances to play professional basketball.

Perla went on to describe how he had paid Cobb after the game at a party at Rick Kuhn's apartment. He also mentioned his trip to Boston for the Fordham game but said nothing about meeting Cobb the night before at Kuhn's apartment and talking about point-shaving. This latter point would be at the center of the case: had Perla approached Cobb in December, or was he still trying to secure Cobb's cooperation in early February? Perla held firm that though he may have talked about Cobb during the February trip, the initial approach had been made in December.

On cross, Golub tried to shake Perla's account by bringing up a trip he made to Boston in October—a time when Cobb claimed he was approached about the Bentley and Stonehill games—but Rocco was adamant that he had mentioned the scheme for the first time to Cobb during the trip in December. Then, Golub pointed out that there was no credit-card charge for plane tickets to Boston during early December, but on redirect Perla explained that he had paid by cash and that he had the ticket at home.

When FBI agent John Bowe took the stand to describe the interview he and partner Gary Kirby had conducted with Cobb at the New Jersey Nets training camp in 1980, Bernstein sensed something did not feel right. Both he and Golub later intimated that the FBI had chosen Bowe to interview Cobb because, like Cobb, Bowe was African-American. It was a well-intentioned ploy that may have backfired.

"He knew nothing about the case," Bernstein recalls. "It was obvious that they had gotten a black agent to interview a black target. It was pretty self-evident."

As Bowe testified, it also became evident that he was unsure just what point-shaving was, and assumed that the fact that Cobb had accepted money from gamblers meant that he had shaved points. But Golub later called Kirby to the stand and introduced into evidence the notes the agent had taken during the interview. The notes said that Cobb said he had accepted money for playing well against Bentley and Stonehill, but that he had refused when Rocco had asked him to lay down for a third, unspecified game.

Kirby tried to counter that he had not written down that Cobb had confessed to point-shaving because, as he told Golub, "I didn't need to. I didn't take down a confession. He said he was involved." On cross, he told Bernstein, "The notes were for my personal use to remember what happened. But it was obvious he said he was involved. That was the whole point of the interview." The damage had been done, though.

• • •

Before Barbara Reed's turn on the witness stand, Bernstein introduced into evidence a receipt for a round-trip plane ticket with Rocco Perla's name on it from Pittsburgh to Boston, leaving on December 9, 1978, for a two-day stay. Golub objected to the introduction of the evidence and moved for a mistrial on the basis that he had not been notified of the existence of the tickets during discovery. But Wexler bought Bernstein's explanation that the government did not have the tickets in its possession during discovery and could not have anticipated Golub raising the issue at trial.

In yet another of many oddities surrounding the entire Boston College case, Reed, who had testified in 1981 on behalf of the government against Rick Kuhn, now would be testifying against the government on behalf of Kuhn's teammate and alleged coconspirator, Ernie Cobb. Preceding her testimony was some creative lawyering by Golub after Bernstein rested the government's case.

In his motion for a judgment of acquittal, Golub raised three points:

- The government's indictment was faulty. Cobb was charged not with sports bribery, but conspiracy to commit sports bribery, and that statute applied only to the person making the bribe. "That statute is not intended to include the player," he said. "He is, if anything, the victim of the conspiracy."

Wexler denied the first part of the motion, saying that when the statute says "individual" it can mean payor or payee. He didn't make a ruling on the substance of Golub's point, preferring to leave it up to the Second Circuit Court of Appeals.

- Golub's second point concerned the trial venue. He argued that if the government was charging Cobb with receiving a bribe to influence the outcome of a game, the trial could not be held in New York because there was no connection there. "There is not evidence that Mr. Cobb altered his play in Brooklyn, that the bribe took place in Brooklyn," he said. "There is no connection with New York."
- He cited case law that said a defendant cannot be connected to an overriding conspiracy through one specific act unless it was shown that he knew what was going on in the overriding conspiracy, or that the act he had engaged in made it clear that there was an overriding conspiracy.

If Cobb had only had an agreement with Perla and Kuhn, then there was no evidence of an overriding conspiracy, which goes back to the venue question. Cobb and Vario had never met, nor did Cobb know about Vario through Perla or Kuhn.

"There has to be a line drawn somewhere as to where the player's involvement ends," Golub summed up.

Bernstein was impressed, if not quite in assent.

"Obviously we think there is no merit to any of the arguments, although they are creative," he said.

Then, it was Winograd's turn. He requested a judgment of acquittal based on the fact that Vario had effectively withdrawn from the conspiracy "sometime in December 1978," a motion that Wexler denied, saying withdrawal would have required an affirmative act, which did not exist.

Wexler then pronounced that the government had shown by a preponderance of evidence that there was a conspiracy and that the defendants were involved to some degree.

• • •

Since her eventful year sharing an apartment with Rick Kuhn in Boston, Barbara Reed had returned to her hometown of Syracuse where she worked as a registered nurse specializing in labor and delivery. She had flown to New York for her trial appearance with her father, John, who was in the gallery on Tuesday, March 20, to see his daughter's testimony.

Under direct questioning from Golub, Reed retraced what she knew about the scheme from the time Rick first mentioned it to her in the fall of 1978 through the end of the season and the Holy Cross game. When she got to the weekend of the Fordham game in early February 1979, she described how she had overheard Rick and Jim Sweeney talking about how they had to keep the ball away from Ernie Cobb, because he shot all the time and was unreliable. She also remembered Kuhn saying Cobb was "too into his own game" to cooperate with "the betting thing," but that the men from New York still wanted Cobb involved.

This testimony was aimed at buttressing Golub's argument that Cobb had been approached in early February, not during December as Rocco Perla was claiming.

Reed also denied Kuhn's claim that he told her to call Tony Perla in Las Vegas before the Holy Cross game and tell him not to bet on the game.

Bernstein did not come to Reed's cross-examination unarmed. First, he got Rocco Perla's December plane tickets in by asking Reed if she remembered Rocco being in Boston in early December, then having her read the dates on the tickets.

Then he cited Reed's grand jury testimony, in which she had said that Rocco and Georgeanne had arrived in Boston and gone straight to the Colonnade Hotel and checked in at 11:43, to raise doubt about her recollection of a meeting between Rocco and Sweeney or Rocco and Rick that evening.

"So, Ms. Reed, you're not really sure, are you, that the conversations that you testified about concerning getting Ernie Cobb in this scheme took place on that weekend in February, are you?" Bernstein asked.

Reed insisted she was correct, and then Bernstein said, "That's not what you told me on the telephone, was it?" Winograd and Golub immediately objected, and Winograd punctuated his objection by banging his hand on the defense table.

"Please get back to your places," Wexler commanded. "If you are going to bang in my courtroom, maybe I won't listen to you."

Wexler concurred with the defense that Bernstein could not insert himself into the equation, unless he wanted to submit to being called as a witness by the defense. When questioning resumed, Bernstein got Reed to admit that she was not one hundred percent sure that it happened on that weekend; however, she did say she was sure it happened after Christmas and before the second Holy Cross game.

Golub rehabilitated her on redirect by eliciting that Reed had already testified at *U.S. v. Burke* in 1981 that the discussions about getting Cobb involved had taken place in February.

• • •

Tuesday, March 20, 1984, was a day Ernie Cobb had been anticipating for three and a half years. During that time he had been interrogated by the FBI, seen his chances at an NBA career bite the dust, had his name and picture splashed in headlines across the country, passed two lie-detector tests, and generally lived under a cloud that had forced him to keep silent instead of screaming to the world how the government and the press had it all wrong, that he would never take money to play below his level.

Not surprisingly, Cobb prepared for his day in court as he would for a big game, by psyching himself up. He was used to performing in front of people; this would be another performance, another chance to prove himself to the people in the stands, though this time it would be a considerably smaller crowd and the stakes considerably higher. While Barbara Reed testified during the early afternoon, Cobb, wearing a natty, navy-blue suit, paced the hallway outside the courtroom and tried to loosen up as he would before a game, stretching his arms and shoulders and slowly rotating his neck.

Then, at 2:55 P.M., it was time to step into the witness box. Partly to put Ernie at ease and partly to demonstrate to the jury how his client had overcome long odds to get to where he was, Golub began by asking Cobb about his childhood and how basketball had been the force that had driven him to succeed in school and eventually earn a college scholarship. The feel-good testimony went on for so long that Wexler ultimately broke in and said, "Can we get on with the case?"

Cobb then described how he had been approached by Rocco Perla after basketball practice one evening in October 1978 and asked how Boston College would fare against Bentley and Stonehill. He then detailed how Rocco had given Laverne Mosley one thousand dollars in an envelope at Boston Garden after the Harvard game. Newspaper reporters immediately saw the next day's headlines. But Cobb explained that he understood that he was being paid for the information he had given Rocco on the two earlier games.

Golub had Cobb go over the approach by Kuhn before the St. John's game, as well as his frustration about not getting the ball enough during the game. In the Holy Cross game, Cobb said, he again refused Kuhn's entreaties to dump the game and ended up nearly saving B.C. with some key baskets near the end of the game.

Anticipating a question Bernstein was sure to ask, Golub asked Cobb why he did not go to Tom Davis or Bill Flynn and tell him about the money he had received from Rocco Perla or the approaches by Kuhn. Cobb portrayed himself as being unaware of any wrongdoing.

"I didn't realize anything wrong was going on at the time. . . . This was Rick and Rocco Perla. Rocco, at that time, was younger than I am. He was on the college campus, and he fit in with the rest of the kids. Rick Kuhn was my teammate for three years. I did not anticipate or see them doing anything wrong."

Golub skillfully framed his questions so that Cobb would come off as a player who only cared about doing his best and was oblivious to the machinations of his teammates. Ernie described his anger at being denied the ball by Sweeney during the UCLA game, and talked about how he got "up" for games against players like Rhode Island's Sly Williams—testimony designed to show that he was not the type to compromise his performance. He also denied shaving points in the Harvard game and claimed he was not aware of any point-shaving taking place during the game.

When Golub started to ask Cobb about his life since being cut by the Jazz, Wexler had had enough.

"Counsel, you have taken us through every phase of his life, his high school, his junior high school, and now we are going through every phase of his life after he graduates," the judge said. "It's a little too much. If you want to cut it short I will let you continue. But I don't want you to go through every phase of his life."

Golub finished by having Cobb reiterate how Rocco Perla had approached him with an offer of money in exchange for beating the point spread against Bentley and Stonehill.

That ended the day's session for the jury, but not for the lawyers, who needed to go over Wexler's charge to the jury, which would follow the closing statements. It was during this discussion that the case took a bizarre twist.

Perhaps sensing that his witnesses had shortchanged him and that the trial was quickly slipping away, Bernstein took a different tack and suggested that Cobb was guilty of taking money to influence his performance *even in the games he had tried to make sure Boston College won.* In other words, if Cobb had taken money from Rocco Perla to cover the spread against Bentley, then he should be considered guilty.

"I disagree with that," Golub said. "If somebody says to a Little League player, 'I will give you an ice cream cone if you get a base hit,' he can be prosecuted under that theory."

Bernstein then offered an example that had Wexler leaning toward his interpretation of the statute.

"Boston College is favored by two points over Bentley. And there are five seconds left in the game," Bernstein said. "Ernie Cobb has the ball, and Boston College is winning by one point. He has agreed he will cover the point spread of two points. If he does nothing and just holds the ball . . . his team will win by one point. On the other hand, if he wants to win the point spread, he may go downcourt despite the coach's instructions . . . and attempt to score another basket. If he missed, the other team could get the ball, run down to the other end and shoot a basket and win by one point."

Wexler agreed, and it seemed Bernstein had scored a major point himself. But Golub was lurking, waiting to pounce. He immediately pointed out that the indictment listed the Harvard, Rhode Island, and Fordham games, none of which Cobb was alleged to have been "influenced" in.

"He is not guilty of the charge the grand jury returned an indictment on," Golub said.

Wexler disagreed, saying, "It is a bribery, although it is a bribery to do something that would normally be the natural instinct. But since he is taking money to do it, it is a bribery."

After throwing other issues back and forth for a while, Wexler tried to get some kind of schedule for the final witnesses and the summations. When he gave Bernstein twenty minutes to do his rebuttal summary, after Golub and Winogard's summaries, Bernstein pleaded for more. "They're going to attack the credibility of every single witness," he said. "I don't think I can defend the credibility of those witnesses in twenty minutes."

"I don't think you can do it in four months," Winograd cracked.

• • •

With its witnesses discredited and its central theory in shambles, the prosecution's last hope was for Bernstein to trip up Cobb on cross-examination, or for Cobb himself to play badly to the jury. But Cobb was determined not to crack. He had gone home to his parents' house in Stamford Tuesday night after his direct testimony and spent the evening reading and talking to Herman Alswanger, his high school coach and mentor. When he arrived at court Wednesday morning for his second day on the witness stand, he was ready.

Bernstein immediately focused on the FBI interview and produced the report made by Bowe and Kirby. Cobb looked at the report and said, "This has nothing to do with what took place."

This earned him a scolding from Bernstein.

"Let me ask the question, okay?" the prosecutor said.

Bernstein continued to hammer Cobb on his differing stories to the FBI during the interview regarding whether he knew about Sweeney's and Kuhn's involvement. But Cobb held firm, though he continued to try and embellish his answers. Wexler finally had to tell him, "Mr. Cobb, you are going to have to answer 'yes' or 'no' when it calls for that. If you can't, say you can't give a yes or no. You cannot give an explanation unless he asks for an explanation."

Cobb admitted that he said Rocco and Kuhn were "involved," but, in his words, not in any point-shaving.

"Nothing to do with the point-shaving scheme?" Bernstein asked. "What were they asking you about?"

"They were asking me if anybody approached me in regard to betting or anything like that. I told them the whole story. Everything that I knew from beginning to end."

Bernstein confused Cobb when he asked him about whether the agents were correct when they testified that he originally denied everything at the beginning of the interview.

"I cannot answer that yes or no. It deserves an explanation, sir," he said. "I will be happy to comment if you give me a chance."

Wexler was not amused.

"Mr. Cobb, the last statement was not called for," he said, and repeated his previous instruction.

At this point, Cobb might have appeared a little too confident, according to Bernstein, who said that after the trial some jurors said they felt his testimony made him come off as arrogant.

Cobb admitted that after he signed the rights statement, he began to tell the agents about Rocco and Kuhn. He repeated that he told the agents that he got the one thousand dollars from Rocco through Laverne. But Bernstein produced the report, which said nothing about Cobb getting the money from Laverne, but instead said Cobb got the money directly from Rocco at the Garden. Cobb claimed he told them the money was from Rocco, but that he actually got it from Laverne.

Then Bernstein pointed out that Tony Perla had testified that there would have been no point spread on the Bentley and Stonehill games.

"I don't know that to be true," Cobb replied.

"Isn't it true that there is no point spread in Las Vegas or anywhere else on the Bentley or Stonehill games?" Bernstein insisted.

"I have no idea, sir."

"When you told the FBI the story about the Bentley and Stonehill games, you didn't want to admit that you had agreed to shave points in the Harvard game, isn't that right, Mr. Cobb?"

"That is not correct, sir."

Cobb denied ever meeting Rocco Perla the week before the Harvard game and stuck to his claim that he only met Rocco at the gym the one time with Kuhn after practice in October, though perhaps he "saw him around" a few other times. He admitted that he had played below par against Harvard, but he considered it just a bad game.

Golub used his redirect to allow Cobb to explain his statements to the FBI.

"I told them that I absolutely had nothing to do with any shaving points," Cobb said. "They showed me some pictures. I said I had never seen any of these men before in my life, and then they asked me had anyone ever approached me, and that's when I told them that, yes, Rick Kuhn and Rocco had approached me and that was the discrepancy between what I told them in the beginning, which was no, I had never seen anyone, that was in regards to the pictures that they had shown me. And that was true, sir."

"Mr. Cobb, did you ever agree to shave points in any Boston College game?" Golub asked, point-blank.

"No, I did not, sir," Cobb replied.

• • •

After the lawyers and Wexler went over a few more charges out of the presence of the jury, Golub addressed the judge's charge on what the conspiracy to influence the games really was. It was here that he reiterated his central point in the case.

The government, Golub said, gave evidence to the grand jury that Cobb engaged in altering the outcome of the Harvard, Rhode Island, and Fordham games. Now, at trial, the government was changing its tune, and, Golub contended, Bernstein should not be allowed to argue this point to the jury.

"The government went to trial on one theory, and I don't think the government should now be allowed to change its theory of the case by, A, altering the games that are involved, and B, saying no, convict him not of shaving points or dumping points but convict him of trying to beat the spread," Golub said.

He went on to point out that if Cobb was supposed to beat the spread to get paid, there would have been an agreement with Rocco Perla to that effect, and there was no testimony from Perla that mentioned any such arrangement.

Bernstein countered that the games now under discussion—Stonehill and Bentley—occurred during the time frame listed in the indictment, and that these games only came into play because of Cobb's testimony. He also charged that the government never specified which games were involved.

"What was peculiar was that we had a purported confession by [Cobb]," Bernstein remembers, "but it was a confession to different games than the ones Henry Hill said he had fixed. And there was no way to reconcile it."

Wexler was unmoved by Golub's argument and denied the request with no explanation. Clearly, though, he had sided with Bernstein's belief that a player could be bribed to win games as well as lose them.

• • •

When Bernstein walked to the podium to give his final summation, he knew the odds were against a conviction. But he was able to retrace the story and connect the dots in such a way that a reasonable person might reach the conclusion that Cobb had indeed shaved points.

There was Rocco Perla's testimony about going to Boston to meet with Cobb, corroborated by Kuhn and buttressed by the airline tickets. There was the fact that Cobb had played poorly against Harvard and admitted receiving one thousand dollars after the game.

"Finally, there is the testimony of Ernie Cobb," Bernstein began. "I submit to you that the version he gives you of what happened during the fall of '78 and the early part of '79 is simply preposterous and unbelievable, and nothing short of that."

Was it believable that Cobb was approached out of the blue by Perla, someone he didn't know, and then, a month later, magically received one thousand dollars from him, Bernstein asked.

"He never has to do anything. He just got the money. That was it. He put it in his pocket, forgot about it. That was it? It is simply preposterous, ladies and gentlemen, and I ask you to reject it.

"He twisted things around so that it would benefit himself. He had to stick with that story about the Bentley game because he knew that the FBI agents were going to be testifying. He didn't have any choice. He had to come up with that story."

When Golub stepped up to the podium, he took exception to Bernstein's characterization of Cobb's testimony.

"I want to evaluate the evidence with you, so we can decide together what is preposterous, who has twisted, where the doubt is," he said.

"The issue in this case is not whether there was point-shaving at Boston College. That's never been the issue. That was proved in 1981. . . . The issue is not whether Tony Perla went to New York, whether he went to Boston on November 16, whether there were any phone calls, whether there were hotel receipts. . . . The issue in this trial is whether Ernie Cobb was involved."

He certainly was not involved during the time period the government was claiming, Golub said, citing Barbara Reed's testimony about Kuhn and Rocco Perla talking about "getting Cobb involved" in February 1979. He also cited Hill's claim in the *Sports Illustrated* article that said the players agreed they "had to have Cobb" *after* the Rhode Island game, implying that he was not on board before the game.

The money did not add up either, Golub continued. The five thousand dollars Kuhn received after the Harvard game divided perfectly into twenty-five hundred dollars each for two players, the fee according to Hill.

"Where was Ernie Cobb's twenty-five hundred dollars?" Golub asked. "Ernie Cobb, the star who, according to Anthony Perla, had told Rocco he only wanted to deal with Rocco, he wanted his money—what happened to Cobb's twenty-five hundred dollars? Well, it never got there, did it?"

Then Golub responded to Bernstein's claim about the Stonehill and Bentley games.

"You know, we can talk all night about whether or not there was a point spread on the Stonehill and Bentley games, because there was no bet on that game. That was the come-on, the lure, 'Let's get Cobb involved, let's get him some money because once he gets some money we can go on to the next step.' It was the lure, the safety approach, the cultivation. And I say to you, five years later, it's easy to call something preposterous but when it happens and someone says, 'Hey, I'll give you one thousand dollars. . . .' Yes, he got one thousand dollars, but that is not the issue and that is not the crime charged. That is not a crime."

What was preposterous and unbelievable, Golub said, was Rocco Perla's story about going to Boston and having lunch with Kuhn and Sweeney at the Chestnut Hill Mall when his plane had arrived at 7:40 on a Saturday night and the mall was closed on Sunday.

Golub picked up steam as he headed down the homestretch.

"You judge who are the people who are convicted of sports bribery and racketeering, who [received] ten-year sentences, who are trying to make a deal, who admit lying under oath—you judge that, whether that is the kind of evidence to convict somebody on, beyond a reasonable doubt, and you judge that against Ernie Cobb's character, against the character of someone who has a tutor for four years so he can make it through high school and learn to read, and goes to college and graduates with his class.

"This isn't a sob story. That's not why I'm saying that. It's because that is what Ernie Cobb did. He didn't have a free ride. . . . That's the kind of person they want to believe would go out on the floor of the Boston Garden in front of seventeen thousand people and throw a game.

"This is Ernie Cobb's chance to clear his name against what the people in this courtroom for the government have said. You are the only ones who can do that for him. I ask you to return a verdict of not guilty. I ask you to clear Ernie Cobb's name."

It was Winograd's turn next, and he began by attacking Henry Hill's credibility before moving on to the slender threads the prosecution had offered to tie his client, Peter Vario, to the conspiracy. There were no phone records, hotel receipts, or airline tickets with Vario's name on them—just the testimony of Hill, Tony Perla, and Paul Mazzei. Besides, he pointed out, it sounded "incredible" that drug dealers like Perla and Mazzei would have to ask Perry and Vario for $150 or $200 to fly to Boston.

"The government is asking you to convict a man based the testimony of rogues, scoundrels, liars, cheats, deceivers, manipulators, people of the worst ilk," Winograd concluded. "Mazzei, Perla, and Hill. . . . When you're a liar, you're a liar. You don't change. People don't change. These men haven't changed. A leopard doesn't change its spots. A lie is a lie is a lie."

Bernstein gave it a game effort in his rebuttal, pointing out that Golub's defense was based partly on what Hill had said in the *Sports Illustrated* article about trying to get Cobb involved in February—in effect, impeaching his own witness, Hill. And the money disparities were not as great as Golub was contending, either, he said; Cobb had received one thousand dollars after the Harvard game and, per Kuhn's testimony, five hundred dollars each from the money orders sent on December 19 and January 8, which made a total of two thousand dollars.

If the money was being used to "cultivate" Cobb and he hadn't done anything wrong to get it, Bernstein asked the jury, why didn't he go to the authorities? Instead, he now was admitting taking the money to cover the point spread, which was a violation—which Bernstein explained by using the example he had used during the discussion with Wexler the day before with the jury absent. "One of you remember that example," he said. "That's how you can take money to be influenced even if you are supposedly trying to win the game."

As for Cobb testifying that he didn't think there was anything wrong with taking the money—"It's unbelievable," Bernstein said. "He's a college kid. He doesn't have much money. Gets a thousand dollars. 'I just didn't give it much thought'? Is that believable?"

The case against both Ernie Cobb and Peter Vario relied on the testimony of some unsavory characters, it was true. But that was how the game worked.

"It's unfortunate that the government has to put witnesses on the stand who are not nice people. But this isn't a nice case," Bernstein said. "There is nothing nice about what happened here. It's a conspiracy. Conspiracies don't include nice people like yourselves. They don't stand out in the public square so that everybody, all the nice people, can hear about it and come in and testify. . . . So, when you have a conspiracy, you've got to use people like Paul Mazzei, Henry Hill, and Anthony Perla."

Holding a pointer as he spoke, Bernstein walked over to a blow-up schedule of Boston College's 1978–79 schedule that had been displayed for the jury.

"The bottom line is this, ladies and gentlemen: Cobb took the money. He admits it. He took it to be influenced. You don't have to find that he was specifically point-shaving in a game. All you have to find is that he agreed—he took the money and he agreed to be influenced. That's it. You can stop right there," he said, slapping the pointer down on the Bentley game for emphasis.

• • •

The jury began its deliberations in *U.S. v. Cobb* on Thursday morning, March 22, after the charge by Wexler. Near the end of the day, forewoman Dorothy Dobbins sent back a note that a verdict had been reached on one of the charges against Cobb and Vario.

This development might have sent a shiver through the defendants and their attorneys, as it could have been assumed that only a guilty verdict on the sports bribery count against the two men would make it necessary for the jury to deliberate on the second count. But within minutes, the jury requested a reading of Rocco Perla's testimony, which made it clear that Cobb's fate still was up in the air.

Golub saw it differently.

"Confident is not the right word, because you're never confident when the jury's out," he says. "But I thought . . . when they had a verdict on one of the defendants, I was fairly confident it was the other guy, and I was fairly confident that it was for acquittal, because it was so fast. Then I began thinking we were going to get an acquittal."

The volume of testimony the jury requested to have read back and the comments made by jurors after the verdict depict a contentious atmosphere in the jury room.

Paul Mazzei's testimony about the meeting at Aqueduct between himself, Tony Perla, Vario, and Richard Perry was read back. So was the entire testimony of John Bowe, the FBI agent who interviewed Cobb in 1980, as well as Henry Hill's testimony, which covered the meeting at Aqueduct. As the day concluded, a request was made to have Rick Kuhn's and Tony Perla's testimony read back the next morning.

By the time Dobbins informed Wexler about the one verdict that had been reached, the discussions had become heated. Ten jurors were voting for acquittal, but two were holding out.

"We had been screaming at each other in the jury room," juror George Samaras, one of the dissenters, later told *Boston Globe* reporter Ron Borges. "We were all talking at once. We needed the night off."

What happened that night could have come straight out of a movie-of-the-week screenplay. It was the third round of the NCAA basketball tournament, and Michael Jordan's North Carolina team was playing Indiana. Jordan was held to thirteen points in the Tar Heels' four-point loss. Samaras happened to see the box score in the paper Friday morning, and he figured if a player of Jordan's caliber could have a subpar game like that in the NCAA Tournament, then it was not unreasonable to expect that the same thing could have happened to Cobb.

When court adjourned the next morning, before the jury listened to a reading of the Kuhn and Perla testimony, another vote was taken and a unanimous verdict was reached.

With the spectators in Courtroom 4 holding their breath, Dobbins read the verdict at 11:30 A.M. She barely got the word "not" out of her mouth when Cobb let out a whoop and the rest of the courtroom broke out in cheers. Cobb leaped up and embraced his mother, Hattie, who dissolved into tears.

Shortly afterward, Cobb left the courtroom for a few minutes.

"I just had to be alone," he told reporters when he returned. "This has gone on for four years. My family has suffered. I have suffered. My parents have suffered. I don't know if the losses can ever be made up . . . not the losses me and my family and friends have suffered. But I don't feel any bitterness toward the prosecution. They were just doing their jobs. I just thank God there is justice."

"I knew he wasn't guilty in any way," Hattie Cobb said about her son. "This has been going on for four years. If he'd been guilty I would have known."

Laverne Mosley, who had accepted an envelope from Rocco Perla containing one thousand dollars at Boston Garden five and a half years ago, was philosophical.

"You really learn who is with you when something like this happens," she told reporters. "While we were at Boston College we learned about the upside of being a celebrity. Now we know about the downside. We're all just glad it's over."

Outside the courtroom, jurors told reporters that they had believed Cobb's story over the stories told by the government's rogues' gallery of witnesses. Central to their verdict was a sense that Cobb was an unwitting accomplice in the scheme.

"We knew he took the money," Samaras said. "But did he take it knowing he had done something wrong? It was a matter of whether Ernie knew what he was doing. We believed what he told the FBI. It was easy to accept that story.

"You couldn't believe Kuhn," he added. "He was taking money from everybody and lying to everybody."

Elissa Sundler, a marketing researcher from Sheepshead Bay in Brooklyn, was the other holdout along with Samaras. "There were doubts," she told reporters. "And to go for a conviction when you have doubts . . ."

Dobbins, the forewoman, bought into Golub's theory that the gamblers were cultivating Cobb.

"I don't think he ever realized what he had done," she said. "We thought he was too naïve to know. We all felt in the end that (the gamblers who had set up the scheme) were trying to set him up by getting him used to taking money."

• • •

Before he left the courthouse, Cobb spoke of renewing his efforts to play in the NBA and of how he would already be playing in the NBA if the FBI had not come to the Nets training camp three and a half years earlier. It was a story he would stick to for the next decade as his NBA dreams gradually faded and disappeared.

CHAPTER SEVENTEEN

Aftermath

The acquittals of Ernie Cobb and Peter Vario were far from the final legal actions taken in the Boston College matter. In particular, Jimmy Burke and an army of attorneys kept the courts busy with motions and appeals even after his original twenty-year sentence was reduced to twelve years by Judge Henry Bramwell in 1984.

In fact, all of the defendants received reductions from Bramwell on April 16, 1984, just weeks after Cobb's acquittal. Rick Kuhn's and Tony Perla's ten-year sentences were reduced to four and six years, respectively, and Paul Mazzei's was reduced to eight years. Rocco Perla, who was universally considered the least culpable of the defendants, had his sentence reduced from four years to time served, plus five years' probation, and was released.

Today, Tony and Rocco Perla live a few miles from each other in the part of Western Pennsylvania where they grew up. Tony, together with his two sons, runs the vending-machine business his family has owned for years. Rocco runs Perla Appliances, in Swissvale, Pennsylvania, a store owned by his father, Rocco Sr., who passed away in February 2000—the same store where he worked in the summer of 1978 when his brother approached him about talking to his high school friend, Rick Kuhn.

Rocco waited until 1999, when his own son was a senior in high school, to tell him that his father had spent time in jail in the early '80s for conspiring to fix college basketball games. It was Rocco's way of preparing him for the day when someone recognized his last name and put the pieces together, but it also has allowed him to talk more openly about it. Now, he even chuckles at some of the absurdities of the events of twenty years ago. A few years ago he got a jolt from the past when he heard Henry Hill's voice coming through his car radio on Howard Stern's show.

Rocco Perla echoes the view of his lawyer, Kerry O'Malley, when he questions a punishment that did not fit the crime.

"At some point we tried to get our lawyers to raise the mentality of the times, which was that the newspapers published point spreads, they ran contests, kids sold pools," he says. "I'm not trying to use that as an excuse, because at the time we certainly knew right from wrong. It was wrong, but we tried to use the 'victimless' scenario: Who's losing here? Are the bookies losing, or the casinos, or are they just balancing their books?"

• • •

Ernie Cobb never realized his dream of playing in the National Basketball Association. After his acquittal in 1984, he played in the Continental Basketball Association for the Albuquerque Silvers and signed the next spring with the Connecticut Colonials of the United States Basketball League. He continued to play in Israel and made a name for himself in the professional league there.

"No one gave him a shot," Herman Alswanger, who still lives in Stamford and is active in running summer camps, remembers. "The papers were kind to him, but it was too late. They liked him once they got to know him; it was that way with Ernie, once you got to know the kid he had a great personality, and he was not a guy who looked for the publicity all the time. He just loved playing the game of basketball."

During one of his stints in Israel, Cobb befriended a young woman from Detroit who worked at a health-food restaurant he frequented, and the two married in 1989. Today, Ernie and Tammi Cobb have two boys and a girl and live near Dimona, in the southern half of Israel about twenty minutes from Beersheba. Cobb teaches high school English and coaches basketball.

When she first met Ernie, Tammi remembers, she was not a basketball fan and knew nothing about the Boston College case. Ernie talked about it all the time, though, and as time went on, she began to see that he was still profoundly affected by it.

"If he sees a ballgame, especially if it's the Nets, he'll say something like, 'That could have been me out there. I'm supposed to be rich, I'm supposed be a millionaire, that should have been me out there. Stuff like that,'" she said. "I said, 'Boy, this is deep.'"

The pain does cut deep for Ernie Cobb, twenty years later. It is evident in his tone when he talks about the events of 1978–79, particularly when he talks about the three and a half years it took him to clear his name in court. He sees himself as a victim of an overzealous prosecution by a government that bent and twisted the facts to try and bring him down, which it succeeded in doing by robbing him of his prime earning years as a basketball player.

"If there was a way, I would really challenge the American system," he says. "Because it was really unjust. I was never compensated. As a result, I had to pick up the pieces and do it on my own. Not to mention the selective prosecution. Because you had Sweeney, who had immunity, and was definitely involved."

Still, Cobb has remade himself and carved out a living in a country far away from the one where the mention of his name still elicits images of shame and scandal. But listening to him makes it clear that this is a consolation prize.

"I feel I deserve certain rewards based on what I've been through and what I've accomplished," Cobb says. "I think the average person might have crumbled under the circumstances. In retrospect, it's made me a better man, and I've benefited a lot from it. It's a fascinating story and I have a lot I'd love to share, but at the same time, it's time for me to get some compensation, because I really felt like I was supposed to have an NBA contract. . . .

"But having said that, I managed to bounce back, and I'm very content and very happy with my life. I'm speaking a foreign language, functioning in a foreign country, and you can't be a slouch to do that. You have to have something on the ball to function over here like I have and to be able to succeed like that. So I've gotten my reward in the end, and I feel like this is the best reward overall. I've been through a lot, and I'm proud of where I am right now."

Unfortunately, perception frequently overrides reality. When news of gambling by Boston College football players broke in 1996, twelve years after Ernie Cobb was acquitted of wrongdoing, *Sports Illustrated*'s Tim Layden wrote, "But as long as nobody shaves points, as B.C. basketball players Rick Kuhn and Ernie Cobb did seventeen years ago, a bullet has been dodged."

• • •

The government's defeat in *U.S. v. Cobb* was the only blemish on Henry Hill's record in ten trials between 1980 and 1985. In 1987, Hill found himself on the other end of a different kind of legal battle.

Wiseguy had come out in January 1986 and was an almost instant bestseller, with more than a million copies in print by the summer of 1987. But the New York State Crime Victims Board ordered Hill and his publisher, Simon & Schuster, to turn over more than ninety-six thousand dollars in profits under the state's ten-year-old "Son of Sam Law," which held that a criminal's book, movie, and television royalties had to be placed in a victims' fund, with any money left after five years going back to the criminal.

Simon & Schuster editor Michael Korda challenged the law in U.S. District Court in Manhattan, joined by several other publishing houses. The challenge was rejected, but the appeal was heard by the U.S. Supreme Court, which struck down the law on December 10, 1991, saying that it violated First Amendment rights and "establishes a financial disincentive to create or publish works with a particular content." By this time, *Wiseguy* had reportedly become required reading at the FBI training academy because of its revelations about the hierarchy and inner workings of an organized crime family. Henry Hill was a winner once again.

Hill's notoriety reached new heights with the release in 1990 of *Goodfellas*, Martin Scorsese's movie based on *Wiseguy*. The point-shaving scheme rates a few frames in the film, during a scene at Robert's Lounge when the camera pans past a television showing a basketball game.

Today, Henry Hill lives near a large body of water far away from the streets of New York City. Contrary to popular perception, he has not been in the Witness Protection Program since 1984, when he was kicked out for repeatedly breaching security. He still uses an alias, but his Brooklyn accent has emerged unscathed by his twenty years of forced exile.

Since hitting bottom in 1987 with a conviction for narcotics trafficking—for which he served no jail time, thanks to a letter from Ed McDonald to the sentencing judge—Hill has turned his life around. He has a son with a woman he has been with since the mid-1980s, and he gets occasional work as a consultant on mob-related television and movie consulting projects, and says his daughters from his previous marriage have received a large advance from a major publisher for a book on their experiences growing up in the Witness Protection Program. He is the embodiment of mobster chic, with a World Wide Web site in the works and a cookbook on the way that trades on his public persona as lovable wiseguy. He considers HBO's series *The Sopranos* the best work television has produced on the mob, but cannot resist qualifying this assessment by adding, "They stole a lot of shit out of *Wiseguy*, I'll tell you that."

Despite the Supreme Court's ruling, Hill is not living off royalties from *Goodfellas* and *Wiseguy* today. Taxes, booze, and drugs took care of that, according to those close to him. The fact that he is living at all is enough of an achievement for someone whose former cohorts are not.

To the sometimes brutal, often funny, and ultimately poignant life of Henry Hill, add this bit of ignominy: He blazed the trail for legions of wiseguy turncoats to follow, a development that has done at least as much to weaken the mob as any piece of legislation. By 1992, ten years after the sentencing of Rick Kuhn, James Burke, Paul Mazzei, and the Perla brothers, there were an estimated fifteen thousand criminals in the federal Witness Protection Program, many of them former mobsters.

"He really is the first modern cooperator that let the door open for all the others who followed," his lawyer, Robert Simels, says. "It was around that time that people decided that *omerta* didn't exist anymore.

"I feel sorry for Henry. I blame the government for the program really having no capacity written into it for retraining or refocusing. . . . They won't create a past for you. So you wind up in Cincinnati, Ohio, applying for a job and they say, 'Where did you work last, can I get a reference?' And you have no references."

• • •

James Burke's numerous appeals of his racketeering conviction in the Boston College case fell on deaf ears. His attorneys argued that the testimony of Rick Kuhn and Tony Perla at Ernie Cobb's trial cast doubt on whether the UCLA and St. John's games had actually been fixed, as Hill had claimed in the first trial, but no one bought it. Instead, Hill's testimony helped the government to convict Burke in 1985 of the murder of Richie Eaton, a drug courier and money launderer whom Burke told Hill he had killed over a cocaine deal.

On April 13, 1996, two days after seven-year-old Jessica Dubroff crashed in a small plane while trying to become the youngest person to fly across the country, James Burke died of cancer in a Buffalo prison at age sixty-four. He had spent the final sixteen years of his life behind bars.

Paul Vario, the reputed Lucchese capo who gave his okay to the point-shaving scheme in the fall of 1978, was serving a six-year sentence at the Federal Correctional Institution at Fort Worth, Texas, for running a protection racket at Kennedy Airport when he collapsed in his cell and died on May 3, 1988. The cause of death was attributed to respiratory arrest.

Richard Perry, who skipped out on the second Boston College trial, pleaded guilty to sports bribery in the Boston College case, and in 1984 was sentenced to one year's probation and a five-thousand-dollar fine. In 1991, through attorney Oscar Goodman, he released his only public statement on his involvement in the scheme.

"I did not serve prison time for this . . . because I advised against the proposal of informant Henry Hill to shave points at Boston College," Perry wrote. "Unlike the other defendants in the case who received substantial prison time, the court recognized that I pled guilty because I was promised probation and a five-thousand-dollar fine.

"Obviously, because of my prior conviction I was concerned that if I went to trial I would be convicted because of prior conduct, or my punishment might be enhanced if I was convicted. I would like to state that I have paid for my mistakes and that I have moved to Las Vegas where gambling activity is legal so as to avoid any problem for myself and my family."

Trouble seemed to follow Richard Perry, though. He brought unwanted publicity to the UNLV basketball program through his involvement with controversial recruit Lloyd Daniels, and made more headlines in 1991 when the *Las Vegas Review-Journal* ran a photo showing him and three members of the UNLV basketball team in a hot tub at Perry's Las Vegas house. By 1992, his name appeared in Nevada's *Black Book*, a listing of people prohibited from entering the state's casinos, and in 1997 he pled guilty to tax evasion and was sentenced to fifteen months in jail after he admitted failing to pay more than two hundred thousand dollars on income earned in 1989, '90, and '91.

• • •

After more than eleven years with the Organized Crime Strike Force, Ed McDonald stepped down in April 1989 and now works as a white-collar criminal defense attorney for a firm in Manhattan. The former prosecutor managed to land himself a minor role in *Goodfellas*, as the lawyer who explains the Witness Protection Program to Henry and Karen Hill, played by Ray Liotta and Lorraine Bracco, a task that in real life was performed by Robert Simels, Hill's lawyer.

Within the last two years, McDonald, who refused several requests to be interviewed for this book, has consulted on a screenplay about the Boston College case with Rick Kuhn, the man he put in prison nearly twenty years ago, and says he has plans to write a book about his experiences as a prosecutor. At a public forum in 1990, McDonald admitted that Henry Hill should have received some jail time as part of his immunity agreement.

Robert Simels has a private practice in New York. He considers his association with Hill a mixed blessing: His initial decision to trade his services for a percentage of the rights to Hill's life story earned him financial rewards, but he suffered a backlash from some of his former clients who disapproved of his involvement with an informant.

"No matter how good an attorney you may be, and how capable you are of representing other people, there are a host of people who, because of my association with organized crime, have never used me again," Simels says. "I'm friendly with them, and many of them have told me they would use me, but because of my connection with Henry, [they won't]."

Associations with organized crime figures proved more problematic for Michael Coiro, the former cop turned lawyer who provided such a vigorous and colorful defense for James Burke in the first Boston College point-shaving trial. In 1987, Coiro was convicted of racketeering and sentenced to fifteen years in prison, stemming from his ties to John Gotti, the infamous "Dapper Don" whom Coiro had represented from the mid-1960s to the mid-1980s. He was sentenced to another twenty-seven months in 1992 for lying in front of a grand jury two years earlier.

Leonard Sharon still follows basketball avidly and occasionally gets up at five o'clock in the morning to play at a local gym in the part of Maine where he teaches law school and has a private practice. He remembers *U.S. v. Burke* as "seven weeks of purgatory," but as a longtime basketball fan he considers his cross-examination of Tom Davis one of the highlights of his career.

Like many people connected to the case, Sharon remains skeptical about some of the claims the government's witnesses made during the trial.

"Let me put it this way," he says. "First of all, if they were shaving, Ricky wasn't the only one. Because these guys were supposed to have invested large (amounts of money). Jimmy Burke was supposed to have bet huge sums of money on the games. If you follow basketball, it's impossible for one guy of Ricky's caliber to affect the outcome of the game. Because he ain't going to touch the ball that much. You're not going to fix a game with your center or power forward, because your guards are going to stop giving him the ball. And he can't dribble it, he can't bring it up. So I think if they were fixing it, there had to be other people involved. I think Sweeney was probably involved if they were fixing them."

Kerry O'Malley and Gary Zimmerman practice law in Pittsburgh. O'Malley admits still being fascinated about the case and is unequivocal in his opinion about the sentences imposed on the defendants.

"The sentences were outrageous," he says. "I thought they were out of line back then. They didn't kill anybody, they didn't hurt anybody. Some of the guys even lost money. But it was Jimmy Burke. He was the reason."

Zimmerman's reputation as a tenacious defender made him a sought-after attorney in the '80s and '90s, and he made a name for himself in several high-profile drug cases. He considers the Boston College case less interesting than some of his other assignments, but he summed up the sentiments of many college basketball fans with the following point:

"Who would have ever thought the kids at Boston College would shave points? Think about that for a minute. Nice Catholic school, a nice program, they have a good coach, a good athletic director, a good recruiting program. They're doing well. Then all of a sudden they have something like this. Who would have ever thought the CCNY guys would have done that? They were the heroes of New York, and then all of a sudden they're shaving points.

"You never know. I've seen some of the best people in the world do some of the most godawful things to others, and I've seen some of the slimiest creeps do some of the nicest things you could ever imagine."

• • •

Dr. Tom Davis survived the pressure-cooker in 1981 when the point-shaving investigation was made public, and coached Boston College to its best season ever the next year, when an overachieving team led by John Garris, John Bagley, and Martin Clark made it to the Elite Eight before losing to a Houston team that featured Clyde Drexler and Akeem Olajuwon. But the residual effects of the point-shaving scandal apparently played a significant part in Davis's departure. He reportedly had already made the decision to leave around the time of Rick Kuhn's sentencing in February 1982.

Davis went to Stanford, coached there for four years and then moved to Iowa, where he became the winningest coach in school history. When he was unceremoniously forced out at the end of the 1998–99 season by Iowa athletic director Bob Bowlsby, he left with a 543–290 career record in twenty-eight seasons.

More than twenty years after the fact, Davis can still remember the sense of disbelief he felt when he heard that three of his players were being investigated for shaving points.

"I actually felt that way about all of them. That was my initial reaction, as I recall. But I think of Jim (Sweeney) more than most, because of the kind of life that he'd been able to lead, in terms of the schools that he'd gone to and the family background and everything.

"But I think if there's a message in there, it is that when you're eighteen, nineteen, or twenty you can make mistakes. It's not unusual. We see it every day, whatever sport. Guys just make really bad decisions, and I think the younger you are, the more vulnerable you are to that."

• • •

Kevin Mackey was the players' choice to inherit Davis's job in 1982, but he was passed over for Gary Williams, Davis's assistant, and instead took over at tiny Cleveland State, where his rise and fall was one of the more well-chronicled tales in college basketball in the late 1980s and early 1990s.

Mackey turned the Cleveland State program around and averaged twenty wins over the next seven seasons, and seemed to have the world by the tail when his team of rejects upset Indiana in the first round of the 1986 NCAA Tournament. But he hit bottom in 1990 when he was arrested outside a crack house in Cleveland and was subsequently fired by the school. He underwent treatment and has resurrected his coaching career in the alphabet soup of basketball's minor leagues, where he continues to win games at every stop—USBL, IBL, IBA, GBA . . . he has won titles in all of them. During the winter of 2000, he coached the International Basketball League's Trenton Shooting Stars, who played their home games barely a mile from Jim Sweeney's parents' house.

Like the man himself, Mackey's take on the 1978–79 season does not adhere to the party line.

"I basically believed it was a case of the guys taking the money; to me, it was that simple," he says. "However, I don't believe the games themselves were affected. Ernie was as poor as a church-mouse, and Rick and Jimmy, they didn't have a lot of money either. They made a bad decision, a wrong decision, they did the wrong thing. I believe they took the money and whatever was supposed to get done was not done.

"This was the kind of guy Ernie was: If two guys were giving him money, he'd tell them two different things. But he'd go out there and play to win."

"I had a lot of respect for (Sweeney). He was a tough kid, I thought he was an overachiever in basketball. Of the three, he probably should have known better . . . but he's a human being. He made a terrible mistake, and he's had to pay for it. I know better than most, that no one gets off scot-free. I wish them all the best."

•　•　•

Despite Judge Bramwell's admonition at the sentencing of Rick Kuhn, the Boston College case did not serve as a warning to future generations of players; or, if it did, not enough of them were listening.

Less than a year after Cobb was acquitted, three Tulane students pleaded guilty to bribing five of the school's basketball players to shave points in two games. One of the players, John "Hot Rod" Williams, was acquitted in 1985 despite the fact that three of his former teammates testified against him. Tulane abolished its basketball program the next year.

Allegations of point-shaving on the 1987–88 North Carolina State team surfaced in 1990 when ABC Television broadcast an interview with a Wolfpack player whose face and voice were disguised to protect his identity. The player, according to a source who knew him at one time, was Kelsey Weems, a point guard on the team from 1985 to 1989. No charges were brought, but the allegations were among a host of other factors that led to the resignation of head coach Jim Valvano in 1990.

In the 1990s, several high-profile cases brought point-shaving to the forefront again. Reports of fixers influencing games at Arizona State during the 1993–94 season and Northwestern in 1994–95 spurred the usual calls for reform. An investigation into the 1996–97 Fresno State team, which covered the spread in only eight of thirty games, is ongoing as of this writing.

Perhaps the most devastating revelation came in the fall of 1996, when it was divulged that a number of Boston College football players had been making illegal wagers, some of them against their own team. Thirteen players were suspended for the final three games of the season. One of the games was against Syracuse. Ironically, B.C. graduate Mike Mayock, one of the only people Jim Sweeney told about the point-shaving scheme in 1979, was by then a broadcaster for CBS, and remembers participating in a make-believe wager on television with broadcast partner Sean McDonough, a Syracuse graduate, before the game.

With casinos popping up on Indian reservations and riverboats across the country, and with the proliferation of sports wagering outlets on the Internet, the culture of gambling is flourishing as never before. In response, the NCAA is pushing two bills in Congress it hopes will stem the tide, though neither had been signed into law by the fall of 2000. A bill that would outlaw sports gambling on the Internet passed the Senate but did not get the required two-thirds majority in the House. A bill that would prevent casinos and sports books in Nevada from accepting legal bets on college and amateur events was languishing in the Senate and was not expected to be considered before 2001.

On the home front, the NCAA has strengthened its own antigambling rules. Under new legislation effective in September 2000, any Division I athlete found to have made an illegal wager with a bookmaker will be suspended for one year, regardless of the amount of money involved.

Players have not been the only sources of suspicion. Indiana coach Bob Knight commented to ESPN interviewer Digger Phelps in early 1999 that the public would be "amazed" if it knew the extent to which referees had been influenced by gambling interests over the years. Knight may have known more than he let on: A few weeks after Cleveland State's win over Indiana in the 1986 NCAA Tournament, Kevin Mackey says he was visited by three FBI agents, one of whom he knew from the Cleveland area, who inquired about one of the referees who had worked the game. When Mackey pressed them, they said that the referee—"the tall one from the West Coast," Mackey remembered—was "tied in," in Mackey's words, with the implication that the Mafia was involved in some way.

Blaine Sylvester, one of the three referees who worked the game and the only one who lived west of the Mississippi, said he was never contacted by the FBI and had no idea why he would have been suspected. Murph Shapiro, who also worked the game and who still referees Division I basketball, remembered nothing unusual occurring during the game and also said he was never contacted by the FBI. Mackey, however, remembers some curious calls that went in Cleveland State's favor, and recalls making remarks to his assistant coaches to that effect.

Through an intermediary, Knight neither confirmed nor denied knowledge of an investigation into the CSU-Indiana game. But beginning in early 2000, the NCAA instituted background checks for all referees working in the NCAA Tournament.

• • •

Chris Foy remembers the last real conversation he had with Jim Sweeney, near the end of the 1980 season. Foy, then a junior, had lost his starting job to newcomer John Bagley despite having worked hard over the previous summer to lose weight and impress Davis, who had suggested that he transfer.

"One time after a game, in the shower, Sweeney looked at me and said, 'You know, you gave up this year,'" Foy recalled. "I said, 'What are you saying?' He said, 'You gave up. You laid down for John Bagley.' And I went up to Sweeney and said, 'Fuck you. I competed as hard as I could. You don't even know what I went through.' That's pretty much the last conversation I had with Jim Sweeney.

"I was bitter that he could have the balls to say something like that to me [after] what he was doing. . . . That kind of left a bad taste in my mouth. But even with the little bitterness I have left, I really think that Jimmy, if he could do it all over again, in a second he would change everything.

"You've got to understand, he *was* Boston College. He loved that school, the school loved him, and to throw it all away on one silly mistake. . . . It's something that you just can't do a take-back on."

• • •

Rick Kuhn was released from prison in 1986. His phone number in the Pittsburgh suburbs is still unlisted after all these years, and he did not return phone messages left on an answering machine requesting an interview for this book.

Kuhn's collaboration with Ed McDonald, the man who sent him to prison, began when both men began appearing at basketball camps to preach the evils of gambling to aspiring college stars.

At a Nike camp run by Sonny Vaccaro at Princeton University in 1990, Kuhn appeared with McDonald on the same bill with filmmaker Spike Lee. Later that day, after recounting his experiences to the audience of campers—one of whom was a high school star from Detroit named Chris Webber—Kuhn told *Newsday*, "I sent myself to prison the night I thought I was bigger than the game, the night I agreed to get involved in the scheme. I made that decision. No one else made it for me. I could have said no. I chose not to. I got thirty-five hundred dollars a game and spent it.

"I didn't think I was hurting anybody. It seemed so harmless. I didn't know about the New York end of it. I was always in contact with friends from Pittsburgh. I didn't know it was going into New York and Vegas. Once the whole thing was laid out to me, I said, 'Man, this thing is bigger than I thought. Man, I really screwed up here.'

"I made a mistake, no doubt about it. It was the biggest mistake of my life. I thought I was invincible—the Pete Rose syndrome. You think you're above everything. You can't be hurt by anything. Let's face it: I made the decision and I put myself in jail. I hurt my family badly."

One of the coaches attending the camp was Dr. Tom Davis, who had not seen his former player since the trial in 1981. The two men spoke briefly, enough for Davis to see that Kuhn's remorse was genuine.

It is possible that Rick Kuhn's second act has yet to be written. The screenplay on which he and McDonald acted as consultants is completed and awaiting a buyer. Twenty years after the fact, Rick Kuhn may finally get his payoff.

• • •

Barbara Reed still works in the health care industry and is happily married, though not to the man she was engaged to at the time of her testimony in *U.S. v. Burke* in 1981. The intervening years have given her a sense of perspective about the events that reshaped her life twenty years ago, but her voice wavers when she recounts some of the more unpleasant details, in particular how her life was threatened before she testified in court. She also says Rick Kuhn did not testify for the government because, he, too, had had his life threatened.

Reed did testify, and it was her testimony that likely sealed her former boyfriend's fate—but in doing so she was forced to endure having details about her personal life and her relationship with Rick printed in newspapers across the country.

Reed has had twenty years to ponder the confluence of events that dragged her out of peaceful obscurity and onto the front pages. Some of the memories are still painful.

"I do think about it," she says. "I think, 'How the heck did I ever get involved in something like this?' You're a young kid in college, and you think you can handle it when you really have no idea. You think you can take in a stray puppy and teach him how good the world can be. . . . I feel I was used. People may not believe me, but I did not know they were shaving points. I worked at night, I was a nurse. I thought the guys were calling every week to see how the team was going to do.

"I'm lucky. I had a pretty strong faith and a good family that stood behind me. I'm proud I told the truth. I hope the whole thing prevents somebody else from being put in that situation."

• • •

Tom Meggers saw Jim Sweeney once since graduating from Boston College, at a B.C. football game in the mid-'90s. The two former teammates shook hands, but Meggers remembers the meeting as being somewhat strained. Like the other players, he still wonders about exactly what transpired during the 1978–79 season.

"It's really kind of a shame, because he was really a great kid," he says of Sweeney. "And I'm not saying he's not now. Someday I would love to have the opportunity to just sit down over a beer and really hear what happened, and why or how he got involved in it. Because obviously he was.

"All I can think, deep down, is that there was something there that he got caught into and he probably couldn't get himself out of it. You do one thing and get deeper into it, and before you know it, there's no turning back. And I'm sure that's probably how it happened."

• • •

Jim Sweeney has not hidden his head in the sand in the years since his testimony helped send his former friend Rick Kuhn to prison. He has not sought publicity either, and he has politely declined numerous requests to be interviewed over the years, usually right after news of another college basketball point-shaving scandal has made national headlines.

Sweeney lives in the South with his wife, Maura, the woman he met on the first day of his sophomore year at Boston College and then married a few months before he testified in *U.S. v. Burke* in 1981. He owns a successful small computer business and is content to live "under the radar," as he terms it. During the 1980s, he embraced the message of Jesus Christ and became a born-again Christian, and he is active in missionary work that has taken him to England, Ireland, and Russia. He says his salvation had nothing to do with the events at Boston College.

His love of basketball has not waned. He played competitively well into his thirties on an AAU team that played exhibitions against college teams, and at forty-two, he still plays in a local league against players who often are nearly half his age.

By any objective measure, Jim Sweeney's life is good. But there is a disconnect between the first half of his life and the second, like a halftime intermission during which the script was hastily rewritten for the second act. For the first twenty-one years, he did little to disappoint those around him who came to marvel at his athletic prowess, engaging personality, and excellence in the classroom. Then, like a light switch being turned off, that side of Jim Sweeney vanished for a lot of people. Today, it is as if Jim Sweeney—Rhodes Scholar candidate, academic All-American, and Naismith Award winner—never existed, replaced instead by a tarnished image fed by the repetition of his name alongside the familiar words: "point-shaving . . . gambling . . . scandal."

"I think of the time as being so small and in such a short window," Sweeney says. "Yet people have such a fascination with it. I met Henry Hill once. I know he was at a game we played, and I may have met him a second time, but after the first time I never wanted to meet him again. But if you added up all the conversations, it would be minutes.

"I basically look at myself with disappointment because I didn't just run away from it. As I testified in court, I never did anything; but I still hold myself accountable. I did meet with those people; I didn't know what to do. Everyone makes mistakes, and I made a big mistake. I let a lot of people down. I look back and say, by the grace of God I was able to move on."

The last time Sweeney saw Rick Kuhn was in District Court in Brooklyn on November 3, 1981, when he looked right past his former friend and gave the testimony that sealed Kuhn's fate. That knowledge—along with the knowledge that he allowed himself to be involved in something he knew was wrong—gnaws at him today when the subject is broached.

"Yes, it has been difficult to live with," he said. "My heart goes out to [Rick]. He was branded as a bad guy, and he wasn't a bad guy. I thought he was unfairly maligned in the papers. . . . They made him out to be a monster, and he wasn't. We all make mistakes, and I'm sure he regrets what happened to him. He just found himself hanging out with the wrong guys. Unfortunately, most of us in life have done it at certain points and looked back and regretted it. But the press really disparaged him. Sure, he was looking to recruit others to do something that wasn't right, but the guy was not a hoodlum or a thief.

"I'm sure he has some sort of ill will (toward me). I wish I could see him. I would hope he'd feel some sort of regret that he initiated this thing, and that he embroiled (me) in it."

• • •

Rick Kuhn's biggest mistake was not dribbling the ball off his foot or throwing the ball into the stands on purpose, it was in assuming that he could cut corners and manipulate the game to serve his ends, modest though they may have seemed at the outset.

Yet when it came time to hold him accountable for his sins, logic went the way of all those errant passes. There is no question that Kuhn suffered unjustly for his connections to individuals of questionable repute, several of whom he still has never met. Needless to say, had it been a couple of Boston College frat boys who paid him to shave points instead of Henry Hill and Jimmy Burke, it is doubtful Kuhn would have been dealt with so harshly. Too, it was Kuhn's misfortune to add another link to a chain that stretches back to CCNY, Kentucky, and LIU, to Jack Molinas, Eddie Gard, Sherman White, and Louis Brown—ghosts from a time when the college game truly was hip-deep in the mire of corruption.

Jim Sweeney and Ernie Cobb, meanwhile, were guilty of letting greed, or perhaps youthful indiscretion, shape their decisions. Either could have blown the whistle at any time during the scheme, but neither did. By accepting money, even if only to keep up appearances, they exhibited, at best, bad judgment by risking losing their college eligibility and all they had worked so hard to achieve. At worst, they succumbed to the same temptations as Kuhn and should count themselves fortunate that they avoided punishment.

Yet they were punished in different ways than Kuhn. Ernie Cobb is consumed with bitterness over the NBA career that he feels he deserved. Jim Sweeney must forever live with the knowledge that he could have stopped it all before it started. On a larger scale, the ease with which such a scheme could be conceived and put into action only serves as a reminder of the fragility of the social contract upon which organized sports is based, that often-shaky foundation of mutually shared values of fair play and sportsmanship. When those values are compromised, as they were in the winter of 1978–79, the contract is broken and the structure loses its integrity. To use a well-worn cliché, all bets are off.

As one former teammate said of Sweeney, "Whether he was afraid or not, he did it. At least that's what the court said. He's admitted it. And what bothers the hell out of me is that with the character that that kid had, he could have stepped above it and gotten out of it and done something and gone to the authorities and stopped it right there, instead of dragging us all down years later.

"And it did drag us all down. My wife had to explain to my thirteen-year-old. I have people ask me all the time about it. 'Were you on that team?' 'Yup, that was me.'"

Boston College

1978–79 SEASON

Date	Opponent	Line	Score	Gamblers' Outcome
Nov. 27	Stonehill	none	BC, 89–76	None
Nov. 30	Bentley	none	BC, 83–79	None

Ernie Cobb claims Rocco Perla paid him one thousand dollars for guaranteeing the outcome of the Stonehill and Bentley games, even though there was no betting line on either game.

| Dec. 6 | Providence | BC –6/7 | BC, 83–64 | Lost |

Cobb scores twenty-five points in the "test" game of the scheme.

| Dec. 16 | Harvard | BC –12/13 | BC, 86-83 | Won |

Rocco Perla gives one thousand dollars to Cobb's girlfriend, Laverne Mosley, after the game. Henry Hill says he gave Rick Kuhn three thousand dollars in a hallway in Boston Garden. Sweeney tells roommate Mike Mayock about the scheme after the game, but decides not to tell coach Tom Davis or athletic director Bill Flynn.

| Dec. 23 | UCLA | UCLA –15/18 | UCLA,103–81 | Won |

Rick Kuhn claims he asked to have his money bet on B.C. for this game; Henry Hill claims the gamblers cleaned up by betting on UCLA.

| Jan. 10 | Rhode Island | URI –13/–15 | URI, 91–78 | Lost/Push |

B.C.'s Vin Caraher scores fifteen points in the final minutes to shrink the final margin from twenty-eight points to thirteen—and, in the process, lose most of the gamblers' money.

| Jan. 17 | UConn | BC –5 | BC, 90–80 | Won |

Hill claims the gamblers bet on B.C. to win, to allay any suspicions by bookies; Kuhn claims he and Sweeney bet their own money on this game.

| Jan. 20 | Holy Cross | BC –5/–2 | BC, 89–87 | Won/Push |

After B.C. opens as a five-point favorite, the line drops to two, indicating heavy money being bet on Holy Cross.

Date	Opponent	Line	Score	Gamblers' Outcome
Jan. 27	UConn	BC –5	BC, 78–77	???

There is confusion over whether this game, the final of the Colonial Classic, was part of the scheme. If any money was bet against B.C., it probably was not significant.

| Feb. 3 | Fordham | BC –10 | BC, 71–64 | Won |

Sweeney misses a foul shot near the end of the game that could have helped B.C. cover the spread, and later makes a joking comment to Rocco Perla about "seeing a pair of concrete shoes" above the backboard while taking the shot.

| Feb. 6 | St. John's | SJ –9–12 | SJ, 85–76 | Push/Lost |

Cobb commits eight turnovers and shoots 1-for-7 from the floor in his worst game of the season. Heavy betting on St. John's pushes the line from nine points up to as high as twelve by game time.

| Feb. 10 | Holy Cross | HC –2/–7 | HC, 98–96 | Lost |

Cobb scores eight points in the final minutes to bring B.C. close; Sweeney says he fouled out intentionally early in the second half to distance himself from the scheme.

| Mar. 1 | UConn | even | UConn, 91–74 | ??? |

Hill claims that the players "convinced" the gamblers to bet one more game; Kuhn says he told Tony Perla to bet on B.C.

Other games: 12/3, LeMoyne (W, 93–70); 12/10, New Hampshire (W, 78–65); 12/12, Vermont (W, 126-89); 12/21, St. Mary's (CA) (L, 79–81); 12/28, Purdue (L, 54–82); 12/29, Harvard (W, 83–78); 12/30, Tennessee (W, 74–72); 1/6, Northeastern (W, 80–68); 1/12, Baltimore (W, 92–72); 1/15, St. Anselm (W, 95–76); 1/17, UConn (W, 90–80); 1/23, Villanova (W, 83–75); 1/26, Massachusetts (W, 82–70); 2/13, Dartmouth (W, 66–56); 2/15, Merrimack (W, 105–73); 2/17, Georgetown (L, 81–84); 2/21, Boston University (W, 99–84); 2/24, Fairfield (L, 81--93).

Legal Terms Glossary

Accomplice—an individual who aids and assists in the commission of a crime.

Admissible evidence—evidence presented for jury consideration that has been deemed relevant, reliable, and material to a case.

Affidavit—a sworn statement signed under oath.

Bribery—the act of giving or receiving compensation to influence a public or judicial official.

Burden of proof—the job of the prosecution to prove that all disputed facts and evidence are true.

Chambers—a judge's private office.

Circumstantial evidence—evidence that infers or suggests, but does not directly prove, a fact.

Coercion—the act of compelling an individual to act in a certain way by using physical force or threat.

Complaint—the initial document filed by a person or government in which claims and charges against another party are outlined. The document also states the legal basis for the accusations. A complaint is needed to begin a lawsuit.

Conspiracy—an unlawful agreement between two or more parties to commit an illegal act.

Corroborate—to confirm or reinforce evidence or another's testimony to be true.

Cross-examination, cross—the opportunity of an attorney to question a witness called to the stand by the opposition, generally after the witness's direct testimony.

Custodial interrogation—the questioning of an individual while he is being held in custody.

Debrief—to question an individual to obtain relevant information or insight.

Defense—the general term that refers to the attorney(s) who represent a defendant and the facts and arguments used to attempt to free the defendant of blame.

Deliberations—the time during which a jury reviews and discusses testimony and evidence in an attempt to render a decision.

Direct Evidence—evidence or testimony that expressly proves a fact.

Direct testimony, direct examination—the initial questioning of a witness by the side that called him to the stand. During this time, the individual can recount his side of the events in question.

District Attorney (DA)—an attorney who is appointed to represent the state and prosecute parties charged with violating laws of the state. In the federal court system, the district attorney is known as a Federal District Attorney, federal prosecutor, government prosecutor, or United States Attorney.

District—the federal court system of the United States is divided into geographically defined districts. Depending on the size of a state, it may have one or more federal districts.

District court—the trial court in which federal court cases are heard.

Equal protection—the guaranty that all

individuals in like circumstances be treated equally and uniformly.

Exculpatory evidence—evidence that can clear or excuse a defendant of guilt.

Extortion—the act of obtaining money, property, or other valuables by threatening to inflict harm on, scandalize, accuse, or expose an individual if payment is not agreed to.

Federal court system—the branch of the Department of Justice of the United States government that has authority over cases that involve the United States Constitution and federal laws. The federal court system is responsible for hearing cases that involve federal crimes such as racketeering.

Federal District Attorney—an attorney in the federal court system who is responsible for prosecuting federal crimes on behalf of the United States in a particular district. A Federal District Attorney is appointed by the president. (also *federal prosecutor, government prosecutor, United States Attorney*)

Felony—a crime considered serious enough to be punishable by death or imprisonment that exceeds a year.

First Amendment—the Amendment to the United States Constitution that states, among other things, that Congress cannot make laws that deprive the freedom of speech or of the press.

Fifth Amendment—the Amendment to the United States Constitution that states, among other things, that in most cases, an individual does not have to answer for a crime unless indicted by a grand jury, nor can an individual be forced to serve as a witness against himself in a criminal case. The Fifth Amendment also promises the right to a fair trial.

Grand jury—a jury of between twelve and twenty-four people that hears the details and accusations of a proposed indictment as presented by the prosecution, and determines whether or not there is sufficient evidence for the accused to be indicted and stand trial. A grand jury does not try cases.

Hung jury—a jury whose members are unable to come to agreement about a verdict. If no agreement is reached, the judge is forced to declare a mistrial.

Immunity, immunity agreement—an agreement between authorities and a witness that stipulates that, in exchange for testimony and information, the witness cannot be prosecuted for a specific crime.

Impeachment—the act of discrediting a witness's credibility by showing that he is untrustworthy, morally unsound, or inconsistent.

Inadmissible evidence—evidence deemed inappropriate that cannot be presented at a trial. Common reasons evidence is ruled inadmissible include: the information has been garnered illegally, is unreliable, or is based on hearsay.

Indictment—a formal accusation, returned by a grand jury, that charges an individual with a felony. Based on the presentation of an indictment, the accused must stand trial.

Interstate commerce—regulated by the federal government, interstate commerce involves commercial trade, economics, services, and transportation between states. Government regulation was established to guarantee fair rates. Extortion and conspiracy with regard to interstate commerce are punishable by fine and/or imprisonment.

Joint motion—a motion requested by multiple parties in a joint trial.

Joint trial—a trial in which multiple defendants have been charged with the same crime and are being tried collectively.

Jurisdiction—the authority of a court to hear a case and render a decision. Jurisdiction is determined by the type of case being tried and the location of the individuals, goods, and properties involved. Federal courts have jurisdiction over trials that involve federal laws and statutes, federal crimes, and individuals in more than one state. State courts have jurisdiction over cases that involve laws passed by state legislature. Jurisdiction can also refer to the geographical region over which the authority of a specific court extends.

Mistrial—the premature termination of a trial caused by a hung jury or by events that threaten an individual's right to a fair trial. A mistrial in criminal cases can lead to a retrial, the dismissal of charges, or a plea bargain.

Motion—a formal request to the court to make a decision or judgment about an issue that surfaces during litigation.

Objection—a protest to the court by an attorney to a question being asked of a witness by the opposing side. Objections are generally made when questions are irrelevant, immaterial, leading, or based on hearsay.

Open court—judicial proceedings that are held in a public forum and are accessible and free to the public. Open court proceedings ensure a criminal defendant's constitutional right to a public trial.

Parole—the supervised early release of a convicted individual from prison that is based on a defined set of conditions.

Party—a participant in a legal proceeding.

Perjury—the crime of lying or making an untrue statement about facts while under oath.

Plea—the formal answer, generally "guilty," "not guilty," or "no contest," of a defendant to each charge of an indictment.

Plea agreement, plea bargain—an agreement in a criminal case between the defense and the government prosecutor that states, in exchange for a guilty or no-contest plea to a specific charge, the government will agree to reduce the severity of the charges against the defendant, dismiss some charges, or recommend a particular

sentence or benefit for the defendant.

Prejudice—a bias or predisposition that hinders an individual's ability to be impartial.

Preponderance of evidence—the greater weight of evidence in terms of presenting a convincing argument. Preponderance of evidence is one side's ability to present evidence as more persuasive and believable than the other side's, causing a judge or jury to decide for one side or the other. The preponderance is based on the merit, not amount, of evidence presented.

Pro bono—literally, "for the good," pro bono describes legal work or attorney assistance provided free of charge to individuals or organizations with limited or nonexistent funds.

Probation—a convicted individual's chance to avoid imprisonment or shorten a prison term, provided he agrees to accept a specified set of conditions. The conditions can include: community service, reporting to a probation office, substance abuse therapy, and agreeing to not fraternize with certain individuals. Violation of the conditions generally results in serving the prison term originally sentenced.

Probative value—the weight of potential evidence or testimony to be used to prove part of a case. A judge may question probative value when the evidence in question may prejudice the jurors and undermine a defendant's right to a fair trial. Examples include testimony that outlines previous convictions and prior activities.

Prosecutorial misconduct—an inappropriate, illegal, or improper statement or action exhibited by a prosecutor.

Racketeering—the federal crime of conspiring to organize for the purpose of committing crimes.

Reasonable doubt—the level of moral certainty a juror must attain to convict a defendant of a crime. If the evidence, lack of evidence, or testimony presented does not morally convince a juror the charge is true, there is reasonable doubt.

Rebuttal—a direct reply or presentation of evidence made to attempt to discredit, disprove, or contradict an argument or evidence presented by the opposition.

Recuse—the act of a judge or prosecutor being removed or removing himself from a criminal trial. This commonly occurs when there is bias or a conflict of interest, such as when there is a prior relationship between the judge or prosecutor and one of the parties involved in the case.

Recross examination, recross—the questioning of a witness about issues that emerged during redirect questioning. A recross examination is conducted by the counsel for the opposing side.

Redirect questioning, redirect—the questioning of a witness about issues that emerged during cross-examination. Redirect questioning is conducted by the side that called the witness to the stand.

Sequester—an act by a judge that limits the contact jurors of a high-profile criminal case have with the public world. When jurors are sequestered, they are generally confined to a hotel when not in court, where they are not allowed access to the news and opinions of family members and the general public. A judge sequesters a jury so its decision regarding the case is based on the admissible evidence and testimony presented in court.

Severance—the division of defendants involved in a joint trial into separate trials. Severance may be granted when the details of a trial suggest a joint trial would be unfair to one or more of the defendants.

Sidebar—a confidential conversation between a judge and the attorneys representing both sides that is not meant to be heard by the jury or trial spectators.

Sixth Amendment—the Amendment to the United States Constitution that states that, among other things, an accused individual has the right of a speedy and public trial by an impartial jury. The Sixth Amendment also ensures the accused has the right to be informed of the nature and cause of the accusations against him, to confront the witnesses against him, and to have the assistance of an attorney for his defense.

Sports bribery—the act of influencing a sporting event in any way by bribery.

State court system—the court system that has authority over cases that involve state laws and state constitutions.

Statute of limitations—a set period of time during which a lawsuit must be filed. When the statute of limitations has expired, a potential claimant forever loses the right to initiate a suit.

Subpoena—a court order served to an individual that requires him to appear at a specific time and place to testify in a trial.

Subpoena duces tecum—a court order served to an individual who possesses books, documents, instruments, or tangible property to be used as evidence in a case. The individual served is required to produce the desired evidence at a specific time and place during a trial.

Summation—the final argument made by an attorney on behalf of his client after all evidence has been presented. The prosecution makes the first argument, the defense follows, then the prosecution has the chance to refute the defense's final argument.

Sustain—the act of a judge agreeing with and supporting an attorney's objection.

Testimony—oral evidence given under oath by a witness.

Trial court—the court where a suit is filed and where a trial is held.

Voir dire—the preliminary questioning of prospective jurors by the judge and the attorneys representing both sides to determine whether or not any of the potential jurors are prejudiced, biased, or knowledgeable of facts detrimental to the case.

Resources

All definitions gleaned from the following text and online sources.

Gilmer, W. *The Law Dictionary*. 6th ed. Cincinnati: Anderson Publishing, 1986.

Amendments to the Constitution
http://www.house.gov/Constitution/Amend.html

Duhaime's Law Dictionary
http://www.duhaime.org/dict-a.htm
Lloyd Duhaime, LL.B.
Duhaime & Company
Victoria, British Columbia

Law.com Dictionary
http://dictionary.law.com
Copyright © 2000 Law.com
Law.com
San Francisco, California

The 'Lectric Law Library Lexicon
http://www.lectlaw.com

Nolo.com Dictionary
http://www.nolo.com/dictionary/wordindex.cfm
Copyright © 2000 Nolo.com, Inc.
Nolo.com, Inc.
Berkeley, California

Index

Numbers in *italics* indicate photographs.